Global Crime Today

Crime is recognised as a constant factor within human society, but in the twenty-first century organised crime is emerging as one of the distinctive security threats of the new world order. As society becomes more complex, organised and interconnected so too does its crime.

Organised crime in the new century will be characterised by a struggle between an 'upperworld', defined by increasingly open economic systems and democratic politics, and a transnational, entrepreneurial, dynamic and richly varied underworld, willing and able to use and distort these trends for its own ends. In order to understand this challenge, this book gathers together experts from a variety of fields to analyse how organised crime is changing. From the Sicilian Mafia and the Japanese Yakuza, to the new challenges of Russian and East European gangs and the 'virtual mafias' of the cybercriminals, this book offers a clear and concise introduction to many of the key players moving in this global criminal underworld.

This book was previously published as a special issue of *Global Crime*.

Dr Mark Galeotti is Director of the Organised Russian & Eurasian Crime Research Unit and Senior Lecturer in International History at Keele University.

Global Crime Today

The Changing Face of Organised Crime

Edited by
Mark Galeotti

Routledge
Taylor & Francis Group

LONDON AND NEW YORK

First published 2005 by Routledge
2 Park Square, Milton Park, Abingdon, Oxon, OX14 4RN

Simultaneously published in the USA and Canada
by Routledge
270 Madison Ave, New York, NY 10016

Routledge is an imprint of the Taylor & Francis Group

Transferred to Digital Printing 2007

© 2005 Mark Galeotti

Typeset in Minion 10.5/13pt by the Alden Group, Oxford

British Library Cataloguing in Publication Data
A catalogue record for this book is available from the British Library

Library of Congress Cataloging in Publication Data
A catalog record for this title has been requested

ISBN10: 0-415-36699-2 (hbk)
ISBN10: 0-415-43667-2 (pbk)

ISBN13: 978-0-415-36699-1 (hbk)
ISBN13: 978-0-415-43667-0 (pbk)

CONTENTS

Introduction: Global Crime Today

Mark Galeotti

If the twentieth century was dominated by cold wars—which periodically erupted into the real thing—and the 'war on terrorism' has become the prevailing preoccupation since 9/11, then the struggle against organised and transnational crime will become a parallel defining security theme of the twenty-first.

The turnover of the global criminal economy is roughly estimated at one trillion dollars, of which narcotics may account for about half. Around 4 percent of the world's population takes illegal drugs, from inhaled solvents to the Asian betel nut. Five main commodities are dominant: opiates such as heroin (14 million users worldwide), cocaine (14 million), amphetamine-type stimulants (30 million), hallucinogens (25 million) and cannabis (140 million) [1]. Up to half a trillion dollars are laundered through the world's financial systems every year. The OECD estimates that the criminal drug industry costs its member states over $120 billion per year, with the USA alone accounting for $76 billion [2]. Furthermore, global organised crime is evolving, embracing new markets and new technologies, and moving from traditional hierarchies towards more flexible, network-based forms of organisation. To an extent, the legitimate world is a victim of its own success: globalisation of the legal economy has also globalised the underworld, prosperity fuels the demand for many illicit services, and improved policing ironically forces criminals to become more organised to survive.

The late Claire Sterling popularised the notion of a 'Pax Mafiosa', that the international organised crime groupings were working together efficiently and harmoniously and, in effect, dividing the globe between them [3]. There is, of course, ample evidence of cooperation: Italian syndicates sell Latin American drugs in Europe, Russians buy stolen cars from the Japanese Yakuza, Albanians move Asian heroin for Turkish drug clans. It would, however, be a mistake to take this too far. Many of these accords are very loose, little more than mutually-profitable trades or temporary alliances of convenience. If anything, there is ample scope for future conflicts within the global underworld, as markets become saturated and the opportunities for further peaceful expansion exhausted.

In many ways, the traditional demarcations between national security and law enforcement concerns are becoming increasingly less meaningful. Serious and organised crime can directly affect national security resources, whether in plundering state budgets (with implications for defence expenditure) to undermining morale and discipline. Beijing's concerns about the criminalisation of its military elites was one of the main reasons behind its efforts to end their involvement in commercial activities. In Russia, penetration by organised crime has had a more direct and immediate impact, with special forces moonlighting as hitmen and weapons being sold, even to Chechen rebels.

In this respect, there is a direct carry-over, organised and transnational crime groupings acting as agents of instability and insecurity. The haemorrhage of weapons from former Soviet military stockpiles, a trade facilitated and often run by organised crime, fuelled the Balkan arms race and put high-order firepower into the hands of every faction, gang and militia. Organised crime is often powerful enough to create its own 'states-within-states', from the poppy fields of Uzbekistan's Fergana Valley to Morocco's cannabis-growing Rif region, undermining the integrity of their host states and of national borders. Of course, crime has long been used as a tactic to fund political insurgency, from Colombia's FARC to the Kurdish PKK. Yet many organisations, such as the remnants of the Peruvian *Sendero Luminoso* and elements of the Northern Ireland paramilitary forces, have in many ways lost their political rationale and become little more than organised crime groupings with a line in anachronistic rhetoric.

As some terrorists become criminals, so too are some organised criminal groupings becoming increasingly political actors, reflected in a range of activities, from lobbying to suborning or corrupting legitimate governments. This kind of criminalisation is already well entrenched in parts of Latin America, Africa and Asia. However, it would be foolish to pretend that this is never a problem in Europe and North America, where it simply tends to adopt more subtle guises [4].

The State of the Underworld

Despite setbacks both in Italy and the United States, the 'original'—Italian—mafia is still perhaps the world's largest and most sophisticated organised criminal phenomenon, both the traditional gangs of the Italian south, rooted in the culture of the 'man of honour,' hard-hit by the Italian state's long-awaited challenge, as well as 'Mafia Incorporated', a vast, multinational commercial enterprise, which pours criminal earnings into both illegal and legal economic activity. Of course, this is distinct from the North American *Cosa Nostra*, twenty-five 'families' and many smaller groups engaged in a wide portfolio of activities, from usury, narcotics trafficking and racketeering, to pornography, fraud and financial manipulation. Similarly, it has suffered serious setbacks but it is too soon to celebrate its demise, not least because the decline of the Cosa Nostra is both cause and result of the rise of a more disorganised, violent and competitive criminal environment rather than necessarily meaning a straightforward victory for law and order.

The main global rivals to the Mafia in terms of spread, organisation and discipline are the Japanese Boryokudan, more commonly known as the Yakuza, and Chinese groupings (the six Triads and analogous mainland structures, such as the Big Circle Boys). The return of Hong Kong to Chinese rule did not, as some observers expected, lead to a Triad exodus. Instead, it has allowed for a new fusion of mainland and expatriate gangs. Thus, while the Yakuza are facing pressure as, mirroring events in Italy, the Japanese state finally began a serious campaign against organised crime, the Chinese gangs are looking increasingly confident.

Of course, organised crime in Latin America and much of Asia is still dominated by the narcotics industry, especially cocaine and heroin production, respectively. The demand for and trade in narcotics are a constant of human history, and will continue into the next century, even if it will also change. The main trends within the global 'narcobusiness' appear to be a geographic shift of production areas, a diversification of products and an intensification of the industry. Diversification and intensification both reflect the shift in the industry to more networked and businesslike approaches, as well as successful law enforcement. The Colombian *narcotraficantes* have, for example, dramatically increased their production of opiates—as well as their dealing in Asian heroin—and also increased their technical and organisational efficiency.

The second most lucrative criminal business, after narcotics, is the trade in people. It is estimated that between four and five million people are smuggled each year, most by choice as they seek a new life elsewhere, but up to a million trafficked against their will, usually to be forced into prostitution or slavery, a trade in misery earning organised crime an estimated $9.5 billion in profits annually [5]. Furthermore, it feeds and services other vices and criminal activities. Illegal migrants may be forced into near-slavery at their destination, made into prostitutes or used as drug 'mules'. This trade is set to continue to increase, both because of the disparity between the economic opportunities available in the world and the fact that war and unrest are unlikely to become a thing of the past, ensuring both 'push' and 'pull' factors. The increasing organisation and sophistication of the people-traffickers only helps ensure that the trade is cost-effective.

Many of the drug- and people-trafficking groupings operate as very loose networks, allowing them to work flexibly across national borders. After all, one by-product of globalisation and the shift from rigidly structured gangs to looser, network-style ones, is the diffusion of the identities of organised crime. Where once a gang might be based on a single ethnic group (or even home region or village), might be identified as such, and might rely on this to provide everything from internal language to operational culture, now there is little reason for such an exclusive approach. Instead, organised crime is becoming increasingly inclusive: people and groups with the right skills, contacts or territory can be accepted into the network so long as they simply prove able to operate within the dominant culture. This is not in essence new: the Cosa Nostra in the USA brought in such non-Italians as 'Dutch' Schultz—actually of German origin—as long they were able to operate 'Sicilian-style.' What is new is the scale at which this is being practised. Even such hitherto exclusive structures as the Yakuza are beginning to bring in outsiders, as Korean gangs begin, in effect, to operate Yakuza 'franchises' on particular territories.

Furthermore, multi-ethnic societies are producing multi-ethnic underworlds. It remains to be seen, for example, whether the federal pressures pushing for greater homogenisation across the European Union will also affect its underworld. Largely, though, what is emerging is not a process of 'gang expansion' but greater traffic between networks of gangs from a variety of ethnic groups. Thus, Turks might use Albanians to move heroin through Italian-controlled channels for distribution in Germany and the Netherlands by local gangs.

The same is true of the newest and most dynamic of the major international organised criminal groupings, the diffuse and entrepreneurial collection of gangs and combines from the former Soviet Union and East Central Europe. Instead of formal structures, these are best understood as loose networks. They may work together in specific cases, and cooperate against common threats, but there is little of the top-down control and coordination visible elsewhere. Inter-ethnic violence and competition in this context are frequent—but cooperation and exchange even more so. This seems very much to be the way organised crime will evolve in the new century, with border- and even continent-spanning networks loosely uniting groups from many separate ethnic groups, or with no real ethnic identity at all.

Indeed, not only does the rise of cyberspace offers many new opportunities to organised crime, from rapid communication to laundering funds through internet banks, it also raises the prospect of, in the future, 'virtual gangs'—if organised crime is moving towards a structure dominated by the flexible, non-ethnic network, then it would be entirely possible not just to use internet to carry out crimes but as the 'turf' of a group. This would be a development of the existing groups of hackers and crackers, as they organised and regularised their operations, to form criminal gangs whose members need never meet or be in the same city or country.

Drivers[6]

This is why it is so important to take into account changes within the wider context in which crime operates. After all, the global underworld is evolving every bit as rapidly as its legal, 'upperworld' counterpart—and to a large extent in response to the same pressures and opportunities. There are many ways of cataloguing them, but broadly speaking, they can be broken down into five main categories:

1. *Technological Drivers.* As technology reshapes the world, so too it reshapes the underworld, from increasing the ease of travel to introducing new illicit commodities to be sold, from counterfeit computer disks to synthetic drugs. The use of controlled, hydroponic cultivation methods has also allowed drugs to be raised in inappropriate climates—it has been claimed, for example, that cannabis is now the single biggest cash crop in the US state of Oregon. Economic and technological change is putting new tools in the hands of the criminals, from internet banking to the security and

flexibility of the digital cellphone. It is also putting unprecedented power into the hands of small numbers of people, even individuals. After all, while much transnational crime is organised, it need not be, as in computer crime. The evolution of technology and the laws relating to it also create new crimes, such as the burgeoning global trade in CFCs (so-called 'greenhouse gases') and toxic waste.

2. *Political Drivers.* Political changes are defining the new global underworld. At its most basic, crime is defined by laws, and laws are defined by states. Political changes at local, state and international levels all provided both opportunities—such as new trades in refugees, CFCs and endangered species—and also barriers and hazards for the criminals. As even countries once considered havens for money-laundering or criminal asylum accept international standards, such havens become fewer and less welcoming. More broadly, organised and transnational crime must and do respond to a whole range of political changes, from the ebb and flow of state power to wars and natural disasters. The collapse of the USSR was a seismic event which unleashed a new and fast-moving form of organised crime onto the world, but the return of Hong Kong and Macao to Chinese control, war in the Balkans and many other geopolitical upsets have all had serious implications for the global underworld. The Balkan wars, for example, made it even harder to block heroin-trafficking routes into Europe from the south-west. The spread of migrants and refugees into the European Union also created new criminal networks, most especially the Albanians who now handle much of the wholesale heroin trafficking for Turkish gangs. Other political processes are opening up new markets and havens to organised crime. The Schengen Accords (which open borders within the European Union) and the expansion of the EU eastwards all have criminal implications, making international criminal traffic within the region increasingly cost-effective.

3. *Economic Drivers.* Organised crime is similarly responsive to its economic environment. Markets open and close: there is no longer the demand for illegal small arms in the Balkans, just as increasing prosperity in China as a result of economic growth has created lucrative new opportunities, from providing passage to Europe to trading in new narcotics. Furthermore, many countries risk becoming 'hooked' on criminal activity such that it acquires a political importance of its own. By 1997, for example, Mexico's narcotics industry was worth an estimated $30 billion in profits—four times the revenue from the country's largest legal export, oil [7]. Even physical and environmental changes can have an impact on the global underworld, especially by changing the economic factors at work. Global warming, for example, will play its part in changing the geography of drug production, and is already permitting the economically viable production of opium and marijuana in new parts of southern Russia.

4. *Enforcement Drivers.* Successful police operations can have both anticipated and surprising effects. US-backed victories against drug cartels in Peru and Bolivia, for example, drove the *narcotraficantes* closer to the USA, into Mexico. On the other hand, pressure on both the Italian and US Mafias has weakened them both and forced them to be more cautious.

5. *Internal Drivers.* The global underworld is also not purely a product of its context, it is also shaped by internal and often contingent factors. Alliances between organisations can avoid conflict and maximise efficiency, just as feuds and competition may shatter an organisation or alternatively elevate a stronger, more effective new organisation in an exercise in social darwinism. Structural changes within the underworld are also of great importance as, reflecting new challenges and opportunities, even the old, monolithic gangs are going 'post-modern', and instead becoming loose networks of semi-autonomous criminal entrepreneurs.

The Future Threat

This collection of articles does not pretend to offer complete coverage on this dynamic global underworld—how could it? Nor on the whole does it adopt the thematic approach that has been used elsewhere to great effect, studying particular commodities or activities (although it does conclude with Tamara Makarenko's sobering assessment of the convergence between crime and terrorism and Peter Grabosky's study of the rise of cybercrime and how it challenges existing concepts of law enforcement). Instead, it concentrates on the main organisations and criminal phenomena, the players, movers and shakers of this new world.

It is clear that organised crime is going through a period of rapid and dramatic change. Globalisation is reshaping the underworld, just as a combination of evolving law-enforcement strategies and technological and social change is breaking down the old forms of organised crime (monolithic and identified by physical 'turf' or ethnic identity), and creating new, flexible networks of criminal entrepreneurs. As Jay Albanese's chapter shows, the decline of the traditional Cosa Nostra in the United States does not, after all, mean an end to organised crime, just the rise of new players. A recurring theme of this book is the way that even the old aristocrats of crime, the Mafia, Triads and Yakuza, are experiencing this process, not so much of disintegration as of decentralisation. Meanwhile, as my own chapter and that by Kelly Hignett demonstrate, 'new bloods' such as the Russian and East European gangs have from the first operated in flexible, entrepreneurial, transnational structures, products as they are of this new era. Bruce Bagley's study of the situation in Latin America underlines the extent to which the underworld of the twenty-first century will therefore be transnational, dynamic, fragmentary, networked and inclusive, requiring law-makers and -enforcers alike to adapt their thinking to keep up.

The political dimension is often crucial, something Letizia Paoli's study of Italian gangs and Peter Hill's analysis of the Yakuza both make very clear. The US government has formally recognised drug smuggling as a national security threat, and however limited its successes, Moscow has also highlighted crime as a challenge in successive security doctrines (although Bertil Lintner's analysis of Chinese crime suggests that Beijing still has some way to go before seriously addressing the problem on a systemic level). Intelligence agencies are not only being deployed against transnational and organised crime, but are developing their own specialists in this field.

Of course, the malign flip-side of this welcome new awareness is the apparent blurring of the boundaries between crime, espionage and statecraft. This is not unprecedented as criminals have often been useful tools for espionage agencies, but involvement with crime becomes not just a short-term expedient but a basic policy. North Korea, for example, is an increasingly important source of narcotics, and hence Raphael Perl's case study is a useful indication of the threat. To an extent this reflects the activities of corrupt 'untouchables' and also desperate and impoverished military and security officers. Yet beyond the criminalisation of North Korean elites, this appears to be turning into a criminalisation of state policy, as drug trafficking becomes embraced as a means of bringing new revenue into this destitute state and developing new intelligence-gathering routes and contacts.

So while it is encouraging that there is a growing global awareness that crime—and transnational and serious crime in particular—is a national security issue, much still needs to be done. Old structures, certainties, feuds and alliances are all coming into question, and the global underworld is changing at an ever-faster rate. To understand these processes is a challenge which requires even greater communication of ideas and insight across the traditional barriers between academic, law enforcement, intelligence and defence communities, and a variety of fora—including *Global Crime*—can help in this vital process.

Notes

[1] For the best and most recent analysis of the problem, see the UN Office on Drugs and Crime, *Global Illicit Drug Trends 2003*.
[2] UNODC *Press Release* 30 October 1997, available at: http://www.unodc.org/unodc/en/ press_release_1997-10-30_1.html
[3] Sterling, *Crime Without Frontiers*.
[4] For a discussion of the interaction between organised crime and legal states and markets, see Galeotti, 'Underworld and upperworld: organised crime and global society'.
[5] See US State Department, *Trafficking in Persons Report 2004*.
[6] This section draws on and develops ideas I developed originally in 'The new world of transnational crime' in *Jane's Intelligence Review*, September 2000.
[7] *The Journal of Commerce*, 7 November 1997.

References

Galeotti, M. (2000) 'The new world of transnational crime', *Jane's Intelligence Review*, September.
Galeotti, M. (2001) 'Underworld and upperworld: organised crime and global society', in *Non-State Actors in World Politics*, eds D. Josselin & W. Wallace, Macmillan.
The Journal of Commerce, 7 November 1997.
Sterling, C. (1994) *Crime Without Frontiers* (Little, Brown).
UN Office on Drugs and Crime, *Global Illicit Drug Trends 2003*.
UNODC *Press Release* 30 October 1997, available at: http://www.unodc.org/unodc/en/ press_release_1997-10-30_1.html
US State Department, *Trafficking in Persons Report 2004*, available at http://www.state.gov/g/tip/rls/ tiprpt/2004/

North American Organised Crime

Jay S. Albanese

The Italian–American mafia is one of the most enduring images of organised crime—and the image often does not distinguish fact from fiction. Consider that the best-selling book about crime in US history is *The Godfather*, a novel, and the movie version is still one of the top grossing films of all time. Likewise, an HBO television program begun in the late 1990s, *The Sopranos*, offered another extremely popular depiction of the life of a mafia family. The show spawned a market for video and DVD versions of old episodes, and a 'Sopranos Tour' that takes tourists to cemeteries, docks, and stores featured in the series. A sporting goods store, *Ramsey Outdoor*, was forced into bankruptcy in an episode of the television show, but the real sporting goods store of that name never went out of business. Nonetheless, its business dropped off

Professor Jay Albanese is Professor of Government & Public Affairs at Virginia Commonwealth University, currently seconded to the National Institute of Justice as head of its International Centre dramatically after the *Sopranos* episode, because viewers apparently believed the television portrayal to be real. The store had to advertise to remind customers that it was still open and that *The Sopranos* was just a TV show[1]. In a similar way, James Gandolfini, one of the featured actors on the show, reported that people claiming to be mobsters occasionally approach him. He said, 'I'd like to think that the smarter mobsters are the ones who don't come up to TV actors'[2].

A Definition of Organised Crime

Separating fictional images of organised crime from the real thing has not been easy. An analysis by criminologist Frank Hagan elicited common elements of the various descriptions of organised crime groups by researchers over time. After discovering that many books failed to provide explicit definitions of organised crime, he found that definitions had been offered by 13 different authors in books and government reports about organised crime written during the previous 15 years[3]. I have updated Hagan's analysis with authors who have attempted to define organised crime in more recent work[4].

Eleven different aspects of organised crime have been included in the definitions of various authors with varying levels of frequency. Table 1 summarises these 11 attributes and how many authors have included them in their definition. As Table 1 indicates, there is great consensus in the literature that organised crime functions as a continuing enterprise that rationally works to make a profit through illicit activities, and that it insures its existence through the use of threats or force and through corruption of public officials to maintain a degree of immunity from law enforcement. There also appears to be some consensus that organised crime tends to be restricted to those illegal goods and services that are in great public demand through monopoly control of an illicit market.

There is considerably less consensus, as Table 1 illustrates, that organised crime has exclusive membership, has ideological or political reasons behind its activities, requires specialisation in planning or carrying out specific activities, or operates

Table 1 Definitions of Organised Crime in the Research Literature

Characteristics	Number of Authors
Organised Hierarchy Continuing	16
Rational Profit through Crime	13
Use of Force or Threat	12
Corruption to Maintain Immunity	11
Public Demand for Services	7
Monopoly over Particular Market	6
Restricted Membership	4
Non-Ideological	4
Specialisation	3
Code of Secrecy	3
Extensive Planning	2

under a code of secrecy. As a result, it appears that a definition of organised crime, based on a consensus of writers over the course of the last 35 years, reads as follows: 'Organised crime is a continuing criminal enterprise that rationally works to profit from illicit activities that are often in great public demand. Its continuing existence is maintained through the use of force, threats, monopoly control, and/or the corruption of public officials.'

Describing Organised Crime in North America

Organised crime can be described either by the activities it engages in or by the groups that are involved. There are advantages and disadvantages to each approach. The offences are finite in any given historical period, and they always involve some variation of provision of illicit goods (e.g. stolen property, drugs), provision of illicit services (e.g. prostitution, gambling, loansharking), and/or the infiltration of business (e.g. extortion and protection rackets). This typology is depicted in Table 2. The essential difference between the major categories of organised crime activity lies in whether or not the activity is consensual or non-consensual, which determines whether or not violence or threats are essential to the crimes, as shown in Table 2.

What changes by region are the kinds of groups that engage in these activities. The history of criminality in a region, its economic standing, geographic location, national and ethnic customs and beliefs, and political climate are all important factors in shaping the kinds of organised criminal groups that develop in a country or region[5].

North American History of Organised Crime

North America includes the countries of Canada, the United States, and Mexico—all geographically large countries with long land borders on the north and south, and massive coastlines providing access to both the Atlantic and Pacific Oceans. Therefore, the countries of North America are accessible to each other by land and also from many locations around the world into multiple cities and border crossings by sea and air. Mexico is strategically positioned, linking South and Central America to the United States. The long Mexican land and water borders make a desirable

Table 2 A Typology of Organised Crime

Type of Activity	Nature of Activity	Harm
Provision of illicit goods and services	Gambling, lending, sex, narcotics, stolen property	Consensual activities No inherent violence Economic harm
Infiltration of legitimate business	Coercive use of legal businesses for purposes of exploitation	Non-consensual activities Threats, violence, extortion Economic harm

launching point for smuggling people and products to the United States and Canada, which have large consumer populations that enjoy a high standard of living and income. As a result, North America's geographic location, land and water border access, links to Central and South America, and high standard of living combine to form a desirable location for organised crime activity.

Organised crime in North America has always been comprised of a variety of groups, both large and small, that emerged to exploit particular criminal opportunities. If the terminology had been in use 200 years ago, early European settlers in North America might have been accused of involvement in organised crime activity for avoiding European taxes, engaging in planned thefts from trains and stagecoaches, and bribing government officials to secure favours. Organised crime, therefore, is characterised by planned illegal acts involving multiple offenders that are ongoing or recurrent, rather than isolated incidents.

Organised Crime in the United States

Public and government attention to organised crime in the US have been dominated by the Italian-American groups since the late 1800s. This attention corresponded to a large immigration wave from Italy during the late nineteenth century, and Italians were blamed for the crime problem a century ago in the US, in much the same way as the newest immigrants are blamed today in many countries for a variety of social and criminal problems. This phenomenon is called the ethnicity trap, in which organised crime is explained in terms of the ethnicity of its members, rather than by the organised criminal conduct itself. This narrow view leads to unwarranted stereotypes of ethnic groups, ignores the fact that organised crime is committed by groups of many different ethnicities, and that the public demand for illicit goods and services drives most organised crime activity regardless of time and place—accounting for the rich variety of groups and conspiracies involved in organised crime over the course of history. Thus, ethnicity does not help explain the presence or absence of organised crime.

A small number of significant events served to reinforce the connection between 'mafia' and organised crime in the United States. In 1890, the police chief of the City of New Orleans was shot, and he implicated Italians in his shooting. No evidence was produced, however, and the Italian immigrants arrested for the shooting were acquitted. A group of citizens stormed the jail, and publicly hanged many of the Italian defendants, illustrating the intense hatred and blame placed on the US's newest immigrants at that time. It was widely believed then that the US somehow imported a mafia from Italy and that many immigrants were criminals.

After the Hennessey incident, however, the term 'mafia' dropped from public view. The term rarely appears again in American newspapers until after World War II. During the 'gangster era' of the early 1900s, which featured such notable figures as Lucky Luciano and Al Capone, the term 'mafia' was not used. These notorious figures, and their contemporaries, were considered city-based gangsters, but the connections among them were not a major concern. America's prohibition of alcoholic beverages during this period was the single most important event during the early 1900s to cause organised crime groups to become more organised and competitive to meet the demand for illegal liquor, despite the legal prohibition. Prohibition combined with the lack of professionalised law enforcement to result in large criminal smuggling and distribution enterprises that were protected by corrupt police and public officials[6].

The concept of mafia returned to the headlines for good with separate events in 1950, 1957, and 1963. In 1950, US Senator Estes Kefauver held televised hearings (at a time when there were only three TV channels to choose from) claiming that organised crime was nationally organised. Although he conducted no actual investigation, and no proof of his claims was offered, the hearings raised public and political awareness of possible connections among local organised crime groups in cities around the United States [7]. In 1957, a group of Italian-Americans were arrested in rural upstate New York in an alleged meeting to discuss leadership after the assassination of Albert Anastasia. Once again, no evidence was produced that such a meeting took place or was even planned, but the possibility resulted in headlines around the US about a 'meeting of the mob', leading to speculation about a mafia organisation [8]. Finally, in 1963, Joseph Valachi became the first 'insider' to testify publicly about the existence of a national conspiracy of organised crime groups. He called it 'Cosa Nostra', a term that police officials at the time admitted they had not heard before. A President's Commission report a few years later concluded that the organisation had changed its name from 'mafia' to 'Cosa Nostra' (an idea since discounted) but whatever the name, Valachi's testimony identified the now familiar family hierarchy of 'bosses', 'underbosses', soldiers', and so forth. A close reading of Valachi's testimony reveals that the 'Cosa Nostra' was not as centralised as later accounts claimed [9]. Essentially, organised crime groups were local in nature, activities were chosen at the local level, and members benefited from their association/reputation with the larger group, and had to pay a percentage of their profits to leaders for permission to operate their illegal enterprises unchallenged. This system remains intact today, although on a smaller scale.

After Valachi's testimony, and its subsequent repetition in national government reports, new laws were passed that permitted the use of wiretap evidence in court against suspects, created a new crime called 'racketeering' which subjected those found to engage in a pattern of criminal activity to prison terms of up to 20 years, and developed witness immunity for testifying, the witness security program, and related tools to make it easier to investigate and prosecute those involved in organised crime activity.

These new legal tools were not widely used until the 1980s and 1990s, when the political will developed to engage in long-term investigations and to seek prosecution of major organised leaders, rather than larger numbers of arrests of lower-level figures. The result of these investigations were the 'mob trials' of the 1980s and 1990s, and became the most significant organised crime prosecution effort in US history. The leaders of many of the more than 20 Italian–American Cosa Nostra groups were successfully prosecuted, and most received significant prison terms [10]. The result has been a decline in the influence of Italian–American organised crime in the US over the last 20 years.

This decline of mafia groups has been offset by the many political, social, and economic changes that occurred worldwide beginning in the 1990s. Migration related to the fall of the Soviet Union, ease of travel and communication, combined with the decline of traditional mafia groups to create new opportunities for organised crime activity. Organised crime in the United States today is a multi-ethnic enterprise, comprised of many different groups, most of them quite small, which emerge to exploit criminal opportunities (e.g. frauds, smuggling, stolen property distribution, and so on). Many of these groups are short-lived, comprised of career criminals who form temporary networks of individuals with desired skills (e.g. forgery, smuggling connections, border and bribery connections, etc.) to exploit a criminal opportunity. These networks often dissolve after the opportunity has been exploited, as the criminals seek new opportunities that may employ different combinations of criminals. For example, an inquiry by the New Jersey State Commission of Investigation found that Cosa Nostra groups have been joined, and in some cases replaced, by 'a chaotic, violent array of ethnic and transnational criminal entities that function under new and different rules.' [11]. Law enforcement officials testify that underworld activities such as gambling, loansharking, and labour racketeering were being supplemented by financial frauds, identity theft, and global money-laundering operations. As a result, organised crime in the US is now the province of more groups than ever before working from both within and outside the US to exploit new criminal opportunities.

Canadian Organised Crime

The primary organised crime groups in Canada are of four types: Asian groups, East European groups, Italian groups, and outlaw motorcycle gangs. Like the United States and Mexico, Canada is a large country, so there is tremendous variation within its borders—from a number of very large metropolitan areas to expanses of rural areas that are hundred of miles across.

Asian organised crime groups have been identified in British Columbia, Ontario, and Quebec, the provinces that contain Canada's largest cities: Vancouver, Toronto, and Montreal. Some of the Asian groups are actually street gangs that engage in drug trafficking or perform criminal activities for more sophisticated organised crime groups. Asian groups on Canada's west coast have been found to be involved in trafficking drugs, firearms, and human beings. The primary drugs trafficked are heroin, cocaine, and ecstasy. Most major heroin seizures involve Asian-based crime groups [12]. Some of these drugs have been subsequently smuggled into the United States by individuals of Chinese descent. Vietnamese-based groups have been found to be extensively involved in large-scale cultivation of marijuana across Canada. In one operation, organised crime members of Chinese descent bought marijuana from Vietnamese-based drug trafficking gangs to transport in the United States [13].

Since a high profile case in 1999 involving four ships and 600 illegal Chinese migrants attempting to enter Canada, there have not been any large-scale human smuggling attempts into Canada by boat. Instead, commercial airplanes are the transport of choice. In one case, two Canadian citizens of Chinese descent were caught trying to smuggle four Chinese nationals across the Niagara River into the US. The Chinese nationals had arrived in Canada via Vancouver airport [14].

Motorcycle gangs continue to be a problem in Canada. In 2003, nine members of the Hell's Angels motorcycle gang were sentenced to prison terms of 10 to 15 years for drug trafficking and conspiracy to commit murder. Four of those sentenced were part of the Nomads branch of the gang. The charges stem from a violent turf war during the 1990s over the control of Quebec's illegal drug market [15].

Like the US, and a growing number of other countries, Canada has established a specialised agency to track financial transactions to uncover money-laundering activities that are designed to cover up the source of illicit income [16]. The immense size of this task is illustrated by the fact that Canada produced an average of 5,700 financial transactions per day during the year 2002–03.

Mexican Organised Crime

The US–Mexican border is crossed illegally by thousands of Mexican nationals going north in search of work. Most are people looking for legitimate opportunities to better themselves and their families, but some are criminals. The major organised crime groups in Mexico are centrally organised, although they operate as competing networks in the illicit drug business from supply, to transit, to destination and buyers. These extended networks are composed of Mexican nationals living in Mexico, Mexican–Americans, and Mexican immigrants living in the United States. They operate primarily in ethnic enclaves in major cities, including Chicago, New York, Los Angeles, and Houston.

There is evidence that Mexican groups cooperate with Colombian, Dominican, Cosa Nostra groups, and others involved in trafficking illegal narcotics. The primary consumers are in the United States and, to a lesser extent, in Canada. Money earned from this activity has been traced to money-laundering enterprises in the Caribbean and several Latin American countries.

Another significant organised crime activity in Mexico is kidnapping for ransom. There have been a number of cases where corporate executives, government officials, and tourists have been kidnapped, and in some cases killed. In most cases it appears that the kidnapping/extortion activity is used as a fund-raising mechanism to support ongoing criminal group activity. According to one estimate Mexico is second only to Colombia in the incidence of kidnappings for ransom [17]. Related to kidnapping is the role of Mexico in the trafficking of human beings from Asia, through Mexico, into the United States. Groups in Mexico, some consisting of non-Mexicans, have been identified in transporting men, women, and children from China and other Asian countries into the US for purposes of prostitution and sweatshop labour [18].

A weak economy has combined with a weak government and weak police presence to create widespread corruption, which has served to insulate organised crime groups from greater disruption. In early 2003, the Mexican Drug Task Force was closed by the President due to allegations of rampant corruption among its officers [19]. Corruption has hampered international efforts to assist Mexico in improving its law-enforcement response to organised crime. Nevertheless, progress has been made in recent years, and Mexican Federal Police killed drug trafficker Ramon Arellano Felix and arrested his brother in 2002. Other important Mexican and joint-US enforcement efforts also have been undertaken [20]. The long-term impact of this and other attempts to thwart Mexican organised crime remains to be seen.

Future of Organised Crime

Organised crime in North America is shaped by the presence of three geographically large countries that share very long land borders, as well as extensive ocean borders along the Atlantic and Pacific Oceans. Therefore, there is great variation within each country of North America, and their land and water access promotes them as routes for trafficking illicit goods and services, and human smuggling.

Organised crime historically has been strongly influenced by the presence of Cosa Nostra groups. Many successful prosecutions of these groups in the late twentieth century corresponded with global political changes around the world that included the fall of the Soviet Union, the emergence of the newly independent states of Eastern Europe, and a growing ease of international travel and communication all over the world.

What might have been localised organised crime problems 100 years ago, have become manifestations of transnational organised crime as criminal groups from Eastern Europe and Asia have found North America to be a desirable market for the provision of illicit goods and services that support organised crime enterprise. Criminal groups within North America also have exploited new opportunities for crime. The growing recognition of the size and importance of organised crime operations emanating from a variety of foreign countries distinguishes concern about organised crime today from the more local concerns about Cosa Nostra groups and other city gangs in years past. For example, an indictment in the US in 2003 describes a sophisticated heroin-trafficking enterprise that linked conspirators in Pakistan, Thailand, Canada, California, and the Washington, DC area of the US. The indictment charged that heroin was shipped into the US and Canada via London from Pakistan and Thailand in a crate of soccer balls and other athletic equipment. Payments for the shipments were made through an underground paperless banking system, known as 'hawala'. In this system money is deposited in one country with a trusted broker and withdrawn the same day from a broker in another country. The system keeps no records and relies upon mutual trust [21]. The transnational nature of this scheme and the manner in which it overlaps legitimate and illicit businesses and launders profits illustrates the growing complexity and transnational nature of organised crime today.

Traditional crimes associated with organised crime include illegal gambling, prostitution, loansharking, drug trafficking, selling stolen property, and extorting money from business owners, but this list is expanding with changes in the global economy, technology, and communications. For example, there are an estimated 1,800 internet gambling sites worldwide that generate a total of $4.2 billion. These sites permit betting from jurisdictions where various types of gambling are not legal, and they provide a forum for money laundering and fraud [22]. Arrests made outside New York City found that a modest home was used to produce 10,000 bootlegged CDs each week and that the owners were connected to known organised crime groups who allegedly helped in the illegal distribution of these CD copies [23]. In another case, the head of a Boston real-estate firm was sentenced to jail for laundering the criminal proceeds of organised crime figure Stephen 'The Rifleman' Flemmi by investing his criminal proceeds in a commercial condominium at the corner of Massachusetts and Commonwealth Avenues in Boston [24]. Therefore, the types of offences associated with organised crime change as opportunities and circumstances change, and they frequently use legitimate businesses to operate their illegal enterprises. It can be said that easy access to the internet and ease of international air travel are as important to the expansion of human trafficking and fraud, as was the invention of the automobile 100 years ago in creating new opportunities for smuggling goods by land across jurisdictions and various types of registration and ownership frauds.

Table 3 illustrates how organised crime has changed in recent years with the advent of globalisation, and ease of communication and travel. Historically, organised crime has been dominated by locally-based activities, whereas now the same underlying activities have increased in scale and in difficulty of detection due to improvements in technology and communication. Intervention and prevention efforts much keep pace in order to limit the opportunities for organised crime groups to form and be successful.

It remains to be seen whether North America can reduce its high demand for illicit products and services, secure its borders from outsiders interested in exploiting the region, and prosecute those individuals and organised crime groups already inside North America. The long-term solution to organised crime is a reduction in demand for

Table 3 The Correspondence between Traditional Organised Crime Activity and Newer Manifestations

Original Activity	Modern Version
Local number gambling	Internet gambling (at international websites)
Heroin, cocaine trafficking	Synthetic drugs (e.g. methamphetamine and Ecstasy—less vulnerable to interruption of supply)
Street prostitution	Internet-based prostitution and trafficking in human beings
Extortion of local businesses for 'protection'	Extortion of larger businesses, corporations, and kidnapping of executives
Loansharking (usury)	Money laundering in cash, precious stones, commodities
Fencing stolen property	Theft of intellectual property, forgery of CDs, software, DVDs

the products and services that fund it, but in the short term, greater efforts in detection and prosecution will be necessary to disrupt more effectively both foreign and North American organised crime groups.

Notes

[1] Sloan, 'Bada Bing's the Real Thing on Sopranos Tour'; 'Neighborhood Report: Little Italy; Looking for Wiseguys in the Land of Checked Tablecloths,' *The New York Times*, 1 December.

[2] 'Family Matters,' *USA Today*, 21 January 2000, p. 4E.

[3] Hagan, 'The Organised Crime Continuum: A Further Specification of a New Conceptual Model'.

[4] Lyman & Potter, *Organised Crime*; Abadinsky, *Organised Crime*; Maltz, 'On Defining Organised Crime'.

[5] Albanese et al. (eds), *Organised Crime: World Perspectives*.

[6] Albanese, *Organised Crime in Our Times*.

[7] Moore, *The Kefauver Committee and the Politics of Crime, 1950–1952*.

[8] New York State Temporary Commission of Investigation, *The Appalachian Meeting*; *US v. Buffalino et al.*

[9] Maas, *The Valachi Papers*; US Senate Committee on Government Operations Permanent Subcommittee on Investigations, *Organised Crime and Illicit Traffic in Narcotics*.

[10] For a summary of the major mob cases of the 1980s and 1990s, see Albanese, *Organised Crime in Our Times*; Jacobs et al., *Gotham Unbound: How New York City was Liberated from the Grip of Organised Crime*; Cowan & Century, *Takedown: The Fall of the Last Mafia Empire*.

[11] Della Santo, 'SCI Says "Nontraditional" Gangs Enter New Jersey Organised Crime'.

[12] Criminal Intelligence Service Canada, *Annual Report on Organised Crime in Canada 2002*.

[13] Organised Crime Agency of British Columbia, *Annual Report 2001*.

[14] 'Immigrant Smugglers Caught in Broad Daylight,' *Edmonton Journal*, 6 May 2002.

[15] 'Hell's Angels Convictions,' *Associated Press*, 25 September 2003.

[16] Financial Transactions and Reports Analysis Centre of Canada, *FINTRAC Annual Report 2003*.

[17] 'Mexico is Run by Organised Crime,' *Agence France Presse*, 1 August 2003.

[18] Zhang & Chin, 'Entering the Dragon: Inside Chinese Human Smuggling Organisations'.

[19] Sandoval, 'Mexican Drug Agency Closed; Agents Suspected of Corruption'; Moloeznik, 'The Challenges to Mexico in Times of Political Change'; Zamora Jimenez, 'Criminal Justice and the Law in Mexico'.

[20] Sandoval, 'Drug Operation between US, Mexico Leads to 176 Arrests This Week'; Weissert, 'Mexico's New No. 1 Drug Kingpin Rose by Eliminating Rivals'.

[21] Gibson, 'Arrests Break International Heroin Ring'.

[22] Malcolm, 'Testimony: Internet Gambling'.

[23] Holloway, 'Arrests Illustrate a Growing Concern over Bootlegged Recordings'.

[24] 'Boston Realtor Sentenced for Laundering Money for Convicted Organised Crime Leader Stephen Flemmi,' *PR Newswire*, 20 December 2002.

References

Abadinsky, H. (1997) *Organised Crime*, 5th edn, Nelson-Hall.

Albanese, J., Das, D. & Verma, A. (eds) (2003) *Organised Crime: World Perspectives*, Prentice Hall.

Albanese, J. (2004) *Organised Crime in Our Times*, Lexis Nexis Anderson.

Cowan, R. & Century, D. (2003) *Takedown: The Fall of the Last Mafia Empire*, G. P. Putnam & Son.

Criminal Intelligence Service Canada, *Annual Report on Organised Crime in Canada 2002* www.cisc.gc.ca (2003).

Crow, K. (2002) 'Neighborhood Report: Little Italy; Looking for Wiseguys in the Land of Checked Tablecloths', *The New York Times*, 1 December.

Della Santo, A. (2003) 'SCI Says "Nontraditional" Gangs Enter New Jersey Organised Crime', *Associated Press*, 29 April.

Gibson, G. (2003) 'Arrests Break International Heroin Ring', *The Baltimore Sun*, 16 September.

'Family Matters,' *USA Today*, 21 January 2000, p. 4E.

Financial Transactions and Reports Analysis Centre of Canada, *FINTRAC Annual Report 2003*, http://www.fintrac.gc.ca/publications/anualreport/2003/menu_e.asp

Hagan, Frank E. (1983) 'The Organised Crime Continuum: A Further Specification of a New Conceptual Model', *Criminal Justice Review*, vol. 8, pp. 52–57.

Holloway, L. (2002) 'Arrests Illustrate a Growing Concern over Bootlegged Recordings', *The New York Times*, pp. C10, 2 December.

Jacobs, J. B., Friel, C. & Radick, R. (1999) *Gotham Unbound: How New York City was Liberated from the Grip of Organised Crime*, New York University Press.

Lyman, M. D. & Potter, G. W. (2000) *Organised Crime*, 2nd edn, Prentice Hall.

Maas, P. (1969) *The Valachi Papers*, Bantam.

Malcolm, J. (2003) 'Testimony: Internet Gambling', in: *US House Judiciary Committee Subcommittee on Crime, Terrorism, and Homeland Security*, 28 April.

Maltz, M. (1985) 'On Defining Organised Crime', in *The Politics and Economics of Organised Crime*, eds H. Alexander & G. Caiden, Lexington Books.

Moloeznik, M. P. (2003) 'The Challenges to Mexico in Times of Political Change', *Crime, Law and Social Change*, vol. 40 (July).

Moore, W. H. (1974) *The Kefauver Committee and the Politics of Crime, 1950–1952*, University of Missouri Press.

New York State Temporary Commission of Investigation, *The Appalachian Meeting* (State Investigations Commission, 1963), 20.

Organised Crime Agency of British Columbia, *Annual Report 2001*. www.ocabc.ca (2003).

Sandoval, R. (2003) 'Mexican Drug Agency Closed; Agents Suspected of Corruption', *Dallas Morning News*, 18 January.

Sandoval, R. (2003) 'Drug Operation between US, Mexico Leads to 176 Arrests This Week', *Dallas Morning News*, 1 August.

Sloan, G. (2001) 'Bada Bing's the Real Thing on Sopranos Tour', *USA Today*, 26 April.

US v. Buffalino et al., 285 F.2d 408 (2nd Cir. 1960).

US Senate Committee on Government Operations Permanent Subcommittee on Investigations (1963) *Organised Crime and Illicit Traffic in Narcotics: Hearings Part I 88th Congress, 1st session* (US Government Printing Office).

Weissert, W. (2003) 'Mexico's New No. 1 Drug Kingpin Rose by Eliminating Rivals', *Associated Press Worldstream*, 25 October.

Zamora Jimenez, A. (2003) 'Criminal Justice and the Law in Mexico', *Crime, Law and Social Change*, vol. 40 (July).

Zhang, S. & Chin, K. (2002) 'Entering the Dragon: Inside Chinese Human Smuggling Organisations', *Criminology*, vol. 40 (November).

Italian Organised Crime: Mafia Associations and Criminal Enterprises

Letizia Paoli

For almost a century the Italian mafia has been regarded—in the United States and elsewhere—as the prototype of organised crime. In Italy itself, however, the identification between mafia and organised crime was frequently questioned and even denied right up until the mid-1980s. For the social scientists carrying out the first field studies in Sicily between the 1960s and the early 1980s, for example, the mafia was simply a form of behaviour and power. That is, they asserted, there were *mafiosi*, single individuals, who embodied determined sub-cultural values and exercised specific functions within their communities, but no mafia organisation existed as such [1]. As late as 1983, Pino Arlacchi's successful book, *La mafia imprenditrice* (*Mafia Business*), opened with the following statement: 'Social research into the question of the mafia has probably now reached the point where we can say that the mafia, as the term is commonly understood, does not exist' [2].

Contrary to what most scholars maintained up to the mid-1980s, judicial inquiries carried out since then have proved that formalised mafia groups do exist. Cosa Nostra in Sicily and the 'Ndrangheta in Calabria are the largest and most stable coalitions and are each composed of about a hundred mafia groups or 'families', as they are called by their members. These are estimated at about three thousand and five thousand males respectively [3].

The first section of this chapter analyses the two above-mentioned mafia consortia, focusing on their internal organisation and culture and singling out their peculiarities vis-à-vis other forms of organised crime. The second section reviews other groups and networks that are—with varying degrees of justification—also routinely described as organised crime. Some final remarks about the future trends of Italian organised crime(s) will follow.

The Organised Crime Core: The Sicilian Cosa Nostra and the Calabrian 'Ndrangheta

At the turn of the twenty-first century, there are more than five hundred witnesses who can confirm the existence of either the Cosa Nostra or the 'Ndrangheta, because they themselves were members. Though it is not possible to establish clear lines of continuity, recent historical research has demonstrated that antecedents of the contemporary mafia associations existed in the 1880s, if not before. The discovery of new documents in archives and a more objective analysis of the already known papers have demonstrated the presence of mafia groups in Sicily and Calabria since the mid-nineteenth century. As the historian Paolo Pezzino puts it, 'if it is true that these sources have to be examined with great prudence, it is also true that the statements on the existence of well structured associations are so many, and finding confirmation in several judicial proceedings, that it would be difficult to deny their reliability' [4].

Secret Brotherhoods

Cosa Nostra and the 'Ndrangheta possess the distinguishing trait of organisations: independent government bodies that regulate the internal life of each associated family and that are clearly different from the authority structure of their members' biological families. Starting from the 1950s, moreover, superordinate bodies of co-ordination were set up—first in the Cosa Nostra, then in the 'Ndrangheta as well. Composed of the most important family chiefs, they are known as 'commissions' [5]. Although the powers of these collegial bodies are rather limited, the unity of the two confederations cannot be doubted. In fact, it is guaranteed by the sharing of common cultural codes and a single organisational formula. According to a model very frequent in pre-modern societies, in fact, the Cosa Nostra and the 'Ndrangheta are 'segmentary societies' [6]: that is, they depend on what Emile Durkheim called 'mechanical solidarity' [7], which derives from the replication of corporate and cultural forms.

Neither Cosa Nostra nor the 'Ndrangheta can be compared to Max Weber's ideal type of legal-rational bureaucracy, as was suggested by Donald Cressey in the late 1960s with reference to the American La Cosa Nostra [8]. Far from recruiting their staff and organising the latter's work according to the criteria and procedures of modern bureaucracies, mafia groups impose a veritable 'status contract' on their members [9]. With the ritual initiation into a mafia *cosca* (group), the novice is required to assume a new identity permanently—to become a 'man of honour'—and to subordinate all his previous allegiances to the mafia membership. If necessary, he must be ready to sacrifice even his life for the mafia family.

The 'men of honour' in Sicily and Calabria are obliged to keep secret the composition, the action, and the strategies of their mafia group. In Cosa Nostra, in particular, the duty of silence is absolute. Secrecy constitutes, above all, a defence strategy. Since the unification of Italy in 1861, mafia groups have been at least formally criminalised by the state and, in order to protect themselves from arrest and criminal prosecution for their continuing recourse to violence, they have needed to resort to various degrees of secrecy.

The ceremony of affiliation additionally creates ritual ties of brotherhood among the members of a mafia family: the 'status contract' is simultaneously an act of fraternisation [10]. The new recruits become 'brothers' to all members and share what anthropologists call a regime of generalised reciprocity [11]: this presupposes altruistic behaviour without expecting any short-term reward. As F. Lestingi, chief prosecutor for the king, pointed out in 1884, mafia groups constitute brotherhoods whose 'essential character' lies in 'mutual aid without limits and without measure, and even in crimes.' [12] Only thanks to the trust and solidarity created by fraternisation contracts does it become possible to achieve specific goals and thus satisfy the instrumental needs of the single members.

As secret brotherhoods using violence, Southern Italian mafia associations have remarkable similarities to associations such as the Chinese Triads and the Japanese Yakuza [13]. With their centuries-old histories, articulated structures, and sophisticated ritual and symbolic apparatuses, all these associations—and the American descendant of the Sicilian Cosa Nostra [14]—have few parallels in the world of organised crime. None of the other groups that systematically traffic in illegal commodities have the same degree of complexity and longevity [15].

The Will to Power

Cosa Nostra and the 'Ndrangheta share another important peculiarity with the Chinese Triads and the Japanese Yakuza. Unlike other contemporary organised crime groups, they do not content themselves with producing and selling illegal goods and services. Though these activities have acquired an increasing relevance over the past 30 years, neither the trade in illegal commodities nor the maximisation of profits has ever been the primary goal of these associations. As a matter of fact, it is hardly possible to single out an encompassing function or goal that characterises the mafia phenomenon, as has been suggested by the supporters of the 'economistic' paradigm [16], and more recently by Diego Gambetta [17], according to whom the mafia is 'an industry of private protection'. Southern Italian mafia coalitions are multifunctional organisations. In the past hundred years, their members have exploited the strength of mafia bonds to pursue various endeavours and to accomplish the most disparate tasks. As early as 1876 the Tuscan aristocrat Leopoldo Franchetti pointed out the 'extraordinary elasticity' of the associations of *malfattori* (evildoers): 'the goals multiply, the field of action widens, without the need to multiply the statutes; the association divides for certain goals, remains united for others' [18].

Within this wide range of functions, there is one that usually has been neglected by late-twentieth-century observers: the exercise of a political dominion. The ruling bodies of Cosa Nostra and the 'Ndrangheta claim, above all, an absolute power over their members. They control every aspect of their members' lives, and they aim to exercise a similar power over the communities where their members reside. For a long time, their power had a higher degree of effectiveness and legitimacy than that exercised by the state. In Western Sicily and in Southern Calabria mafia associations successfully policed the general population, settling conflicts, recovering stolen goods, and enforcing property rights. Even today, although most mafia rules are no longer systematically enforced, mafia families exercise a certain 'sovereignty' through a generalised system of extortion. As a state would do, they tax the main productive activities carried out within their territory, which usually corresponds to a village or town, or to a neighbourhood in larger cities. Cosa Nostra and 'Ndrangheta members have not only enjoyed high-level political connections up to the present, but the Italian state and the mafia long shared power in considerable parts of Sicily and Calabria and the power of mafia groups was accepted and even legalised by government representatives [19].

In the second half of the twentieth century, Southern Italy's mafia associations participated in at least three plots organised by right-wing terrorist groups; since the late 1970s Cosa Nostra has assassinated dozens of policemen, magistrates, and politicians. The mafia challenge to state power reached a climax in the early 1990s. In 1992, Cosa Nostra murdered the Palermitan Judges Giovanni Falcone and Paolo Borsellino in two spectacular bomb explosions. In 1993, in an effort to demonstrate the national power of the mafia, a series of bombings occurred—for the first time out of traditional mafia strongholds—in Rome, Florence, and Milan [20].

Despite their power, mafia fraternities have not been able to guarantee themselves a monopoly in any sector of the illegal economy outside of Southern Italy. In the early 1980s, Cosa Nostra families played a pivotal role in the transcontinental heroin trade from Asia to the United States via Sicily. But in the second half of that decade, the Cosa Nostra lost this position after being targeted by law-enforcement investigations and replaced in the US market by a plethora of Mexican, Chinese, and, more recently, Colombian heroin suppliers [21].

Despite the growing relevance of economic activities, 'the mafia has not become a set of criminal enterprises.' [22] Its history as well as its cultural and normative apparatus prevent this transformation and today constitute a constraint as much as a resource. By building a strong collective identity, shared cultural codes and norms enhance group cohesion and create trustful relationships among mafia members. The reliance on status and fraternisation contracts, which are non-specific and long-term, produces a high degree of flexibility and makes the multifunctionality of mafia groups possible. The same shared cultural codes and norms also represent, however, a powerful brake on entrepreneurial initiative. The prohibition on exploiting prostitution, for example, which exists in both confederations [23], has blocked the entrance of the Sicilian and Calabrian *cosche* into what has become a most profitable illicit trade: the smuggling of humans and the exploitation of migrants in the sex industry or the informal economy.

Especially constraining is one of the preconditions for recruitment: only men born either in Sicily or in Calabria or descending from mafia families can be admitted as members. This rule has long prevented Cosa Nostra and 'Ndrangheta groups from adding new members with the experience necessary to compete in the black markets for arms, money and gold. Rigid recruitment criteria have also hampered the geographical expansion of mafia power. Cosa Nostra, for example, prohibits families settling outside of Sicily. This self-imposed rule, which aims to strengthen the cohesion of the mafia consortium, has limited its involvement in the international narcotics trade—currently the largest of the illegal markets. 'Ndrangheta families, thanks to their extensive branches in Northern Italy and abroad, played a larger role in narcotics trafficking in the 1990s, importing large quantities of cocaine and hashish from Latin America and North Africa; today, however, the 'Ndrangheta faces new competition from foreign and Italian traffickers with more direct connections to drug-producing and transit countries.

The 'will to power' of the mafia associations also negatively affects security and business decisions, as a Palermitan prosecutor pointed out in 1992:

> The true goal is power. The obscure evil of organisation chiefs is not the thirst for money, but the thirst for power. The most important fugitives could enjoy a luxurious life abroad until the end of their days. Instead they remain in Palermo, hunted, in danger of being caught or being killed by internal dissidents, in order to prevent the loss of their territorial control and not run the risk of being deposed. Marino Mannoia [a former mafia member now co-operating with law-enforcement authorities] once told me: 'Many believe that you enter into Cosa Nostra for money. This is only part of the truth. Do you know why I entered Cosa Nostra? Because before in Palermo I was Mr. Nobody. Afterwards, wherever I went, heads lowered. And to me this is priceless' [24]

As a result, ever since the early 1990s Cosa Nostra and 'Ndrangheta families have extracted a growing percentage of their income from entrepreneurial activities that depend on the exercise of regional political domination. They practise systematic extortion in their communities and, thanks to intimidation and collusion with corrupt politicians, they have struggled to control the market for public works [25].

Unlike other Western forms of organised crime, the meaning (and danger) of Sicilian and Calabrian mafia associations cannot be limited to their involvement in illegal markets. Their peculiarity lies in their will to exercise political power and their interest in exercising sovereign control over the people in their communities.

Other Forms of Organised Crime in Italy

In addition to the Sicilian Cosa Nostra and the Calabrian 'Ndrangheta, two other clusters of crime groups are usually referred to as organised crime in Italy: 1) the 'galaxy' of mafia-like and gangster-like groupings in Campania, collectively known as camorra and 2) the multiplicity of criminal groups, gangs and white-collar criminal networks operating in Apulia.

The Camorra

The camorra consists in a variety of independent criminal groups and gangs. Some of them are well-established family businesses that, as much as Sicilian and Calabrian mafia groups, claim to exercise a political dominion over their neighbourhoods and villages and systematically infiltrate local government institutions, at some point enjoying the protection of high-level national politicians as well. Other camorra groups are less lasting formations that have developed around a charismatic chief, usually a successful gangster. Finally, there are also loose gangs of juvenile and/or adult offenders, which—according to police sources—rather belong to the sphere of common crime than to that of organised crime [26].

To strengthen their legitimacy and cohesion, many of the above groups frequently resort to the symbols and rituals of the nineteenth-century camorra. This was an organisation sharing several cultural and organisational similarities with its Sicilian and Calabrian counterparts, though it distinguished itself by its concentration in the city of Naples and its plebeian background. Unlike Cosa Nostra and the 'Ndrangheta, however, the contemporary Campanian underworld does not directly derive from its nineteenth-century forerunner. As Isaia Sales puts it, 'if camorra means a criminal organisation that ruled over Naples' popular and plebeian strata, we can safely say that it started and ended in the nineteenth century' [27].

The Camorra was 'born again' in the 1960s, thanks to the expansion of smuggling in tobacco and later, in drugs. In the 1980s, several camorra groups and short-lasting coalitions of groups (above all, the Nuova Camorra Organizzata and the Nuova Famiglia) then gained great wealth and power with the appropriation of the public money flows invested in Campania after the earthquake of 1980 [28]. Despite their extensive infiltration of the legitimate economy and the public administration, however, contemporary camorra groups have not succeeded in establishing stable co-ordination mechanisms such as those of the nineteenth-century camorra or of the Sicilian and Calabrian mafia associations. As a result, Campania has had the highest rate of murders and violent crime in all of Italy for more than a decade.

The heterogeneity and anarchy of the Campanian underworld are also proved by the great variety of entrepreneurial activities the local crime groups are involved in. The most powerful camorra clans are still able to condition the local legitimate economy, despite the devastating investigations conducted by law enforcement agencies in the 1990s. The smaller groups and gangs engage in all sorts of illegal activities—from extortion to fraud, from drug trafficking and dealing to loansharking, from counterfeiting to the exploitation of prostitution—and are ready to resort to violence whenever they see their 'turf' and activities being threatened [29].

So-called Apulian Organised Crime and Other Groups

The development of Apulian 'organised crime' goes back to the 1970s, when the region became Italy's major import point for smuggled cigarettes and was 'colonised' by neighbouring mafia and camorra groups. In the following years, indigenous crime groups and gangs sprang up in different parts of Apulia. The most successful of these collective actors was long the Sacra Corona Unita ('United Holy Crown'), a consortium of about ten to fifteen criminal groups and gangs from Southern Apulia, which was founded in 1983 [30]. Contrary to the accounts of the media, the Sacra Corona Unita never controlled the whole of Apulian organised crime; despite its imitation of the 'Ndrangheta's structure and rituals, its cohesion and stability have always been much lower. Today, after the defection of some of its leaders and the arrest of most of its members, the Sacra Corona Unita no longer exists as a single viable organisation [31].

Notwithstanding the decline of the Sacra Corona Unita, illegal business activities go on. Up to few years ago tobacco smuggling was the main source of revenue for most Apulian criminal enterprises. Since the early 1990s these have diversified their investments, exploiting their strategic geographical position to smuggle drugs and migrants from the close Balkan countries. In the last few years, as the improved co-operation of Italian and Albanian police forces resulted in an intensified repression of tobacco smuggling, Apulian crime groups have also started to engage in extortion, usury, robberies and counterfeiting, to compensate for their loss of revenues.

The members of Italy's four major domestic crime 'clusters' are the privileged addressees of charges pursuant to Article 416bis of the Italian penal code, that defines the offence of 'membership in a mafia-type delinquent association' (*associazione a delinquere di stampo mafioso*) and represents the most stringent legal translation of the concept of organised crime in the Italian legal system [32].

A few other criminal coalitions and gangs located in Eastern and Southern Sicily and in Northern Calabria, such as the Stidda in the Agrigento and Caltanissetta provinces or the Laudani, Cursoti and Pillera-Cappello in Catania, are also occasionally referred to as organised crime or mafia. Their internal cohesion and political and economic resources are much lower than those of Cosa Nostra or 'Ndrangheta families, though Sicilian groups have from time to time been able to threaten the supremacy of the local Cosa Nostra families due to their larger number of members and their readiness to use violence [33].

The New 'Foreign Mafie' and Inconspicuous Players

The expressions 'organised crime' and '*mafie*' are also increasingly used to refer to foreign criminals operating in Italy. For example, the last bi-annual reports on the activities of the Direzione Investigativa Antimafia, a police body specialising in the fight against organised crime, all contain a chapter devoted to '*criminalità organizzate straniere*' (foreign organised criminalities) [34].

As a matter of fact, Italy has over the past 20 years undergone a process of internationalisation and ethnicisation of its illegal markets. This trend, which started in other Western European countries in the 1950s, took place very rapidly in Italy from the mid-1980s on, when Italy, too, became the destination of considerable migration flows. All over Europe, the internationalisation of illegal markets was strongly accelerated in the 1990s by the European integration process and the abolition of border controls as well as by the radical transformations that occurred in what was once called the 'Second World': the former Soviet Union and Eastern Europe. Paradoxically, in Italy the internationalisation of illegal markets was also favoured by the successes of the law enforcement forces, that in the 1990s dismantled the most consolidated branches of mafia groups in the Centre and North of Italy. The empty spaces, once controlled by the powerful clans of the Calabrian 'Ndrangheta and the Sicilian mafia, are today occupied by various groups and gangs of different ethnic origin and make-up [35].

As a result, today in Milan as in Rome, Frankfurt, London or Amsterdam, illicit goods and services are offered and exchanged by a multiethnic variety of people. Next to *mafiosi* and local criminals, one finds illicit entrepreneurs coming from all parts of the world. A few of these 'ethnic' criminals—in particular the Chinese ones—tend to exercise a sort of political power within their own communities [36]—much like the Sicilian and Calabrian *mafiosi* in their strongholds. However, most of the foreign criminal groups and actors active in Italy cannot claim to exercise a political authority. They merely content themselves with making fast money by trading in illicit commodities and/or reinvesting dirty money from their home countries in the European Union and, specifically, in Italy.

Their internal composition is also much different from that of Southern Italian mafia families. Foreign crime groups and gangs active in Italy hardly have the longevity and organisational complexity of Southern Italian mafia associations. Some of them are family businesses or organisations cemented by profit-making or by shared revolutionary or ideological goals; many more are loose gangs, founded on ties of friendship and locality. These are usually small, ephemeral enterprises that can be most correctly described as 'crews': loose associations of people, which form, split, and come together again as opportunity arises. In crews, positions and tasks are usually interchangeable and exclusivity is not required: indeed, many crew members frequently have overlapping roles in other criminal enterprises [37].

Illegal market groups and crews are by no means composed exclusively of foreigners. At all levels of Italy's illegal markets we also find people belonging to the mainstream population with no previous underworld connections. It is enough to say that two of the largest cocaine importers operating in Milan, italy's second largest city, in the late 1990s were neither mafia members nor foreigners, but Italians who merely belonged to the sphere of white-collar crime. The first was a Milanese, who invested money earned from loansharking in the drug business and was able to import 600–800 kilograms of cocaine directly from Colombia each time. The second was a former bank manager from Naples, who was responsible for several 400–700-kilogram cocaine shippings. Both of them supplied a plurality of wholesale traffickers, including members of Southern Italian mafia groups, who resided in several parts of the country [38].

As such, the 'new' illegal market players fit better into the 'entrepreneurial' definitions of organised crime that are *en vogue* in Northern and Central Europe than into the mafia-centered understanding of organised crime that is widespread in Italy [39]. Despite the lack of empirical proof, however, foreign illicit entrepreneurs are all too frequently labelled as mafia and are believed to be organised in the same way as Cosa Nostra and the 'Ndrangheta. Sooner or later—in Italy and elsewhere—we will have to discuss seriously these assumptions and the opportunity of employing the instruments developed in anti-mafia campaigns in the fight against this 'other' form of organised crime, which—if we take the Italian understanding of the concept as a parameter—is not as organised as it is very often made out to be.

Future Trends

Whereas the new Italian and foreign players are likely to expand their activities on Italy's illegal markets, the future of the Sicilian Cosa Nostra and the Calabrian 'Ndrangheta is more uncertain.

Far from expanding outwards, Cosa Nostra groups and, to a lesser extent, even those of the 'Ndrangheta have in the last fifteen years receded into their territories, avoiding international competition. Today they obtain a growing and preponderant quota of their revenues by manipulating the tendering process of public works and imposing generalised extortive regimes on all the economic enterprises of their areas. Instead of creating stable 'enterprise syndicates' [40] capable of operating on international illegal markets, both Sicilian and Calabrian mafia families tend to fuse entrepreneurial action with the action typical of 'power syndicates' and thus to concentrate on those profit-making activities that are more directly advantaged by the control of a territory and collusion with politicians and government officials. Though the relationship with the latter has lost its rooting in a common *Weltanschauung* and is accepted by shrinking portions of public opinion, Cosa Nostra and 'Ndrangheta *cosche* have become even more dependent on the decisions made by public, local and central administrations. These administrators are thus today largely arbiters of both the judicial and the economic-financial lots of mafia coalitions.

It is, above all, to condition the outcome of the pending trials, to amend heavy first-degree sentences in appeal trials and to improve the detention conditions of their imprisoned members that the Cosa Nostra and 'Ndrangheta families need politicians and public officials to comply with them. The manipulation of state decision-making processes, however, does not merely have judicial goals, as mafia families count on their ramifications in the state administration to improve their financial lot as well.

All Sicilian and Calabrian mafia families place their hopes for economic recovery in the gaining of public contracts, which have just started to be distributed once more, especially in the South, after the sharp drop following the Tangentopoli ('Bribesville', initially an allusion to Milan) inquiries [41]. Between 2000 and 2006, Sicily and Calabria are respectively disposing of €9,000,000,000 and €5,000,000,000 coming from the EU funds of Agenda 2000. Apparently, the *cosche* intend to acquire—directly and through front-men—a substantial portion of these funds and of the sums that are being distributed by the central government and the local administrations. Unaware of being wiretapped, a Sicilian 'man of honour' recently stated: 'They say we should not make any fuss, they recommend that we all avoid making noise and attracting attention, because we have to get all this Agenda 2000...' [42]

What is at stake was clearly singled out in the report on the DIA's activities in the second half of 2000: 'if Cosa Nostra relies on dragging the public funds foreseen for large-scale construction works in order to recover definitively, preventing it from implementing this project could plunge it into one of the most serious crises it has ever known' [43]. Unfortunately, this awareness does seem to shared by the cabinet headed by Silvio Berlusconi, set up in June 2001. As the Minister for Public Work, Pietro Lunardi, officially stated a few months afterwards, while talking about the huge public investments foreseen for the construction of a bridge over the Messina straits, 'in Southern Italy there is the mafia and we need to come to terms with it' [44]. Incompetence or mafia collusion? It is hard to say. There can be no doubt, however, about the following point: even more than in the past, mafia associations' survival now seems to depend on how their relationships with politics and different sectors of the public administration are set up in the future.

If mafia groups do not receive the political support they desperately need, in the long-term Italy might end up having the same type of organised crime that is widespread in the rest of Europe: namely, a myriad of criminal enterprises selling prohibited commodities with no ambitions to exercise a political power of any sort.

Notes

A longer version of this article is published in Fijnaut and Pauli (eds) *Organised Crime in Europe: Concepts, Patterns and Policies in the European Union and Beyond*, Springer.

[1] See Hess, *Mafia and Mafiosi: the Structure of Power*; Blok, *The Mafia of a Sicilian Village, 1860–1960: A Study of Violent Peasant Entrepreneurs*; Schneider and Schneider, *Culture and Political Economy in Western Sicily.*

[2] Arlacchi, *Mafia Business: The Mafia Ethic and the Spirit of Capitalism.* See also Catanzaro, *Men of Respect. A Social History of the Sicilian Mafia*, 3.

[3] Paoli, *Mafia Brotherhoods: Organized Crime, Italian Style*, 24–32.

[4] Pezzino, 'Stato violenza società. Nascita e sviluppo del paradigma mafioso', 954. For a similar opinion, see also Lupo, 'Il tenebroso sodalizio'. Un rapporto sulla mafia palermitana di fine Ottocento.

[5] Paoli, *Mafia Brotherhoods*, 40–64.

[6] Smith, *Corporations and Society*, 98.

[7] Durkheim, *The Division of Labor in Society*, 176–7.

[8] Cressey, *Theft of the Nation.*

[9] Weber, *Economy and Society*, 72.

[10] *Ibid.*

[11] Sahlins, *Stone Age Economics*, 193–200.

[12] Lestingi, 'L'associazione della Fratellanza nella provincia di Girgenti', 453.

[13] Murray, *The Origins of the Tiandihui. The Chinese Triads in Legend and History*; Kaplan, *Yakuza: Japan's Criminal Underworld.*

[14] Paoli, *Mafia Brotherhoods*, 3–12.

[15] Paoli, 'The Paradoxes of Organised Crime'.

[16] Catanzaro, *Men of Respect*; Santino & La Fiura, *L'impresa mafiosa. all'Italia agli Stati Uniti.*

[17] Gambetta, *The Sicilian Mafia. The Business of Private Protection.*

[18] Franchetti, *Condizioni politiche ed amministrative della Sicilia*, 100.

[19] Paoli, *Mafia Brotherhoods*, chapters 4 and 5.

[20] Stille, *Excellent Cadavers: The Mafia and the Death of the First Italian Republic.*

[21] Paoli, *Mafia Brotherhoods*, 215–7.

[22] Becchi, & Turvani, *Proibito? Il mercato mondiale della droga*, 156.

[23] Falcone with Padovani, *Men of Honour: The Truth about the Mafia*, 115.

[24] Scarpinato, 'Mafia e politica', in *Mafia. Anatomia di un regime*, 45.

[25] Paoli, *Mafia Brotherhoods*, 218–9.

[26] Ministero dell'Interno, *Rapporto sul fenomeno della criminalità organizzata (anno 2000)*, 60–5.

[27] Sales, 'Camorra', 468.

[28] Sales, *La camorra. Le camorre*; Monzini, *Gruppi criminali a Napoli e a Marsiglia. La delinquenza organizzata nella storia delle due città (1820–1990).*

[29] Ministero dell'Interno, *Rapporto*, 60–75.

[30] Massari, *La Sacra corona unita: potere e segreto.*

[31] Ministero dell'Interno, *Relazione semestrale sull'attività svolta e i risultati conseguiti dalla Direzione Investigativa Antimafia nel primo semestre del 2002*, 57–64.

[32] Ingroia, *L'associazione di tipo mafioso.*

[33] Ministero dell'Interno, *Rapporto 2001* and *Relazione semestrale 2002.*

[34] See, for example, Ministero dell'Interno, *Relazione semestrale sull'attività svolta e i risultati conseguiti dalla Direzione Investigativa Antimafia nel secondo semestre del 2000* and *Relazione semestrale, 2002.*

[35] Paoli, *Pilot Project to Describe and Analyse Local Drug Markets—First Phase Final Report: Illegal Drug Markets in Frankfurt and Milan*, 110–15.

[36] See Suchan, 'La criminalità organizzata cinese in Toscana'.

[37] Paoli, 'Flexible Hierarchies and Dynamic Disorder: The Drug Distribution System in Frankfurt and Milan'.

[38] Paoli, *Pilot Project*, 110–15.
[39] See Paoli, 'The Paradoxes of …' cit., and Fijnaut & Paoli (eds), *Organised Crime* in *Europe: Concepts, Patterns and Policies in the European Union and Beyond*, Springer.
[40] Block, *East Side—West Side: Organizing Crime in New York*.
[41] Barbacetto et al., *Mani Pulite: la vera storia*.
[42] *La Repubblica*, 6 February 2001, 15; see also Consiglio Superiore della Magistratura, *Verifica della evoluzione delle forme organizzativo-dirigenziali di Cosa Nostra al fine di un'eventuale elaborazione di proposte per attuare strategie di contrasto. Risoluzione approvata dall'Assemblea Plenaria nella seduta antimeridiana del 7 giugno 2001*, 13–15.
[43] Ministero dell'Interno, *Relazione 2000*, 16.
[44] *La Repubblica*, 23 August 2001, 2.

References

Arlacchi, P. (1988) *Mafia Business: the Mafia Ethic and the Spirit of Capitalism*, Oxford University Press.
Barbacetto, G., Gomez, P. & Travaglio, M. (2002) *Mani Pulite: la vera storia*, Editori Riuniti.
Becchi, A. & Turvani, M. (1993) *Proibito? Il mercato mondiale della droga*, Donzelli.
Block, A. A. (1983) *East Side–West Side: Organizing Crime in New York*, Transaction Books.
Blok, A. (1988) *The Mafia of a Sicilian Village, 1860–1960: a Study of Violent Peasant Entrepreneurs*, Polity Press.
Catanzaro, R. (1992) *Men of Respect. A Social History of the Sicilian Mafia*, The Free Press.
Consiglio Superiore della Magistratura (2001) Verifica della evoluzione delle forme organizzativo-dirigenziali di Cosa Nostra al fine di un'eventuale elaborazione di proposte per attuare strategie di contrasto. Risoluzione approvata dall'Assemblea Plenaria nella seduta antimeridiana del 7 giugno 2001. Relatore: G. Natoli.
Cressey, D. (1969) *Theft of the Nation*, Harper and Row.
Durkheim, E. (1964) *The Division of Labor in Society*, The Free Press [1893, 1902].
Falcone, G. & Padovani, M. (1993) *Men of Honour: The Truth about the Mafia*, Warner.
Fijnaut, C. & Paoli, L. (2004) eds, *Organised Crime in Europe: Concepts, Patterns and Policies in the European Union and Beyond*, Springer.
Franchetti, L. (1993) *Condizioni politiche ed amministrative della Sicilia*, Donzelli.
Gambetta, D. (1993) *The Sicilian Mafia. The Business of Private Protection*, Harvard University Press.
Hess, H. (1973) *Mafia and Mafiosi: the Structure of Power*, Saxon House.
Ingroia, A. (1993) *L'associazione di tipo mafioso*, Giuffré.
Kaplan, D. & Dubro, A.(2003) *Yakuza: Japan's Criminal Underworld*, University of California Press.
Lestingi, F. (1884) 'L'associazione della Fratellanza nella provincia di Girgenti', *Archivio di Psichiatria, Antropologia Criminale e Scienze Penali*, vol. 5, p. 453.
Lupo, S. (1988) '"Il tenebroso sodalizio". Un rapporto sulla mafia palermitana di fine Ottocento', *Studi storici*, vol. 29, no. 2.
Massari, M. (1998) *La Sacra corona unita: potere e segreto*, Laterza.
Ministero dell'Interno (2001) *Rapporto sul fenomeno della criminalità organizzata (anno 2000)*, Camera dei Deputati.
Ministero dell'Interno (2002) *Relazione semestrale sull'attività svolta e i risultati conseguiti dalla Direzione Investigativa Antimafia nel secondo semestre del 2000*.
Ministero dell'Interno (2002) *Relazione semestrale sull'attività svolta e i risultati conseguiti dalla Direzione Investigativa Antimafia nel primo semestre del 2002*.
Monzini, P. (1999) *Gruppi criminali a Napoli e a Marsiglia. La delinquenza organizzata nella storia delle due città (1820–1990)*, Meridiana Libri.

Murray, D. H. (1994) *The Origins of the Tiandihui. The Chinese Triads in Legend and History*, Stanford University Press.

Paoli, L. (2000) *Pilot Project to Describe and Analyse Local Drug Markets—First Phase Final Report: Illegal Drug Markets in Frankfurt and Milan*, EMCDDA.

Paoli, L. (2002) 'Flexible hierarchies and dynamic disorder: the drug distribution system in Frankfurt and Milan', *Drugs: Education, Prevention and Policy*, vol. 9, no. 2.

Paoli, L. (2002) 'The paradoxes of organised crime', *Crime, Law, and Social Change*, vol. 37, no. 1.

Paoli, L. (2003) *Mafia Brotherhoods: Organized Crime, Italian Style*, Oxford University Press.

Pezzino, P. (1987) 'Stato violenza società. Nascita e sviluppo del paradigma mafioso', in *La Sicilia*, eds M. Aymard & G. Giarrizzo, Giulio Einaudi Editore.

La Repubblica, 6 February 2001.

La Repubblica, 23 August 2001.

Sahlins, M. D. (1972) *Stone Age Economics*, Aldine Atherton.

Sales, I. (1993) *La camorra. Le camorre*, Editori Riuniti.

Sales, I. (2001) 'Camorra', *Appendice 2000*, Treccani.

Santino, U. & la Fiura, G. (1990) *L'impresa mafiosa. all'Italia agli Stati Uniti*, Angeli.

Scarpinato, R. (1992) 'Mafia e politica', *Mafia. Anatomia di un regime*, Librerie Associate.

Schneider, J. & Schneider, P. (1976) *Culture and Political Economy in Western Sicily*, Academic Press.

Smith, M. G. (1974) *Corporations and Society*, Duckworth.

Stille, A. (1995) *Excellent Cadavers: The Mafia and the Death of the First Italian Republic*, Jonathan Cape.

Suchan, P. (2001) 'La criminalità organizzata cinese in Toscana', in *Mafie nostre, mafie loro. Criminalità organizzata italiana e straniera al Centro Nord*, eds M. Massari & S. Becucci, Comunità.

Weber, M. (1978) *Economy and Society*, eds G. Roth & C. Wittich, University of California Press, [1922].

Globalisation and Latin American and Caribbean Organised Crime

Bruce Bagley

Organised crime [1] flourishes best in the contexts provided by weak states [2]. The longstanding institutional weaknesses of most states in Latin America and the Caribbean, in combination with the existence of a highly lucrative underground drug trade in the Western hemisphere, make the countries in that corner of the world system not only especially prone to indigenous organised crime, but also attractive targets for transnational criminal enterprises. Indeed, the dubious practice of a number of the states in the region (e.g. Dominica, Panama, Uruguay and Paraguay) of 'selling' citizenship literally provided an open invitation to foreign crime groups to establish themselves in the hemisphere. As Tom Farer notes, when states are weak, but act as if they were strong '...spewing out laws and regulations purporting to regulate, inhibit, and tax private activity...' without the will or capacity

Professor Bruce M. Bagley is Professor of International and Latin American Studies at the University of Miami.

to enforce the law, they inevitably create spaces or niches between reality and legality that can be and frequently are exploited by organised crime in an unfortunate implication of globalisation [3].

In broad strokes, globalisation refers to the 'shrinkage' of distance on a global scale through the emergence and thickening of 'nets of connections'—economic, technological, social, political and environmental [4]. Of course, as many sceptics have noted, the recent transformations in the world system are by no means completely new [5]. What is novel about them in the contemporary period is their extensity, intensity, velocity and impact on states and societies around the globe [6]. Transnational criminal organisations have been able to exploit the increased ease of international travel, the liberalisation of emigration policies, the expansion of international trade, the spread of high technology communications systems and the under-regulation of international financial networks (via sophisticated money-laundering techniques) to extend their criminal enterprises well beyond the borders of their own country [7].

For historically weak states such as those in Latin America and the Caribbean, their accelerating insertion into the global economy over the last several decades, with particular intensity in the post-Cold War era, has generally required painful fiscal austerity measures on the part of national governments and a severe 'downsizing' of the state in general. Under the banners of the 'Washington consensus' and neo-liberal market reforms, state penetrative, extractive and regulatory capacities throughout the region (never particularly strong) suffered dramatic erosion in the aftermath of the 1982 regional debt crisis. As a result, state authorities in the 1990s often found themselves bereft of the financial and institutional resources essential for combating the rise and expansion of transnational organised criminal activity within their national territories. Law-enforcement agencies throughout Latin America and the Caribbean remain woefully inadequate, underfunded and corrupt. Courts and prison systems are outdated and overwhelmed. And high-level political corruption has continued, or even worsened in many cases, despite the neo-liberal belief that wholesale liberalisation would—once the initial transition phase had been completed—'... reduce the range of illicit and concealed profit opportunities available to the holders of political power' [8]. Ill-prepared as they were in the past to combat transnational organised crime, following almost two decades of neo-liberal reforms most states in the region are even less capable today.

The tendency of neo-liberal reforms to exacerbate the gap between rich and poor in many Latin American and Caribbean countries and to heighten the poverty and misery of those subordinate classes not effectively linked to export sectors—the principal 'losers' in the processes of globalisation—quite predictably has generated rising resistance to globalisation among the disadvantaged and intensified popular demands for policy reforms and fuller democratisation across the region. Yet, in the context of globalisation, the scope of autonomous state action in most developing countries is significantly constrained and ameliorative policies are often viewed as inefficient and unacceptable. Confronted with the overwhelming power of globalised production and international finance, including heavy international debt burdens, most Latin American and Caribbean political elites have been reduced to negotiating from positions of weakness the terms of their progressive national integration into the global capitalist system. Unable to oppose stronger transnational forces and unwilling to adopt more flexible systems of democratic political representation designed to modernise and legitimise the state, governmental and party elites have generally striven, instead, to preserve the fundamental structures of power and domination intact while resisting grass-roots pressures for greater socio-economic equality and democracy via selective state cooptation (to restrict mounting dissent) and systematic state coercion (to repress outbreaks of protest and praetorianism) [9].

In most of Latin America and the Caribbean, the dynamics of globalisation over the last two decades have resulted in almost ideal conditions for the rapid penetration and spread of transnational organised crime. On the one hand, the hundreds of millions of under- or unemployed poor provide a vast seething cauldron in which criminality of all sorts can and does incubate and multiply [10]. Indeed, engagement in criminal activities, including forms of organised crime, on the part of many of the disadvantaged in the region can be seen as a rational survival strategy in the face of otherwise severely limited life opportunities. On the other hand, the weak, often corrupt, and frequently illegitimate states typical throughout the hemisphere have routinely proved unable to address adequately the desperate needs of these 'marginalised' segments of their populations or to prevent the spread of common criminality. They have been even less able to halt the rise or impede the spread of more sophisticated and technologically adept transnational organised crime [11].

Russian Mafia Activities in Latin America and the Caribbean

Thus, as well as considering the overall situation in Latin America and the Caribbean, this article will particularly consider the scope and impact of the post-Cold War wave of Russian transnational organised crime to illustrate this phenomenon. Although the evidence currently available in the public realm is primarily journalistic and often anecdotal, it is, despite these limitations, sufficient to support the conclusion that the linkages or 'strategic alliances' between various Russian organised crime groups and major transnational criminal organisations in Latin America and the Caribbean in 2001 were already substantial and expanding rapidly. Moreover, it raises the spectre that, at least in some key countries in the region (e.g. Colombia, Mexico and Brazil), the alliances between home-grown and Russian criminal organisations may provide domestic criminal and/or guerrilla groups with access to the illicit international markets, money-laundering facilities and illegal arms sources that could convert them into major impediments to economic growth and serious threats to democratic consolidation and long-run stability at home.

Given their common interests in illicit profits and avoidance of national and international law-enforcement authorities, there is a 'natural' tendency for Russian (or Italian, Asian, or North American) criminal organisations to forge alliances or partnerships with their South American and Caribbean counterparts when operating in the region. Such links allow the Russians, along with other transnational crime groups, to carry out criminal activities in the region with a relatively low profile, to avoid detection by authorities, and to reduce their risks of arrest, infiltration, and loss of profits.

According to Interpol, in Latin America and the Caribbean to date the Russian mafia has been primarily attracted to and involved in activities such as drug trafficking, money laundering, and arms trafficking [12]. Although Russia and Eastern/Central Europe only account for approximately 10 percent of world drug sales (approximately $15 billion total), the market there is growing fast and the profits are already huge [13]. The drug market is even bigger in Western Europe (perhaps $50–60 billion), where the Russians are also deeply engaged. Closely linked to their drug-smuggling activities is their growing involvement in arms trafficking into Latin America, often in arms-for-drugs deals with drug-trafficking rings (or cartels) and guerrilla organisations. Finally, in light of weak state enforcement and regulatory capabilities throughout the former Soviet Union and the incipient institutionalisation of the financial and banking systems in Russia and most of Eastern Europe, Russian criminal organisations, working under 'thieves-in-law' sponsorship and protection, have been able to offer relatively low-risk money-laundering services to a variety of South American drug traffickers, sometimes charging as much as 30 percent of the proceeds [14].

Alongside these three core criminal activities, there is also some (admittedly spotty) evidence of expanding Russian involvement with other Latin American criminal enterprises such as prostitution, international traffic in women, child pornography, usury, extortion, kidnapping, credit-card fraud, computer fraud, counterfeiting, and auto theft, to mention only the most prominent. The actual extent of Russian mafia involvement in such criminal activities in Latin America is, of course, difficult to specify with precision and undoubtedly varies from country to country. The sections that follow provide summary descriptions of the principal features of Russian criminal activity in the major countries and sub-regions of Latin America and the Caribbean.

Mexico

Mexico has become an increasingly important source of narcotics trafficked to the USA and beyond, an economy dominated by seven principal Mexican criminal organisations or cartels. Over the past five years, Pacific Ocean smuggling routes have increasingly supplanted the more closely monitored and congested Caribbean as the cocaine traffickers' most lucrative smuggling option. More than half of all the cocaine entering the United States is now believed to come up the Pacific side. Seizures of South American cocaine bound for Mexico and the United States more than doubled between 1999 and 2000 alone. This upsurge in confiscations was both a function of the overall increase in drug flows through the eastern Pacific, especially from Colombia, and a result of a major redeployment of the US Coast Guard's Pacific Coast forces away from their traditional mission of fisheries enforcement to support for US military counter-drug operations. It also reflects the greater cooperation and information sharing between US law enforcement and the Mexican navy evident in the last two years [15].

Nonetheless, drug traffickers' techniques in the Pacific are even more challenging to law enforcement authorities than those traditionally employed in the Caribbean. First, the Pacific is open ocean and hence much more difficult to patrol than the smaller and more confined Caribbean. Second, cocaine in the Caribbean is usually transported in open speedboats that are relatively easy to detect because of their oversized engines and extra fuel containers. In the Pacific, in contrast, cocaine is commonly hidden in the hulls of fishing boats or on board huge container ships that are inherently more difficult to identify and search [16].

In May 2001, the US Coast Guard seized a Russian/Ukranian-manned, 152-foot, Belize-flagged fishing trawler named the *Zvezda Maru* off the Pacific coast. It was loaded with 12 tons of Colombian cocaine, providing dramatic new evidence of Russian mafia involvement in drug trafficking in Mexico [17]. The US authorities maintain that the crew, comprising eight Ukrainians and two Russians, must have had the permission of the Tijuana cartel (led by the infamous Arellano Felix clan) to ship so much cocaine to the West Coast [18]. According to San Diego-based DEA agent Errol Chavez, the nationalities of the crew are an 'indication that there is direct involvement or some kind of association between Russian organised crime and members of the Arellano Felix organization' [19]. Previous revelations in November 2000 by the Mexican Attorney General's office to the effect that Mexican authorities had uncovered proof that Tijuana's Arellano Felix gang had provided Russian military hardware and cash to Colombia's FARC guerrillas in exchange for large shipments of cocaine also pointed to a pattern of deepening Russian mafia involvement in the Colombian–Mexican drug connection [20]. US officials in Southern California reportedly suspect that the crew belonged to a Russian organised crime syndicate based in Los Angeles, where between 600 and 800 known Russian crime figures live, mostly in the North and West Hollywood areas. Prior to this May 2001 seizure, however, Mexican authorities claimed that Amado Carillo Fuentes (alias 'El Senor de los Cielos' or Lord of the Skies) of the Juarez cartel had forged the only known Mexican–Russian criminal alliance just prior to his death in 1997 [21].

Central America

In the early 2000s, conditions in Central America (Panama, Costa Rica, Nicaragua, Honduras, El Salvador, Guatemala and Belize) were particularly conducive to international organised crime, owing to the widespread poverty in the sub-region (up to three-quarters of the roughly 30 million Central Americans live on less than two dollars per day) and the weakness and illegitimacy of political institutions throughout the Isthmus. Drug trafficking is Central America's most profitable criminal enterprise. In 2000 the DEA reported that of the estimated 645 metric tons of cocaine smuggled into the United States some 425 metric tons passed through the Central America–Mexican corridor [22].

This huge volume of Colombian (and to a lesser extent Peruvian) cocaine shipped through the sub-region has fuelled an explosion of some 2,000 youth gangs and related gang violence in recent years, especially in Nicaragua, Honduras, El Salvador and Guatemala [23]. The combined gang membership in these four countries is estimated at about 400,000 youths, composed primarily of males between 12 and 24 years old. Honduran police, for example, have confirmed the existence of 489 different youth gangs and Guatemalan officials have identified some 500 in their country with more than 100,000 active members in all. Many of these gangs, or *maras* as they are known in the sub-region, are led by youths or adults who previously belonged to gangs in the United States but were convicted of felonies and deported back to Central America. A number of these gangs, such as El Salvador's ruthless and widely feared 'Mara Salvatrucha', also have branches in major American cities, engage in drug and arms trafficking, and carry out contract murders for Mexican and Colombian drug organisations [24].

These linkages with Colombian and Mexican cartels have allowed the Central American gangs to upgrade their arsenals and build more sophisticated criminal organisations than ever before. As a result, violent local Central American gangs with international connections, financed and armed by drug money, are currently challenging—and sometimes overwhelming—civilian law-enforcement agencies throughout the Isthmus [25].

The governments of the sub-region have attempted to contain their spiralling crime waves, but they each face serious national budgetary constraints that have (and will for the foreseeable future) limit their capacity to respond effectively. The Salvadoran and Honduran governments opted in 2000–1 to draw on their military forces to reinforce their inadequate civilian law enforcement institutions. After a bloody prison riot in June 2001, Guatemalan President Portillo declared that his government would seek augmented security assistance from the US, the UK and Israel, among others. Both the Nicaraguan and Costa Rican governments have also recently pledged to crack down on criminal activity in their countries as well. As a result, civilian law enforcement throughout Central America is likely to become progressively more militarised over the next few years. However, national economies across the sub-region are so hard-pressed that increased budgetary outlays on security and law enforcement will inexorably reduce social spending. Such reductions, in turn, could prove socially explosive and politically destabilising. Moreover, heightened military involvement in the fight against drug trafficking and organised crime in the sub-region could lead to the contamination and corruption of their armed forces, as it has in Mexico, Peru, Bolivia and elsewhere in Latin America during the last two decades [26].

Colombia and the Andes

Despite the US government's provision of almost one billion dollars in counternarcotics aid to Colombia during the 1990s, by 1999 Colombia had become the premier coca-cultivating country in the world, producing more coca leaf than both Peru and Bolivia combined. This explosive expansion occurred in spite of a permanent Colombian National Police eradication program that sprayed a record 65,000 hectares of coca in 1998 alone (approximately 50 percent more than the total for 1997). Concomitantly, Colombia also maintains its status as the world's principal cocaine-refining nation, producing 680 metric tons of cocaine base in 2002 [27]. The country also became an important source of both marijuana and heroin. During the 1990s Colombian production of opium poppy (the raw material for heroin) also skyrocketed from zero in 1989 to 61 metric tons in 1998. While these production totals meant that Colombia still ranked as only as a relatively minor player in the world heroin market (less than 2 percent of total global supply), they did enable it to become the major heroin supplier to the eastern part of the United States by the end of the decade, exporting an estimated 6 metric tons of pure heroin yearly. A study by Colombia's National Association of Financial Institutions (ANIF) estimated that the country's total earnings from the illicit drug trade amounted to approximately $3.5 billion in 1999. This figure placed drug earnings close to the $3.75 billion made from oil—the country's top export—and more than two and a half times earnings from coffee exports.

These dismaying statistics notwithstanding, it would be inaccurate to conclude that the US-sponsored 'War on Drugs' in the Andean region as a whole was a total failure during the 1990s. In contrast to the Colombian situation, coca cultivation has decreased in Peru and Bolivia, to a large extent thanks to the disruption of the 'air bridge' that had permitted Colombian trafficking organisations earlier in the decade to transport coca paste or 'base' from these two central Andean countries into Colombia, where it was subsequently refined into cocaine and then smuggled into the US. The air bridge effectively collapsed in late 1995 after the Peruvian air force, under orders from President Alberto Fujimori, began to shoot down suspected trafficker airplanes flying between Peru and Colombia. Combined with the more aggressive eradication efforts undertaken by both the Peruvian and Bolivian governments (with US financial backing) since 1996, alternative development programs began to enjoy considerable success among the coca-cultivating peasants in both countries. Despite reversals at the turn of the millennium, the result of a sudden rise in the price of coca leaf (which stimulated renewed peasant cultivation) and increased domestic consumption and processing, progress continues to be made in Peru. Coca cultivation was down 15 percent in 2003, although there are still extensive areas of high-density coca cultivation in the Monzon and Apurimac/Ene river valleys [28].

With the air bridge down, however, the Colombian traffickers rapidly expanded coca cultivation in Colombia, thus leading to Colombia's progressive displacement of Peru and Bolivia as the major coca cultivating country in the world during the late 1990s. Furthermore, while cultivation and smuggling expanded exponentially in Colombia over the decade, the combined efforts of the US and Colombian governments did succeed in partially disrupting the drug-trafficking activities of the country's two most notorious drug-trafficking rings, the Medellin and Cali cartels. Although remnants of both continued to operate at lower levels of activity (sometimes from jail) during the late 1990s, the dismemberment of these two powerful and violent transnational drug-trafficking organisations over the early and mid-1990s constituted important achievements. This should not, however, obscure the underlying reality of the ongoing explosion of drug cultivation and drug trafficking in Colombia over the second half of the 1990s, nor distract attention from the accelerating political corrosion that flowed from the country's still-flourishing illicit drug trade. In practice, rather than curbing the nation's booming drug traffic, the deaths, extradition or incarcerations of the two principal cartels' 'bosses' created only temporary and relatively minor disruptions in the contraband flow of drugs from Colombia to the US and European markets. Indeed, the vacuum left by partial demise of the Medellin and Cali cartels was quickly filled by the rise and proliferation of scores of smaller, less notorious (but equally violent) trafficking organisations or *cartelitos* throughout Colombia that engaged in both cocaine trafficking and the even more lucrative and rapidly expanding heroin trade. Unlike the Medellin and Cali cartels, however, these new, smaller trafficking groups have maintained relatively lower profiles, often operating from bases located in Colombia's many 'intermediate' or secondary cities and small towns where they could bribe and intimidate local officials to gain 'protection' for their activities in relative anonymity.

After all, Latin American narcotic traffickers have reacted to increased pressure from law enforcement not only by adopting new structures but also by diversifying. Throughout the 1990s and into the early 2000s a booming trade in the 'designer' or 'club' drug commonly known as ecstasy (MDMA) burgeoned in the United States and in many cities in Latin America, providing additional profit-making opportunities. For the last decade, Israeli and Russian MDMA trafficking organisations have dominated the MDMA market in the United States. But the high profitability of the trade has begun to attract other drug-trafficking organisations based especially in Colombia, the Dominican Republic, Mexico and Asia. Such groups, possibly through temporary alliances or via ecstasy-for-cocaine deals, are likely to make inroads into Israeli and Russian control of the MDMA trafficking networks during the next few years.

Dominican drug-trafficking organisations in alliance with Colombian cartels have been deeply involved in the cocaine trade along the US east coast for more than a decade. In the mid-1990s, the Dominicans became the first Latin American smugglers to assume a major role in MDMA distribution. Some Colombian and Mexican crime groups have also become involved in recent years. MDMA traffickers targeting US or Latin American markets commonly employ couriers or 'mules' travelling by plane from Europe to cities such as Miami, Santo Domingo, Bogota, or Mexico City, but larger quantities shipped by sea on cargo vessels have been confiscated as well. The couriers either ingest (swallow) MDMA pills wrapped in plastic balloons or condoms or strap them to their persons or luggage.

They have also responded by deepening their relationships with gangs from the former Soviet Union. Russian mafia groups operating out of Los Angeles, New York, Miami and Puerto Rico, among other US cities, have formed a variety of alliances with Colombian trafficking organisations since at least 1992 to acquire cocaine for delivery to Europe and the territories of the former Soviet Union and to provide arms to

Colombian *narcotraficantes* and guerrilla organisations [29]. Indeed, US undercover operations since the mid-1990s have detected various attempts by Russian crime groups to sell Colombian drug traffickers submarines, helicopters and surface-to-air missiles [30]. At least two Russian combat helicopters, along with quantities of small arms, were sold to the Cali cartel in the mid-1990s. In the late 1990s Russian vessels docked repeatedly at the Caribbean port of Turbo in northern Colombia to offload shipments of Russian AK-47 assault rifles and rocket-propelled grenades for the FARC guerrillas and, possibly, for right-wing paramilitary bands, in exchange for cocaine. The discovery of a partially built submarine, based on Russian plans and specifications, in a suburb just outside of Bogota in late 2000 added to speculation about a growing Russian connection with the Colombian drug trade, even though no direct involvement of Russian criminal figures in this case was ever demonstrated [31].

However, it is clear that Russian gangs have become closely linked with Latin American criminals, including terrorists. This was evident in a new Russian smuggling ring that opened up during 1999–2000, which linked corrupt Russian military figures, organised crime bosses, diplomats and Colombia's FARC guerrillas. It moved regular shipments of up to 40,000 kilograms of cocaine to the former Soviet Union in return for large shipments of Russian and Eastern European weaponry. The scale of these arms-for-cocaine smuggling operations underscores the enormous challenge law-enforcement authorities face in Russia and throughout the independent states of the former Soviet Union, where in many cases Soviet-era intelligence operatives made virtually seamless transitions from Cold War espionage or military intelligence operations into organised crime [32]. According to US intelligence officials: 'The source of the weapons [smuggled into Colombia from Russia] is both organised crime and military. There is a tremendous grey area between the two in Russia and the Ukraine' [33]. According to US intelligence officials, this major Russo–Colombian smuggling operation reportedly worked as follows:

1. Russian-built IL-76 cargo planes took off from various airstrips in Russia and the Ukraine laden with anti-aircraft missiles, small arms and ammunition.
2. The planes, roughly the size of Boeing 707s, stopped in Amman, Jordan, to refuel. There, they bypassed normal Jordanian customs with the help of corrupt foreign diplomats and bribed local officials.
3. After crossing the Atlantic, the cargo jets used remote landing strips or parachute airdrops to deliver their cargo to the FARC.
4. The planes returned loaded with up to 40,000 kilos of cocaine. Some was distributed as payment for the diplomatic middlemen in Amman and sold in the Persian Gulf. The rest was flown back to the former Soviet Union for sale there or in Europe [34].

A senior US intelligence source identified Luiz Fernando Da Costa (alias Fernandinho or Fernando Beira Mar), one of Brazil's biggest drug *capos* until his capture by Colombian military forces in early 2001, as a key player involved in the delivery of these Russian arms shipments to the FARC. Within Colombia, Fernandinho apparently coordinated the arms deliveries to the FARC through his base in the town of Barrancomina, Vichada, also the headquarters for the FARC's 16th Front led by Tomas Medina Caracas (alias el Negro Acasio) and a major FARC-run cocaine-processing centre [35]. Da Costa also ran arms into Brazil and Colombia out of the town of Pedro Juan Caballero in Paraguay where he worked with Fuad Jamil, a Lebanese businessman operating in the same Paraguayan town. Indeed, US sources claim that Hezbollah, the Iranian-backed, Lebanon-based, militant Shiite organisation best known for its guerrilla activities against Israeli troops in southern Lebanon, may also have been involved. Hezbollah has roots among the Arab immigrant communities of Paraguay, Ecuador, Venezuela and Brazil and frequently uses legitimate business operations to cover illegal arms transfers [36]. In other words, this was a truly global criminal network, servicing a wide range of criminal actors, from local crime bosses all the way to international terrorism. Nor is this confined to Colombia. The involvement of former Peruvian National Intelligence Director Vladimiro Montesinos (*Servicio de Inteligencia Nacional*—SIN) in dealing Russian black-market arms acquired in Amman, Jordan, leaked out in July 2000 and led ultimately to the collapse of Peru's Fujimori government in November 2000 [37].

Cuba

In contrast to the weak, democratic and capitalist states of the insular Caribbean that proved uniformly easy prey for transnational organised crime during the 1990s, the highly centralised and authoritarian Communist state of Fidel Castro's Cuba remained largely immune from criminal penetration over the decade. In the late 1980s, the Cuban government had been linked with Colombian drug traffickers when General Arnoldo Ochoa, a prominent and popular Cuban military commander in Angola, and other Cuban officers under his command reportedly engaged in drug-smuggling activities to underwrite their poorly funded troops in Angola and, allegedly, to enrich themselves personally. Prior to Ochoa's high-profile 1989 trial in Havana on drug-trafficking charges and his subsequent conviction and execution, Fidel and his brother Raul, head of the Cuban Armed Forces, were widely rumoured to have at least condoned Ochoa's drug-smuggling activities as a way of circumventing the US embargo against Cuba and obtaining badly needed hard currency to support the Cuban military presence in Africa. Whether such accusations against the Castro brothers were true or not remains unresolved. Whatever the truth of the matter, however, Ochoa's considerable following among Cuban troops in Angola and among veterans at home, the increased autonomy from the Castros and the Cuban high command that drug money conferred upon him, and the intense international opprobrium that accompanied international revelation of high-ranking Cuban military officers' roles in illicit drug-trafficking operations, in combination apparently led the Castro regime to put an end to Cuba's involvement in the trade by the early 1990s.

Without massive Soviet subsidies to keep the Cuban economy afloat (estimated as high as $10 billion annually at the outset of the 1980s), during the 1990s Fidel and the Cuban Communist leadership were forced to seek out foreign investment from Europe (especially Spain) in the state-owned tourist industry to help diversify the failing national economy. One consequence of the growth of foreign tourism in Cuba over the decade was the emergence of an illegal drug market (along with prostitution) to service the burgeoning tourist trade. Small Cuban criminal gangs working with traffickers from Colombia, neighbouring Caribbean countries such as Haiti, the Dominican Republic or Jamaica, and even Mexico smuggle drugs into Cuba for distribution and sale within the country or for transit on to Europe. Cuba's repressive state security apparatus has, however, been quite successful both in preventing the rise of powerful domestic organised crime groups and in disrupting efforts by Russian or other transnational criminal organisations to use Cuban territory as a transit point for large scale drug trafficking into Europe.

Nonetheless, given the Cuban economy's severe economic problems over the decade, including the scarcity of expensive imported petroleum, the Cuban Navy and Coast Guard have been unable to afford the equipment or fuel needed to patrol Cuban waters out to the 12 mile territorial limit effectively. The resulting gaps in Cuban coastal patrols have allowed Colombian traffickers to use Cuban waters as a handy drop-off point for drug shipments (drugs are either tossed over the side of ships or parachuted from a low-flying airplane into the sea) destined for the US market. After a prearranged drop, US-based traffickers operating 'fast boats' pick up the drugs and transport them into South Florida, avoiding detection by US authorities under the cover of darkness or in the confusion of weekend and holiday pleasure-boat traffic. Although the Cubans repeatedly approached Washington with proposals for closer US–Cuban cooperation and information-sharing in the area of drug trafficking during the 1990s, their offers were regularly rebuffed by hardliners in the US Congress who reject out of hand any form of collaboration with the Castro regime, including cooperation in the area of drug control.

Despite some 30 years of close Cuban–Soviet relations during the Cold War following the Cuban revolution in 1959, the 1991 collapse of the USSR, the concomitant end of Communist party rule in Russia and the progressive termination of former Soviet subsidies to Cuba under Russia's first president, Boris Yeltsin, severely strained Cuban–Russian relations over the 1990s. Ironically, this also helped immunise Cuba against the Russian criminal penetration which has become such a feature in the rest of the region. Latent Cuban antipathy toward Russians, unmistakably present among Cubans even at the high point of Cuban–Soviet cooperation in the 1970s and 80s, grew more palpable over the 1990s, effectively making Cuba an inhospitable prospective host country for Russian criminal organisations seeking to establish themselves in the Caribbean [38]. The wariness and vigilance of the Cuban state in the wake of the Ochoa affair regarding any involvement of Cuba in international drug trafficking also militated against the establishment of Russian mafia operations in Cuba. Finally, the US embargo against Cuba and the country's limited participation in the global capitalist economy meant that Cuba held little attraction for Russian criminals intent upon establishing bases for their transnational criminal activities in the region.

Instead, the microstates of the Caribbean have proved especially attractive to Russian criminal syndicates. Already entrenched in Europe, where there is a lucrative growing market for cocaine, and in Russia and other former Soviet Bloc countries, Russian criminal organisations increasingly resorted to use of various Caribbean nations as both transit points for drugs and arms smuggling activities and as easy-access money-laundering sites for their expanding international operations from the mid-1990s on [39]. With strict bank secrecy laws and lax financial enforcement mechanisms, Caribbean islands such as Antigua and Aruba, where Russians opened several offshore banks in the mid-1990s, offered attractive havens for laundering large sums of money from Russian mafia operations. Panama, Costa Rica and the Cayman Islands have also served as Russian money-laundering sanctuaries as well [40]. Intensified US government and international pressures on these Caribbean and Central American havens over the late 1990s and early 2000s have made operations more difficult for Russian *blanqueadores* (launderers) in recent years but have by no means halted Russian (and other international organised crime) laundering activities in the sub-region altogether [41].

Brazil and the Southern Cone

Brazil's continuing role as a major narcotic transit point has resulted in cheap cocaine flooding the country. Along Brazil's long, unprotected borders with Bolivia, Peru and Colombia, refined cocaine costs just $2,000 per kilo or less. In Brazil's major urban areas such as Rio de Janeiro or Sao Paulo a kilo goes for as little as $4,000, or 80 percent less than the street price in New York or Chicago [42]. As a result of surging drug trafficking, violent crime rates have soared in Brazil's major urban centres and many of the country's sprawling urban slums have become armed camps run by 'drug commands' or gangs that often act as alternative governments in their neighbourhoods. Drug-related corruption has also permeated the Brazilian national economy and political system. In 2001, a Brazilian congressional investigation into corruption linked 827 prominent Brazilians to drug trafficking and money laundering, including two national congressmen, 15 state legislators, four mayors, six bank directors and scores of police officers and judges [43].

This environment of pervasive official corruption has proved highly propitious for the rapid expansion of Russian organised crime groups alongside Brazil's own home-grown criminal organisations. Since the mid-1990s there have been a variety of press reports hinting at growing Russian organised crime involvement in drugs and arms trafficking and money laundering in Brazil and the four Southern Cone countries (Argentina, Paraguay, Uruguay, Chile). The half dozen or so highly publicised arrests of Russian and other former Soviet Bloc crime figures that have taken place in recent years in the nations of the sub-region have lent some credence to these journalistic alarms [44]. Nonetheless, a mid-2000 report on the Russian mafia prepared by Argentine national security officials found that there was no credible evidence indicating that Argentina had yet been seriously affected by Russian criminal organisations. According to one highly placed

Argentine Interior Ministry source: 'If you ask me officially, I would have to say that there is no record of the presence of the Russian mafia in Argentina. The truth is that no one investigates mafias in Argentina, but that does not mean that they are not here' [45].

Russian mafia presence in Argentina (specifically Chechen gangs) has been linked primarily to the use of Argentina as a transit country for Andean cocaine shipments to Europe (in fishing trawlers and cargo ships), arms trafficking to Brazil and Colombia, and money laundering. In the so-called 'tri-border' area where Argentina, Brazil and Paraguay abut, Argentine intelligence sources have detected contacts between Chechen separatist groups and 'Islamic terrorists' and suspect Chechen use of these networks for arms-smuggling purposes [46]. The Argentine border with Paraguay is notorious for contraband of all types and provides virtually ideal conditions for Russian mafia operations [47].

In June 2000 the Brazilian daily newspaper *O Globo* reported growing participation of Russian mafia groups in the recruitment of Brazilian women for prostitution in Europe, especially Spain, and Israel. Russian criminal networks were also reported to be responsible for the smuggling of Russian AK-47s and Soviet rocket launchers into the *favelas* of Rio and Sao Paulo in exchange for Colombian cocaine. General Rosso Jose Serrano, former head of the Colombian National Police, claimed that Russian criminal networks were also smuggling arms through Brazil to Colombia using the same contraband routes that had been developed for smuggling cocaine out of Colombia to Brazil and on to Europe [48].

Uruguay reportedly became the preferred site for Russian money-laundering activities in the Southern Cone during the 1990s because of the country's comparatively weak banking regulations. Lax Uruguayan law enforcement has allowed Russian mobsters to take control of a number of Uruguayan banks and to obtain Uruguayan visas and passports with relative ease. The Russian mafia also reportedly uses the Bolivian banking system for laundering purposes for the same reasons [49].

Conclusions

Traditional and longstanding patterns of patrimonial rule, personalism, clientelism, and bureaucratic corruption throughout Latin America have encouraged and facilitated organised crime groups' resorts to the favoured tactics of bribery, blackmail and intimidation to maintain and protect lucrative narcotics businesses. Time and again, many (although certainly not all) police and customs officials, military officers, judges, politicians, and businessmen have proved susceptible to such enticements in large and small countries alike throughout the region [50].

The Russians are just the latest transnational criminal groups attracted to the region, but even for those Latin American countries not engulfed in civil wars such as the one raging in Colombia, their illegal arms trafficking and arms-for-drugs deals in alliance with local criminal gangs significantly increase the firepower available to violent elements of society and make them more difficult and dangerous for law enforcement to control. Brazil's *favelas*, for instance, have become virtual war zones, at least in part as a result of Russian drug- and arms-trafficking links with local criminal organisations in that country. Likewise, the Central American *maras* have become progressively better armed and threatening to social stability and state security throughout the Isthmus as a result of their linkages with Russian (along with Mexican, Colombian and North American) transnational organised crime groups.

The Russian mafia is not, by any means, the only source of weapons in the region. The United States itself is a major purveyor of small arms throughout Latin America and the Caribbean and elsewhere in the world [51]. But given the political chaos and relative availability of black-market arms in Russia and most other former Soviet Bloc countries, Russian crime groups enjoy significant comparative advantages in this clandestine market and thus have emerged as major players in the international illicit arms trade [52]. The consequences for Latin America and the Caribbean are visible on a daily basis in the surging rates of gang warfare and violent crime registered in every major urban area in the region.

Therefore, in the future, indigenous and foreign-based transnational crime networks in Latin America and the Caribbean could become more directly threatening to state security throughout the region and in the United States itself. Networks initially created to move drugs and light arms might conceivably be reconfigured to move heavy weapons such as fighter aircraft or submarines, to disseminate nuclear, chemical or biological weapons of mass destruction, or to smuggle contract assassins and/or members of the Al Qaeda terrorist network, if there was enough profit to be made in doing so [53]. In late October 2001, for example, rumours surfaced in both the Colombian and US press that some Colombian drug traffickers had been approached by representatives of 'Arab groups' with a proposal to pay the traffickers to mix cocaine with anthrax before smuggling it into the United States. US authorities immediately dismissed such reports as lacking in credibility. While such reconfigurations are conceivable, unless the profits involved promised to be so huge as to make them irresistible, the logic of the underground marketplace—high profits and limited risks—militates against transnational organised crime groups participating in such terrorist schemes. Drug traffickers are not, as a rule, interested in destroying their own markets or exposing themselves to intense international persecution. To date, there is no credible evidence that such reconfigurations have yet occurred anywhere in Latin America or the Caribbean [54].

As with other forms of transnational organised crime around the globe, to meet the growing mafia challenge successfully will require major institutional reforms in areas such as law enforcement, money laundering, border control, and anti-corruption measures at the individual country level and sustained multilateral cooperation and intelligence-sharing among state law-enforcement agencies at the sub-regional, regional, and international levels [55]. It will also require a much clearer understanding on the part of political elites and law enforcement officials in every Latin American and Caribbean country of the transnational nature of the threats they face in their own nations and the consequent need to revise traditional and antiquated notions of national sovereignty and deeply ingrained but increasingly dysfunctional pseudo-nationalist rejection of international cooperation To date, neither the requisite country reforms nor adequate multilateral-level coordination, much less the needed changes in mind-set, have been forthcoming [56]. As a result, criminal organisations have been able to spread across the entire region virtually unfettered for more than a decade.

Initial developments in the international arena in response to the devastating 11 September, 2001, terrorist attacks on the United States suggest that a new momentum behind greater multilateral cooperation might materialise in coming months and years. Specifically, the additional impetus given by the United States to the multilateral aspects of law enforcement in its prosecution of the 'war ' on global terrorism could ultimately usher in a new era of international coordination against terrorism and organised crime. To combat this new stage of global terrorism effectively will unquestionably require the construction of new, multilateral mechanisms for the international monitoring and policing of terrorist movements, illegal weapons sales, illicit capital flows and money laundering.

The two common elements shared by global terrorism and transnational organised crime—money laundering and proliferation—may finally catalyse serious and sustained multilateral coordination in international law enforcement. The current enthusiasm for multilateral efforts could, however, quickly evaporate. The real key to success in both the 'war' on terrorism and the fight against transnational organised crime will be whether or not the international community has the will and capacity required to design and institutionalise effective systems of multilateral coordination and cooperation over the long haul. The states of Latin America and the Caribbean will be called upon to play major roles in this process. Failure to act promptly and effectively is likely to carry a high price tag in terms of the erosion of domestic prosperity and stability within individual nation-states and the imposition major costs on recalcitrant states via international pressures and sanctions applied either unilaterally by the United States or multilaterally by the international community.

Notes

[1] The Federal Bureau of Investigation (FBI) defines organised crime as '. . .a self-perpetuating, structured and disciplined association of individuals or groups, combined together for the purpose of obtaining monetary or commercial gains or profits, wholly or in part by illegal means, while protecting their activities through a pattern of graft and corruption.' Center for Strategic & International Studies (CSIS), Russian Organised Crime. (Washington DC, 1997: 23–4).Transnational crime is defined as crimes or offences whose inception, prevention, and/or direct or indirect effects involve more than one country. Mueller, 'Transnational Crime: Definitions and Concepts', 14.

[2] The term 'weak' state as used here refers not to the type of regime—e.g. authoritarian or democratic—or to the form of government—e.g. unitary or federalist—nor to institutional arrangements—e.g. presidential or parliamentary political systems. Rather, it refers to the institutional capacity of the state, whatever its form, to penetrate society, extract resources from it and regulate conflicts within it. Specifically, the term refers to the ability of state authorities to govern legitimately, to enforce the law systematically, and to administer justice effectively throughout the national territory. Understood in this fashion, Latin America has produced no

strong states. Not even the Mexican state during the 71 years of single-party domination and inclusionary authoritarianism under PRI rule nor the Brazilian state during the decade plus of military rule and bureaucratic authoritarianism can be accurately classified as strong states according to this definition. Of course, the weak/strong dichotomy encompasses an underlying continuum or range of possibilities. Some Latin American and Caribbean states are clearly weaker than others. Thus, it is valid to argue that both the Mexican and Brazilian states are 'stronger' than, say, the Haitian or Paraguayan states.

[3] Farer, 'Conclusion: Fighting Transnational Organised Crime: Measures Short of War', 251.

[4] Keohane, 'Governance in a Partially Globalized World', *The American Political Science Review*.

[5] Arrighi, 'Globalization, State Sovereignty, and the "Endless" Accumulation of Capital'.

[6] Held et al., *Global Transformations: Politics, Economics and Culture*, 1–31.

[7] For analyses of the impact of globalisation on transnational organised crime see Passas, 'Globalization and Transnational Crime: Effects of Criminogenic Asymmetries'; and Williams, 'Organizing Transnational Crime: Networks, Markets and Hierarchies'. Russian money launderers amply demonstrated their financial sophistication by successfully obscuring their illicit transactions within the larger movement of capital into and out of emerging markets by timing them to the speculative capital shifts that occurred during the Mexican peso crisis (1995), the Thai bhat crisis (1997) and the Turkish lira crisis (2001), among other recent currency crises.

[8] Whitehead, 'High-level Political Corruption in Latin America: A "Transitional" Phenomenon?' See also Manzetti, 'Market Reforms Without Transparency', 130–72; and Jarquin & Carillo-Flores, 'The Complexity of Anti-Corruption Policies in Latin America', 193–204.

[9] Mittleman, 'The Dynamics of Globalization', 6–10. Cox, *Production, Power and World Order: Social Forces in the Making of History*.

[10] Of the 500 million people who reside in Latin America, 89 million live in extreme poverty and almost one half are considered poor. According to the United Nations Economic Commission for Latin America and the Caribbean, the proportion of people living in poverty decreased modestly in Latin America in the 1990s after the disastrous 'lost decade' of the 1980s, but the World Bank's World Development Indicators 2004 Survey has found the overall proportion living in poverty hardly changing in the period 1981–2004. World Bank 'Dramatic Decline in Global Poverty, but Progress Uneven', 23 April 2004, http://web.worldbank.org/WBSITE/EXTERNAL/NEWS/D,,contentMKD:20195240~menuPK:34459~pagePK:64003015~piPK:64003012~thesitePK:4607,00.html

[11] Of course, only a small proportion of the poor in Latin America (as elsewhere around the globe) resort to criminality of any sort and even smaller numbers actually become involved in organised crime. In fact, the poorest of the poor are generally ill-equipped to engage in organised criminal enterprises because such activities require relatively higher levels of education, technical know-how, access to financial resources, and familiarity with bureaucratic-administrative procedures and police and political contacts than the abjectly poor have at their disposal. For a discussion of the characteristics of modern large-scale criminal organisations see Paoli, 'Criminal Fraternities or Criminal Enterprises'.

[12] Gomorra/Grupo Reforma, 'Redes de la mafia globalizada en Mexico'.

[13] *The Economist*, 'A Survey of Illegal Drugs: Stumbling in the Dark'. Speaking to a special meeting of the Russian Security Council on September 28 2001, President Putin stated that the drug problem in Russia has become so serious that it '...threatens the country's national security both directly and by providing funds to terrorists.' Russia registered 243,000 drug-related crimes in 2000, 12,000 of which were committed by organised gangs. Yasmann, 'Putin Says Drug Problem Threatens Russian National Security'.

[14] BBC, 'Q&A: Who's behind Russia's money laundering?'

[15] Moore, 'Cocaine Seizures by US Double in Pacific Ocean: S. American Cartels Abandon Caribbean for More Lucrative Route'.

[16]   *Ibid*: A24. DEA officials estimate that 65 % of the cocaine produced in South America reaches US cities via the US–Mexico border and is smuggled across by Mexican cartels (based principally in Tijuana, Juarez, Sinaloa, Matamoros, and Guadalajara) acting in alliance with Colombian suppliers. Seper, 'Mexicans, Russian Mob New Partners in Crime'; Joyner, 'Tambien en Estados Unidos hay cartels de la droga'.

[17]   A previous bust of a ship called *Forever My Friends* by the US Coast Guard in the eastern Pacific on March 6 2001 involved ten Russian crew members smuggling 8 tons of cocaine to Mexico. CNN.com/US, 'Ship and Suspects in Major Cocaine Bust Arrive at San Diego'.

[18]   Gardner&Fuentes/Grupo Reforma, (2001), 'Operan los Arellano con mafia rusa-DEA'; Stratfor.com, 'Accord with US Won't Stop Mexico's Drug Cartels'.

[19]   Peters, 'Mexico: Drug Trafficking in the Pacific Has a Distinct Russian Flavor'.

[20]   *Ibid.*

[21]   Barajas/Grupo Reforma (2001), 'Desconocen vinculos Arellano-rusos'.

[22]   Stratfor.com (2001), 'Special Report: Central America's Crime Wave'.

[23]   Much of the tidal wave of violent crime engulfing Central America's fragile democracies, discouraging foreign investment and slowing economic growth is directly related to youth gang activity. In El Salvador, for example, National Police authorities reported 735 homicides between January and April 2001, of which 599 were related to gang violence and drugs. The Salvadoran government estimates that crime costs the country the equivalent of 13% of GDP annually. Stratfor.com, *Ibid.*, 2.

[24]   *Ibid*: 2.

[25]   *Ibid*: 2–3.

[26]   *Ibid*: 3; Bagley, *Myths of Militarization: The Role of the Military in the War on Drugs in the Americas*, 16–23.

[27]   US State Department, *International Narcotics Control Strategy Report 2003*.

[28]   US State Department, *International Narcotics Control Strategy Report 2003*.

[29]   The first 'summit' meeting between the Cali cartel and Russian mafia capos reportedly took place in Moscow in late 1992, although there is evidence that Colombian cocaine was being shipped by the Cali cartel to Russia and other East Bloc countries as early as 1991. Clawson, & Lee III, *The Andean Cocaine Industry*, 87. Prior to the forging of this Russian connection, in the late 1980s and early 1990s the Cali cartel had first established '. . .a very effective alliance with Sicilian criminal organisations that was instrumental in opening up the European market for Colombian cocaine. It allowed the use of existing drug distribution routes in Europe, and was effectively a strategic alliance that allowed Colombian trafficking organisations to diversify into a new market at a time when the US cocaine market had become saturated.' Williams, *op. cit.*, 64. For a detailed discussion of the nature of the alliance between the Colombian cartels and Italian crime groups, see Clawson and Lee, 62–89.

[30]   In a February 1997 meeting between a Russian mobster (Ludwig Fainberg, a.k.a. 'Tarzan') and representatives of the Cali cartel that took place at a Russian mob-owned strip club called Porky's located in Miami, Florida, Tarzan offered to provide a $5.5-million Soviet Tango-class diesel submarine, along with a full crew, to the Cali cartel for use in transporting cocaine from the Pacific coast of Colombia to Mexico or California. Fainberg was, however, subsequently arrested and the deal was never consummated. Semana (1997), 'La cocavodka' *Revista Semana* No. 805; Navarro, 'Russian Submarine Drifts into Center of Brazen Drug Plot'; Drummond, 'Enter the Redfellas: Are Russian Mobsters Dallying with Drug Lords?'

[31]   Lackey with Moran, 'Russian Mob Trading Arms for Cocaine with Colombian Rebels,'; Semple, 'The Submarine Next Door'; Semana, 'Investigacion: Yellow Submarine'. In April 2001, Colombian police reportedly seized one and a half pounds of enriched uranium of a type used in Soviet submarines that may have been obtained from elements of the Russian mafia. Campbell, 'Bogota Police Foil "Atom Bomb" Sale'.

[32]   Waller, 'The KGB & Its "Successors"'; Staar, 'Russia's Military: Corruption in the Higher Ranks'.

[33] MSNBC, *op. cit.*: 6.

[34] MSNBC, *op. cit*: 2. Hundreds of thousands of kilos of Colombian cocaine at US $50,000 per kilo in Europe were reportedly smuggled via this route in 1999–2000.

[35] *Ibid.*: 3; Semana, 'Narcotrafico: La prueba reina'.

[36] MSNBC, *op. cit.*: 3–4. Semana, 'Frontera investigada'.

[37] In the first six months following Fujimori's fall, 18 generals and more than 70 of his government's high-ranking military and intelligence officials were arrested and jailed for corruption, drug smuggling and arms trafficking.

[38] The rancor between Castro's Cuba and Putin's Russia boiled over in public on October 17, 2001, when President Putin, without consulting Havana, suddenly announced that Russia would close its large eavesdropping center in Cuba. The Lourdes base, one of the last relics of the Cold War still in operation in Cuba, was built by the Soviet Union in 1964 and housed an estimated 1,500 Russian and Cuban military personnel. Putin's decision to close the Cuban facility, along with a similar Pacific electronic reconnaissance post at Cam Ranh Bay in Vietnam, left Cuba no room for negotiations. Putin unilaterally declared that the posts were to be closed for budgetary reasons, because of their declining significance for Russia in the post-Cold War era, and to shift Russian military assets to the fight against international terrorism. Cuba's anger reflected its frustration at yet another economic blow from Russia, which had paid $200 million annually in rent for use of the Lourdes facility. Glaser, 'Russia to Dismantle Spy Facility in Cuba'; Sullivan, 'Cuba Upset By Closure of Russian Spy Base'.

[39] Around 200 metric tons of cocaine are smuggled into Europe annually, despite seizures of dozens of tons en route. AFP 'European Trade in Cocaine on the Increase'.

[40] Farah *op. cit.*: A16; Roberts, 'Small Places, Big Money: The Cayman Islands and the International Financial System'; Maingot, 'The Decentralization Imperative and Caribbean Criminal Enterprises', 143–70.

[41] See, for example, Naylor, *Hot Money and the Politics of Debt*; Grosse, *Drugs and Money: Laundering Latin America's Cocaine Dollars*; Blum, 'Offshore Money', 57–84. Blum is particularly critical of Panama: 'Free-trade zones such as the Colon free-trade zone in Panama have become centers for illegal commercial and financial activity. One of the most important branches of the BCCI was in the Colon free-trade zone, which was then and continues to be a center for the smuggling of goods and weapons all over the hemisphere.': 83.

[42] A recent UN Report estimated that about 900,000 out of Brazil's population of 170 million regularly use cocaine (0.7%). Although this percentage falls short of the US consumption rate of around 3% (5.3 million), it exceeds consumption rates in European nations such as France or Germany and makes Brazil the second largest cocaine-consuming nation in the world. Faiola, 'Cocaine a Consuming Problem in Brazil: Drug-fueled Violence Turns Slums into Urban Battle Fields'.

[43] Faiola, *Ibid.*, A01.

[44] Stratfor.com, 'Paraguay's Drug Trade Perilous Target for US'; O'Donnell, 'La Argentina en la mira de la mafia rusa'.

[45] O'Donnell, *Ibid.*, 2.

[46] The Paraguayan city of Ciudad del Este, located in the tri-border area some 350 km from Asuncion, is often labeled the contraband capital of South America. It has a population of approximately 500,000, of whom perhaps 30,000 are Muslims, mostly of Arab descent. There is a drug trafficking–Islamic fundamentalism connection not only in the case of the Taliban but also in the case of the Chechen separatists fighting for independence from Russia. General Shamil Basayev, the Jordanian-born fundamentalist leader of the Chechens, was trained in Afghanistan and had direct connections to Osama bin Laden in the 1980s. To finance their separatist movement, Basayev and his Chechen followers transported Afghani heroin through Abkhazia (a renegade province of Georgia that broke away with Russian military help in 1993)

to the Black Sea or through Turkey to Cyprus and then on to Europe. In light of their goal of political independence, the Chechens can be differentiated from most other Russian organised crime groups. Nejamkis/Reuters, 'Preocupa presencia arabe en Paraguay'; LaFraniere, 'Georgia Dispatches Troops Toward Separatist Region: Russia Bolsters Border with Abkhazia after Violence'.

[47] The Paraguayan Consul in Miami from June 1999 to May 2001, Carlos Weiss, is currently under arrest, accused of having sold more than 300 passports, visas and cargo shipment authorisations at up to $8,000 apiece before he was fired in May. Some who received these documents are suspected of possible involvement in the terrorist attacks on the World Trade Center and on the Pentagon on September 11, 2001. According to a report by the Justice Department's inspector general released in February 2000, the Border Patrol '...cannot accurately quantify how many illegal aliens and drug smugglers it fails to apprehend.' Grimaldi et al., 'Losing Track of Illegal Immigrants'; Reyes, 'Atentados en EU reviven un escandalo en Paraguay'; Rohter, 'Terrorists Are Sought in Latin Smugglers' Haven'.

[48] O'Donnell, *op. cit.*, 2.

[49] O'Donnell, *op. cit.*, 3. For an analysis of the evolution of drug trafficking and international criminal activity in Bolivia from the 1950s through the 1990s, see Gamarra, 'Transnational Criminal Organisations in Bolivia', 171–92. Personal interviews conducted by the author with high-ranking officials in Bolivia during July 2001 revealed that, despite the recent dramatic declines in Bolivian coca production under former President Banzer (who resigned from office on September 6, 2001, owing to severe illness from cancer), Russian and Italian mafia gangs—in conjunction with Peruvian and Bolivian traffickers—continue to use contraband routes across northern Bolivia to smuggle Peruvian and Bolivian cocaine into Brazil and, thence, on to cargo ships bound for Europe, especially Spain and Portugal, and Russia.

[50] For an analysis of the relation between political corruption and governability with specific reference to the Colombian case, see Cepeda Ulloa, *Corrupcion y gobernabilidad*. For analyses of the impact of organised crime on democratic governance in Mexico, see the essays in J. Bailey & R. Godson (eds), *Crimen organizado y gobernabilidad democratica: Mexico y la franja fronteriza*.

[51] According to the Small Arms Survey, a Geneva-based organisation, the US is the leading exporter of small and light arms in the world, selling about $1.2 billion of the $4 billion to $6 billion worldwide total in 1998. Lynch, 'US Fights U.N. Accord to Control Small Arms: Stance on Draft Pact Not Shared by Allies'; Weiner & Thompson, 'US Guns Smuggled Into Mexico Aid Drug War'.

[52] See Naylor, 'The Rise of the Modern Arms Black Market and the Fall of Supply-Side Control', 220–2.

[53] See Clawson & Lee, *op. cit.*: 89; Anderson, 'International Terrorism and Crime: Trends and Linkages'.

[54] Reyes, 'Denucian mezcla con cocaina en Colombia'.

[55] For detailed discussions of how to respond more effectively to the challenges of transnational organised crime at the international level see de Gennaro, 'Strengthening the International Legal System in order to Combat Transnational Crime', 259–68; Godson, & Williams, 'Strengthening Cooperation Against Transnational Crime: A New Security Perspective', 321–55.

[56] For examples of the difficulties that continue to plague effective international law enforcement efforts on different fronts see Wechsler, 'Follow the Money', 40–57; Joseph, 'Money Laundering Enforcement: Following the Money', 11–14; and Williams, 'Organised Crime and Cybercrime: Synergies, Trends and Responses', 22–6.

References

AFP. (2001) 'European trade in cocaine on the increase', Yahoo! News, August 8, http://sg.news. yahoo.com/o10808/1/1aolu.html

Anderson, J.H. 'International terrorism and crime: trends and linkages.' William R. Nelson Institute for Public Affairs, James Madison University. http://www.jmu.edu/orgs/wrni/it.htm

Arrighi, G. (1997) 'Globalization, state sovereignty, and the "endless" accumulation of capital', Fernand Braudel Center, Binghamton, NY, http://fbc.binghamton.edu/gairvn97.htm.

Bagley, B. (1991) *Myths of Militarization: The Role of the Military in the War on Drugs in the Americas*, Coral Gables.

Bailey, J. & Godson, R. (eds) (2000) *Crimen organizado y gobernabilidad democratica: Mexico y la franja fronteriza* Mexico DF.

Barajas, A./Grupo Reforma (2001) 'Desconocen vinculos Arellano-rusos', *Reforma*, May 18.

BBC (1999) 'Q&A: who's behind Russia's money laundering?', BBC Online Network, October 19, http: www3.thny.bbc.co.uk/hi/English/world/Europe/newsid_434000/434691.stm

Blum, J. (1999) 'Offshore money', in *Transnational Crime in the Americas*, ed. T. Farer, New York.

Campbell, M. (2001) 'Bogota police foil "atom bomb" sale', *The Sunday Times* (London), April 29, p. 22.

Cepeda Ulloa, F. (2000) *Corrupcion y gobernabilidad*, Bogota.

Clawson, P. L. & Lee, R. W., III (1998) *The Andean Cocaine Industry*, New York.

CNN.com/US. (2001) 'Ship and suspects in major cocaine bust arrive at San Diego', CNN. com., May 14, http://www.cnn.com/2001/US/05/14/cocaine.seizure.txt/index.html

Cox, R. (1987) *Production, Power and World Order: Social Forces in the Making of History*, New York.

Drummond, T. (1997) 'Enter the redfellas: are Russian mobsters dallying with drug lords?', *Time*, vol. 150, no. 2, p. 14.

The Economist (2001) 'A survey of illegal drugs: stumbling in the dark', *The Economist*, July 28, p. 3.

Faiola, A. (2001) 'Cocaine a consuming problem in Brazil: drug-fueled violence turns slums into urban battle fields', *The Washington Post*, July 8, A01.

Farer, T. (1999) 'Conclusion: fighting transnational organised crime: measures short of war', in *Transnational Crime in the Americas*, ed. T. Farer, New York.

Gamarra, E. A. (1999) 'Transnational criminal organisations in Bolivia', in *Transnational Crime in the Americas*, ed. T. Farer, New York.

Gardner, R. & Fuentes, V./Grupo Reforma (2001) 'Operan los arellano con mafia rusa-DEA', *Reforma*, May 14.

de Gennaro, G. (1998) 'Strengthening the international legal system in order to combat transnational crime', *Transnational Organized Crime*, vol. 4, no. 3, p. 4 (Autumn/Winter).

Glaser, S. B. (2001) 'Russia to dismantle spy facility in Cuba', *The Washington Post*, October 18, A34.

Godson, R. & Williams, P. (1998) 'Strengthening cooperation against transnational crime: A new security perspective', *Transnational Organized Crime*, vol. 4, no. 3, p. 4 (Autumn/Winter).

Gomorra, D./Grupo Reforma (2001) 'Redes de la mafia globalizada en Mexico', *Reforma*, vol. 16, de mayo.

Grimaldi, J. V., Fainaru, S. & Gaul, G. M. (2001) 'Losing track of illegal immigrants', *The Washington Post*, October 7, A01.

Grosse, R. E. (2001) *Drugs and Money: Laundering Latin America's Cocaine Dollars*, Westport, Connecticut.

Held, D. et al. (1999) *Global Transformations: Politics, Economics and Culture*, Stanford, CA.

Jarquin, E. & Carillo-Flores, F. (2000) 'The complexity of anti-corruption policies in Latin America', eds J. S. Tulchin & R. H. Espach.

Joseph, L. M. (2001) 'Money laundering enforcement: following the money', *Economic Perspectives: An Electronic Journal of the US Department of State*, vol. 6, no. 2 (May).

Joyner, A. (2001) 'Tambien en estados unidos hay cartels de la droga', *Milenio Diario de Mexico*, p. 18, Septiembre.

Keohane, R. O. (2001) 'Governance in a partially globalized world', *The American Political Science Review*, vol. 95, no. 1, March.

Krauss, C. (2001) 'Economic pain spreads from US across Latin America', *The New York Times*, p. 14, October.

Lackey, S. & Moran, M. (2000) 'Russian mob trading arms for cocaine with colombian rebels', MSNBC.com., April 9; http://www.msnbc.com/news/391623.asp?)m = − 13N

LaFraniere, S. (2001) 'Georgia dispatches troops toward separatist region: Russia bolsters border with abkhazia after violence', *The Washington Post*, October 12, A29.

Lynch, C. (2001) 'US fights U.N. accord to control small arms: stance on draft pact not shared by allies', *The Washington Post*, July 10, A01.

Maingot, A. P. (1999) 'The decentralization imperative and caribbean criminal enterprises', in *Transnational Crime in the Americas*, ed. T. Farer, New York.

Manzetti, L. (2000) 'Market reforms without transparency', eds J. S. Tulchin & R. H. Espach.

Mittleman, J. H. (1997) 'The dynamics of globalization', in *Globalization: Critical Reflections*, ed. J. H. Mittleman, Boulder, CO.

Moore, M. (2000) 'Cocaine seizures by US double in pacific ocean: S. American cartels abandon aaribbean for more lucrative route', *The Washington Post*, September 3, A24.

Mueller, G. O. W. (1998) 'Transnational crime: definitions and concepts', *Transnational Organised Crime*, vol. 4, no. 3, p. 4 (Autumn/Winter).

Navarro, M. (1997) 'Russian submarine drifts into center of brazen drug plot', *The New York Times*, March 7, A22.

Naylor, R. T. (1994) *Hot Money and the Politics of Debt*, Montreal.

Naylor, R. T. (1998) 'The rise of the modern arms black market and the fall of supply-side control', *Transnational Organised Crime*, vol. 4, no. 3, p. 4 (Autumn/Winter).

Reuters Nejamkis, G. (2001) 'Preocupa presencia arabe en Paraguay', *El Nuevo Herald*, 25 de septiembre.

O'Donnell, S. (2000) 'La Argentina en la mira de la mafia rusa', in: *La Nacion*, September 24, vol. 1, http://www.lanacion.com.ar/00/09/24/G01.htm

Paoli, L. (1998) 'Criminal fraternities or criminal enterprises', *Transnational Organized Crime*, vol. 4, no. 3, p. 4 (Autumn/Winter).

Passas, N. (1998) 'Globalization and transnational crime: effects of criminogenic asymmetries', *Transnational Organized Crime*, vol. 4, no. 3, p. 4 (Autumn/Winter).

Peters, G. (2001) 'Mexico: drug trafficking in the pacific has a distinct Russian flavor', *San Francisco Chronicle, May*, p. 30.

Reyes, G. (2001) 'Atentados en EU reviven un escandalo en Paraguay', *El Nuevo Herald*, September 20.

Reyes, G. (2001) 'Denucian mezcla con cocaina en Colombia', *El Nuevo Herald*, October 24.

Roberts, S. (1995) 'Small places, big money: The Cayman islands and the international financial system', *Economic Geography*, vol. 1, no. 3 (July).

Rohter, L. (2001) 'Terrorists are sought in Latin smugglers' haven', *The New York Times*, September 27.

Semana, 'Investigacion: Yellow Submarine', *Revista Semana*, http://216.35.197.109/archivo/articulo_view.asp?id = 2785

Semana, 'Narcotrafico: la prueba reina', *Semana*, http://216.35.197.109/archivo/articulo_view.asp?id = 5628

Semana (1997) 'La cocavodka', in: *Revista Semana*, No. 805, Octubre 5–12.

Semana (2001) 'Frontera investigada', in: *Revista Semana*, Octubre 22.

Semple, K. (2000) 'The submarine next door', *The New York Times Magazine*, December 3.

Seper, J. (2001) 'Mexicans, Russian mob new partners in crime', *Washington Times*, August 13.

Staar, R. F. (1998) 'Russia's military: corruption in the higher ranks', in: *Perspective*, IX/2 (November–December), http://www.bu.edu/iscip/vol9/Staar.html

Stratfor.com, 'Paraguay's Drug Trade Perilous Target for US', Stratfor.com. http://www.stratfor.com/latinamerica/commentary/0108141600

Stratfor.com. (2001) 'Accord with US won't stop Mexico's drug cartels', Stratfor.com, July 31.

Stratfor.com. (2001) 'Special report: central America's crime wave', Stratfor.com, August 29, p. 2–3, http://www.stratfor.com/premium/0108/29.htr.

Sullivan, K. (2001) 'Cuba upset by closure of Russian spy base', *The Washington Post*, October 19, p. A26.

US State Department *International Narcotics Control Strategy Report 2003*.

Waller, J. M. (1994) 'The KGB & its "successors"', *Perspective*, IV/4, (April–May), http://www.bu.edu/iscip/vol4/Waller.html.

Wechsler, W. F. (2001) 'Follow the money', *Foreign Affairs*, vol. 80, no. 4 (July/August).

Weiner, T. & Thompson, G. (2001) 'US guns smuggled into Mexico aid drug war', *The New York Times*, May, p. 19.

Whitehead, L. (2000) 'High-level political corruption in Latin America: A "transitional" phenomenon?', in *Combating Corruption in Latin America*, eds J. S. Tulchin & R. H. Espach, Washington DC.

Williams, P. 'Organizing Transnational Crime: Networks, Markets and Hierarchies', *Transnational Organized Crime*, Vol. 4 no. 3, p.4 (Autumn/Winter).

Williams, P. 'Organised Crime and Cybercrime: Synergies, Trends and Responses', *Global Issues: An Electronic Journal of the Department of State*, 6/2: 22–6.

Yasmann, V. (2001) 'Putin says drug problem threatens Russian national security', *RFE/RL Security Watch*, vol. 2, no. 39, October 10.

The Russian 'Mafiya': Consolidation and Globalisation

Mark Galeotti[1]

In 1985, any suggestions that there was a widespread criminal subculture in Soviet Russia were generally treated as implausible and exaggerated; in discussions with a senior Soviet police officer who wrote a report on organised crime in the USSR that year, I was told that it was a 'waning and scattered negative social phenomenon'. By 1995, the Russian 'mafiya' [2] was considered one of the dominant powers within not just Russia (even the Kremlin accepted the apocryphal estimates that it controlled 40 percent of the economy) but the global underworld, and it had become a staple of

Dr Mark Galeotti is the Director of the Organised Russian & Eurasian Crime Research Unit (ORECRU) at Keele University the post-Cold War thriller. At this time, it still seemed to be able to operate with virtual impunity within Russia, and protection racketeering, contract killing and turf wars were both rife and overt. By 2005, though, this is likely to have changed considerably, even if this change will represent less of an improvement than might be hoped. Two forces are changing the Russian underworld. First of all, it is maturing, as larger, more professional networks eliminate or incorporate the myriad gangs that emerged in the freewheeling days of the early Russian state. Secondly, President Putin is a rather different figure to his predecessor, and he is embarked upon a state-building programme intolerant of the kind of open anarchy that characterised the early 1990s.

Even so, one of the most distinctive things about Russian organised crime is precisely how disorganised it is. It ranges from swaggering Chechen gangsters to seemingly-legitimate Russian entrepreneurs whose business empires have been built on the back of money laundering and rigged privatisation auctions. Along with overtly criminal activities such as protection racketeering, drug smuggling and prostitution, most are also involved in much legal business. Indeed, the most important criminal godfathers now work mainly within the legal or largely-legal sectors. They may secretly transfer their funds to offshore havens, fiddle their taxes, pay off local officials or establish illegal cartels, but they have long since hived off their protection rackets and narcotics rings to hungry protégés. Further, if one looks as the so-called 'oligarchs' and the business empires currently dominating Russia, few do not have skeletons in their cupboards, and in some cases still sitting in their boardrooms. Although there is a tendency on the part of some of the larger and more settled corporations to begin to adopt Western standards of corporate governance, in the main there is still frighteningly little to distinguish the criminal from his legitimate counterparts. Both tend to be flexible, able and entrepreneurial. The criminals simply see crime often simply as the quickest and fastest route to money, power and security, but have no objection to working licitly if the balance of danger against opportunity is right.

The Shape of the Beast

As befits a criminal culture which, for all its deep roots, has really come to age in the past two decades, Russian organised crime is a distinctive, even post-modernist phenomenon, characterised by loose and flexible networks of semi-autonomous criminal entrepreneurs and with an especially keen awareness of the political environment in which it operates. The Soviet underworld built on a criminal culture which dated back over a century, that of the so-called *vorovskoi mir*, or 'thieves' world', which had its own language (known as *fenya*) and code [3], but this was reshaped by the experiences of Stalinism and shortage. Under Stalin, as the Gulag prison camps swelled with the millions of political prisoners, criminals were in effect co-opted as auxiliaries of the State, to keep the 'politicals' in line. This ran counter to the traditional code of the *vorovskoi mir*, but the opportunities in collaboration were too tempting, and a bloody hidden war fought in the camps led to victory for the 'scabs', who thus learned the invaluable lesson that power, profit and protection could all be obtained through corrupted minions of the State. This lesson was put to good use when the camps were opened after Stalin's death and the 'scabs' colonised the rest of the Soviet underworld and reshaped the *vorovskoi mir* in their image. From the 1960s onwards, organised crime would flourish thanks to the growing corruption of the Communist Party élite and the extent to which the underground economy became tacitly accepted by the State as a way of bypassing the bottlenecks of the official, planned economy and pacifying the hungry masses by providing limited access to scarce goods and services.

The criminals thus at once were able to prey on black-market entrepreneurs, but also to act as their middlemen with corrupt elements within the national and local élites. However, they were in many ways the weakest element of this unholy trinity, depending on the black-marketeers for income and the Party bosses for security. As the Party collapsed in the 1980s, though, they were able to emerge from the shadows and assert their dominance over both their erstwhile partners. Mikhail Gorbachev's ill-advised anti-alcohol campaign was every bit as helpful for organised crime as Prohibition had been in the United States, as ordinary citizens turned to the criminals to supply them with drink. Meanwhile, Gorbachev's early steps towards economic liberalisation created thousands of small businesses which were perfect targets for protection racketeering (not least because most Soviets, police included, resented the new breed of entrepreneur) and also legitimate front organisations. Gorbachev's later attempts at more comprehensive political reform fragmented the Party and triggered the attempted conservative coup which led to the collapse of the Soviet state in 1991.

The new Russia was born bankrupt and in crisis, overshadowed by the fear of a Communist resurgence, which helps explain the heedless privatisation campaigns which transferred so many public assets into the hands of the corrupt and the criminal—it seemed more important to transfer resources from the State's hands than ask to many questions about their new owners. Organised crime was able to capitalise on the new opportunities and, freed from the fear of the State or the need to pander to Party bosses who put a premium on the semblance of public order, could do so openly. This was the era of '*mafiya* chic' in which mobsters and their molls and hangers-on revelled in their new wealth and freedom, while turf wars were fought out with car bombs and firefights, with the police unable or unwilling to intervene. Meanwhile, in Chechnya, a tradition of freewheeling banditry, the opportunities provided by organised crime and the promise of freedom from bitterly resented Russian rule served to turn it into a veritable 'free criminal zone'. The subsequent Russian invasions of 1994 and 1999 were essentially products of politics and imperialism rather than police actions, and did little to quell a criminal phenomenon that, by then, had largely outgrown the Chechen highlands [4].

Meanwhile, the structure and culture of the *vorovskoi mir* also changed to reflect its new environment. Attempts at drawing up formal structures for *mafiya* groups have tended to represent them as classic pyramidal hierarchies, with godfathers at the top, a larger number of lieutenants below and then street operatives, but these do not match the realities on the ground. For a start, there is no rigid chain of command. There are certainly key figures within the *mafiya*, including the *vory v zakone* ('thieves-within-code'), who are figures of authority within the *vorovskoi mir*, who may have little direct power but are held in respect and often act as mediators and arbitrators, and the *avtoritety* ('authorities'), who are more conventional criminal leaders. However, even an *avtoritet* is unlikely to have much of a personal gang of his own. Instead, he is merely a powerful, wealthy and influential member of a criminal network. After all, Russian organised crime is best understood as a series of loose and flexible networks of semi-independent criminal entrepreneurs and gangs. Despite official reports which talk of over 4,000 organised crime gangs in Russia, most of these operate within larger networks. Instead, Russia has 12–15 major *mafiya* structures, each of which brings together myriad small crews, local gangs and even individuals. None of these larger networks has a single leader as such, though they may be associated with a few specific figures of particular authority and power. Indeed, there is a great resistance to the very concept of a single 'boss'. This was, for example, one of the contributing factors behind the assassination of Georgian kingpin Otari Kvantrishvili in 1994. He was briefly considered the most powerful criminal in Moscow, but as he tried to assert his personal control throughout and beyond his network, he ran up against this centrifugal tendency, and his murder appears to have been carried out with the blessing of most of the other senior criminals in the city, including his own lieutenants.

Secondly, most *mafiya* figures and crews have very broad criminal and even legal interests. There are specialists, ranging from assassins and computer crackers to money launderers and counterfeiters, but they tend to operate largely on the peripheries of the networks, as freelance service providers. The mainstream criminals will seek to establish a wide range of functions and businesses within the network. For a relatively new or unsophisticated criminal, this may be essentially simple, such as collecting protection money from market traders, selling counterfeit goods and running errands for a more established criminal. However, as the criminal becomes more successful, he will probably develop a 'portfolio' of business stretching from the entirely criminal through to the essentially legitimate. Of course, organised crime does not 'own' Russia [5] but what it does not control outright, it can influence. A concept pioneered by Russian scholar Vadim Volkov is that of 'violent entrepreneurship', the process of translating coercive muscle into economic power [6]. Thus today's *mafiya* is also a much-prized service provider. Central to this is the notion of a *krysha*, a 'roof' or 'protection', which is a very important, but also complex and sometimes ambiguous concept. The term is used for a whole range of separate activities, from the simple—and parasitic—extortion of protection money, to rather more positive services. A 'good' *krysha* provided by the more entrepreneurial gangs will not only protect you from other criminals, it will also provide a range of other services, from debt recovery (handled far more quickly and efficiently than Russia's corrupt and inefficient courts) to an inside track on whom to bribe within the local authorities to get things done. This helps explain why an estimated 70–80 percent of firms pay an average of 10–20 percent of their profits for this 'roof'.

Even the old organising principles of ethnic ties or place of origin are breaking down. Many gang or network names relate to the place where they first formed or where their original leaders came from, but these often have little bearing on their present location or operation. St Petersburg's dominant *Tambov* group is named after the city where its first members used to live, just as few members of the *Solntsevo* grouping, the main gang in Moscow and the most internationally-spread of all the Russian networks [7], still live or work in the suburb the gang was named after. As for ethnic ties, even the so-called 'Chechen mafiya' now includes Georgians, Dagestanis, Kazakhs and even Slavs. As a result, many of these networks have lost the personal or regional loyalties that held smaller gangs together, and never acquired the sort of traditions and mythology which plays in important role in criminal cultures such as the yakuza or mafia. With little holding them together beyond self-interest and fear of reprisals in case of disloyalty, they are also prone to division and redefinition, as components choose to move into another network as the balance of opportunities seems to shift. This helps explain the relative instability of the *mafiya* and its tendency towards internal bloodletting.

Globalisation: Import–export

The Russian *mafiya* moved quickly to establish itself as an international phenomenon. As well as the realities of the modern global economy, to an extent this reflected the degree to which they were actively sought out as partners and consumers by other transnational criminal networks (especially the Italians), and the uncertainties facing Russia itself. In the early 1990s, the fear of some communist or ultra-nationalist coup leading to purges and renationalisation did not seem implausible, and so it was important for the criminals to acquire foreign property and bank accounts to permit a rapid and comfortable escape if need be.

The entrepreneurialism of Russian organised crime groups certainly extends to their international operations. It is fair to say that there is not a criminal activity with which they are not in some way involved. They are also involved in a wide range of legal businesses or the 'mainly-legal' (such as factories producing legal goods, but with illegal immigrant labour). Today Russian-based groupings are reckoned to operate directly in almost 70 countries. However, in an age of cyberbanking, telecommunications and globalised economies, there are few parts of the world in which their influence is not felt.

Mafiya groupings continue illegally to export money, natural resources and weapons. With thousands of guns going missing from Russian military arsenals annually, and at least twice as many from factories, it is hardly surprising that the country's own underground weapons market has become saturated. Russian guns, from ageing AK-47s intended for military reservists to the latest assault carbines, are finding their way onto the international market. This has clear implications for international security. According to US Congressman Benjamin Gilman, 'Russian organised crime elements have become virtual arms bazaars for the Colombian narco-guerrillas' [8].

On the whole, export quantities of most licit and illegal goods handled by the criminals have fallen since the 'free-for-all' years of the early 1990s, although capital flight remains a serious problem. This is, it is important to stress, a two-way process: there is also a thriving illegal import trade into Russia of a wide variety of goods, from stolen cars to computers. But the main expansion has been in Russia's export and through-trade in narcotics. Russia's role is particularly important as a route for opiates from Afghanistan, especially now that traditional routes via the Middle East and Turkey are coming under pressure. Up to three-quarters of the heroin in Russia comes from Afghanistan, which also accounts for a similar proportion of the world's opium. To a considerable extent, this reflects the growing scale of the domestic market for narcotics. Russia may have as many as 6.5 million drug users (4.5 percent of the total population), of whom 2 million are addicts, and not only is the number of users growing, the proportions both using serious drugs such as heroin and also who are considered addicts are both rising [9]. Heroin consumption is estimated as having grown fully 2300 percent in a four year period, 1998–2002. The average number of crimes connected with drug trafficking has topped 200,000 per year, while two-thirds of all thefts and robberies are connected with drugs. Official alarm is such that in 2003, Putin decreed the creation of a new State Committee for Combating the Illegal Trade in Narcotics and Psychotropic Substances (GKBNONPV—*Gosudarstvenny komitet po borbe s nezakonnym oborotom narkotikov i psikhotropicheskikh veshchest*, generally rendered simply as GKN, 'State Narcotics Committee') under Viktor Cherkesov, one of his most trusted security officers.

This is not just a national but an international problem, as the trade routes do not simply supply Russia's own gangs and addicts but continue on into Europe and the rest of the world. The key hubs remain Moscow, St Petersburg, the Siberian city of Yekaterinburg and the Baltic exclave of Kaliningrad, but others are less predictable. The town of Kimry in Tver region, for example, has emerged as a central transportation point, through which flows more than half of all heroin reaching Moscow. The town itself has a population of only 57,000 but an estimated 7,000 drug addicts, 13 percent of the total and the highest proportion in all Russia. To a large extent this reflects its position as the closest city to the capital beyond the Moscow district, a two-hour journey by commuter train. Not only has it been used for decades as a 'dumping ground' during the regular campaigns by the Moscow authorities to purge the city of so-called 'undesirables' such as petty criminals, vagrants and travellers, creating a thriving semi-criminal subculture, but it also means that police investigations are complicated by jurisdictional disputes between Moscow and Tver. Whether as cause or effect, the buoyant trade in narcotics (not just heroin, but also marijuana, MDMA and stolen medical drugs) has also corrupted the local police force, which has become infamous for its close links with the traffickers, even to the extent of impeding attempts by regional police to mount raids against them. The reason why it is worth dwelling for a moment upon the unfortunate town of Kimry is that while it may be an extreme case, there are similar towns and cities throughout Russia. Many other towns around the Moscow region have a similar pedigree and function, and the main overland routes westwards include several settlements infamous as waystations, such as Chelyabinsk, Kazan and Samara.

This has now become a settled and diversified criminal business. The presence of relatively efficient and secure trafficking routes via Russia has tempted other groupings. An increasing proportion of Latin American cocaine is reaching Russia by sea and, especially, by air, either for local distribution or, more often, subsequent transfer to European markets. Russian criminals are, for example, especially significant in Mexico, and their contacts in the Tijuana/Baja California/San Diego area allow them to carry out much direct smuggling into the USA. However, as an offshoot of this they have begun also sending cocaine which they acquire as payment for their services back to Russia to be sold on by members of their criminal networks, especially in Moscow and Yekaterinburg.

As will be discussed later, the scale of narcotic trafficking risks upsetting the present uneasy but useful status quo between state and underworld and between the key criminal groupings. The increasing wealth and power of the drug traffickers, and their ability to infiltrate, subvert and dominate local police and political establishments, also raises the spectre of 'criminal secession'—a further weakening of central control over the regions and even the rise of safe havens for criminals and terrorists within Russia, as Chechnya had become. President Putin noted in 2003, for example, that not a single drug-related crime had apparently been prevented in the Karachay–Cherkessia, Altay, Kalmykia and Karelia regions in 2002. This is given a particular significance by the fact that, far from being narcotics-free, some of these regions are instead falling ever more closely into the hands of criminal groupings. The Republic of Karachay–Cherkessia, for example, has reportedly become something of a criminal haven. Likewise, not all narcotics in Russia have been imported. Marijuana is widely grown, with total crop areas of perhaps 1 million hectares, especially in regions such as Buriyatiya and Tyva [10].

Globalisation: Money and Movement

As a result of their operations, as well as their control of or influence over many of Russia's notoriously under-regulated banks, *mafiya* gangs are also major users and also providers of money-laundering services. They account for a growing share of the approximately $500 billion laundered globally every year: estimates from the G7 group of industrialised nations are that more than $20 billion are laundered in Russia annually. In part, this is the laundering of funds generated by both licit and criminal activity. But the *mafiya* also acts increasingly as a third-party laundry for other criminal groups, thanks to its ability to work through the Russian state and private banking systems, up to a quarter of which are reckoned to be under its control. The scale of this industry is best illustrated by the case of the Bank of New York, which became public in 1999 and is currently under intensive investigation. Between 1996 and 1999, it is alleged that it illegally handled moneys from Russia which were the proceeds of organised crime, tax-dodging capital flight and, especially, embezzled government funds. Estimates of the sums involved range from $7 billion to as much as $15 billion, and around ten Russian banks and up to 50 major companies are involved, from the UK to China, Germany to Australia.

Much of this money inevitably goes through or into seemingly entirely legitimate businesses and investments. While often much less sophisticated in its methods than the Italian Mafia, the Russian gangs are also keen to acquire stakes in or control of overseas firms and, in particular, real estate. In part, this is because they may represent valuable investments in their own right. But they are also security, so that if Russia ever goes through a serious campaign against the *mafiya* or a catastrophic economic collapse, the criminals will have nest eggs abroad. Thus, their economic security is guaranteed, and these assets may even help them win foreign citizenship or the protection of governments prepared to close a blind eye to much-needed foreign investment. In early the 1990s, for example, many former Warsaw Pact states, desperate to rebuild their economies, made little secret of the willingness to excuse much in the name of inward investment.

The flexible and entrepreneurial nature of these criminal organisations is strongly visible in the way they have spread. The first wave of expansion was largely to areas with sizeable Russian communities or, as in the case with many former Warsaw Pact or Soviet states, where they had existing contacts with local criminals and corrupt officials. The Baltic states, Poland and Hungary were all early targets, soon to be followed by a drift into Austria and Germany (where they were able to capitalise on existing contacts in the east). Today, they are active throughout the states of the former Eastern bloc and also in northern Europe, although in many instances they have lost the early dominance they acquired in the 1990s. A combination of tough law enforcement, the rise of even more hungry and violent rivals (especially Albanians and other Balkan gangs [11]) and a deliberate policy of franchising out street operations to local and immigrant gangs to lower the Russians' profile have all contributed to limiting this threat.

While extending their operations and contacts across northern Europe and into Scandinavia, post-Soviet gangs have also begun to drift southwards. Italy has experienced some penetration, although a combination of a powerful domestic underworld and a police force well-prepared to combat organised crime poses some formidable challenges. Thirteen members of the *Solntsevo* network, including middle-ranking leader Viktor Yesin, were arrested in Italy in 1997. France, Spain, Portugal and Greece, though, have all experienced the slow rise of *mafiya* activity and investment (again, especially in the form of acquiring property). Indeed, *mafiya* involvement is visible all around the Mediterranean. Cyprus has become a key money-laundering centre, as well as a congenial haven for many Russian businesses, expatriates and holidaymakers. Israel, thanks to its Law of Return, allowing Jews (or those able to claim to be Jews) immigration rights, as well as the lack of effective laws against racketeering and money laundering, has also experienced a serious influx of Russian crime.

In the United States, the *vor v zakone* Vyacheslav Ivankov, known as 'Yaponchik' ('Little Japanese') arrived in New York's Brighton Beach in 1992 and began suborning or eliminating local émigré godfathers until his arrest in 1995. The Brighton Beach

Organizatsiya ('Organisation') was soon brought back into the fold of the global Russian *mafiya*. However, it is important to stress that this did not mean in any meaningful way that it suddenly became any more organised or else 'run from Moscow'. Instead, it means that the existing networks of Brighton Beach crime simply became integrated into the wider, transnational networks of such organisations as *Solntsevo*. New York remains a focus for *mafiya* operations, and the cradle of cooperation with the Cosa Nostra, especially over fuel excise tax scams, defrauding the government of tax due on the sale of gasoline and diesel fuels. However, criminals from Russia and other post-Soviet states have not confined themselves to taking a bite out of the Big Apple. Ten alleged members of the so-called 'Tatarin Brigade', charged with kidnapping, armed robbery and other crimes in December 1999, also operated in Pennsylvania and Florida. Overall, at least a dozen major networks are now operating across the United States, in up to 20 cities, especially New York, Boston, Los Angeles, San Francisco, Cleveland, Miami and Denver. Indeed, they also operate north of the border: Canada is suffering a steady growth in *mafiya* activity, again largely in cooperation (or at least a state of non-competition) with the Cosa Nostra.

Elsewhere in the world, Russian criminals have penetrated in a more piecemeal fashion, generally exploiting a particular contact or opportunity. While the *mafiya* buys and swaps cocaine from the drug cartels, there have been only limited inroads made into Latin America, although individual groups are ensconced in cities ranging from Buenos Aires to Havana. In Africa, though, there is a little more direct opportunity for the Russians. Gangs have begun operating in South Africa and neighbouring countries, making use of the chaos in the region to establish casinos for money laundering, to sell weapons and narcotics and to muscle into the diamond trade. Some *mafiya* groupings, especially those closely linked to serving and former military personnel, also appear to have played a role in supplying military weapons and mercenaries in several conflicts.

Asia, though, offers both greater opportunities and also challenges. On the whole, the Russians prefer to cooperate with rather than challenge major existing organisations. Given the domination of the Japanese Yakuza, Chinese Triads, Golden Triangle drugs trafficking networks and the like over the Asian underworld, this has limited their opportunities. Nevertheless, there have been attempts to penetrate various markets. In Macao, the *mafiya* proved unsuccessful when it took on well-connected local triads, but elsewhere they have generally picked their targets with more care. Several Australian cities now have small-scale *mafiya* operations, while even in Japan, Russian groups have moved from simply supplying prostitutes for yakuza-run brothels to running their own rings.

Yet it is important to put the *mafiya* in context. In overall terms, Russia and post-Soviet organised crime is still definitely less powerful than such established counterparts as the Mafia, the Yakuza and the Triads. However, the flexible and diffuse structure of the *mafiya* makes it very responsive to new threats and opportunities and impossible to 'decapitate'. While this does mean that they are prone to internecine conflict and simple disorganisation, they also have great flexibility and survivability. There is no real prospect either that their foundations in Russia will be seriously undermined in the near future nor, indeed, that this would kill off organisations which by now are truly multinational. They will continue to spread wherever they see opportunities, consolidate their power where they can, coexisting with indigenous criminal groups where they must. Indeed, it is the question of their relations with other criminals which will prove a key issue in the next stage of their evolution.

Consolidation

Like any competent predator, the *mafiya* is very sensitive to changes in its environment. Two major such changes have had a particular impact: the August 1998 economic crash (which led to a unilateral devaluation of the ruble and widespread imiseration throughout the country) and the rise of Vladimir Putin (who became acting president at the end of 1999, followed by his victory in the presidential elections of 2000).

The crash and the ensuing economic crisis acted as a significant spur to the consolidation of organised crime in Russia. The early 1990s had been marked by overt gang wars, which tapered off in most parts of the country by 1994 as pecking orders were established, turf boundaries agreed and new 'rules of play' developed. The immediate aftermath of the 1998 crash allowed a (relatively) bloodless new round of consolidations. After all, the larger groupings, whose resources can be counted in dollars and property, in political patronage and overseas connections, weathered the crisis without undue difficulty. They were thus able to use it as a useful opportunity, snapping up bankrupted businesses and offering loans in return for influence. The same was true of their expansion within the underworld: smaller gangs which relied instead on the rubles they could earn from smaller-scale protection racketeering and street sales of drugs and other illicit goods and services experienced the same problems as their legitimate counterparts. Some voluntarily joined larger networks to survive; others were forced to do so. Either way, the result was to consolidate the networking of Russian organised crime, such that while gangs in lesser cities and regions remain largely autonomous, they are now generally linked with one of the larger networks, gaining protection, access to higher-order criminal services and new commodities (such as a wider range of drugs), in return for a proportion of proceeds and a willingness to engage in reciprocal assistance.

Moscow's complex criminal mosaic is still dominated by the *Solntsevo* grouping, although it and its allies and clients are balanced by the power of Chechen and other North Caucasian gangs and other ethnic Russian groups, forming a (currently) stable triangular balance of terror. Of course, there is considerable marginal change, not least because of the relatively loose and unstructured nature of these networks. Small groups may rise and fall, shift their allegiances, gain or lose turf, but this has no real impact on the overall picture. There is a similar equilibrium in St Petersburg between the *Tambov* gang, which is especially dominant in the city's fuel industries and protection rackets, and gangs concentrating on smuggling and narcotics, respectively. Further east, the capital of Siberian crime is undoubtedly the city of Yekaterinburg, while the Russian

Far East remains dominated by the loose network known grandly as the Far Eastern Association of Thieves, overseen until his death in 2001 by the senior *vor v zakone* Yevgeny Vasin ('Dzhem'). Nevertheless, this region is characterised by the very number and variety of its gangs, including increasing numbers of ethnic Chinese groupings within the legal and illegal immigrant community. In Southern Russia, an uneasy mix of Slav and North Caucasian gangs periodically explodes into local conflict. The Slavs are largely dominated by gangs based in individual towns and cities and others within the Cossack community. The North Caucasians include a wide range of nationalities, including, above all, the Chechens, but also with powerful Ingushetian, Dagestani, Ossetian and Azeri gangs. In the face of Slav hostility, though, these gangs often cooperate, despite their numerous practical and historical differences.

The Return of the State

The other factor helping shape the environment in which Russian organised crime must operate is the rise of President Putin, a man with a rather sharper vision of what kind of a state he feels Russia needs. When he was elected in 2000, in part on a law-and-order platform, the underworld feared a crackdown—there was a sudden flurry of activity as funds were transferred to off-shore havens and properties abroad bought up to provide bolt-holes for future escape. This proved unnecessary as it soon became clear that while Putin would not countenance open challenges to state authority—including overt gang violence—he did not at the time plan any direct campaign against organised crime. Thus, the first few years of his presidency saw police budgets continue to fall in real terms, their resources instead being diverted to fight the war in Chechnya [12]. However, Putin has increasingly begun to come to terms with the fact that his real control over Russia depends not just on his political mandate but controlling the *Mafiya*.

It contributes to what Prosecutor-General Vladimir Ustinov called Russia's culture of 'rampant corruption,' which he estimates costs the country $15 billion each year [13]. It has helped to arm the Chechen rebels who look set to continue their campaign against Russian occupation forces for the foreseeable future. It has made Russia a hub for the global narcotics trade, a money laundry and a haven for intellectual property piracy, with goods, software and recordings counterfeited for both domestic and export markets. More broadly, he has come to appreciate that crime—both organised and disorganised—is, after all, a national security issue on many levels, from the way it usurps or weakens the powers of the formal government through to the direct impact it has on border security and state budgets. Putin has thus begun to realise that beneath this more orderly façade, the battle is not being won but lost.

The Future: Order but not yet Law

Russian organised crime has adapted to its circumstances, as much in today's free market as under Stalin. As a new generation of criminal leaders rises—generally younger, better-educated and more business-minded than their predecessors—this has led to speculation that these *avtoritety* are replacing the old godfather class of the *vory v zakone*, who were, after all, very much products of the Gulag prison system, guardians of the traditional rules of the underworld. In many ways the *vory* are out of place in today's Russia. The *avtoritety*, for example, shun the tattoos which were such a mark of the *vory*, make less use of *fenya*, their distinctive argot, and are comfortable moving between the overtly criminal and seemingly legitimate worlds. However, the evidence suggests that, for the moment at least, the *vory* still fulfil an important role, as arbiters, co-ordinators and respected elders. Thus, when *avtoritety* have a dispute that they cannot resolve between them, rather than resort to violence (which can, after all, be bad for business), they can instead refer to an impartial *vor* for resolution. Similarly, *vory* can and do hold gatherings, known as *skhodky*, at which *avtoritety* or their representatives can meet in a neutral setting to resolve issues of wider policy or respond to new challenges. Such *skhodky* were, for example, instrumental in avoiding a turf war in St Petersburg in 2002 over sales in counterfeit goods. In this way, the seemingly fragmentary and conflict-prone *mafiya* has been able to use these traditional leaders in a new way to avoid unnecessary and potential dangerous internal disputes.

However, this is an equilibrium under constant threat, and as of the end of 2004, Russian police officers are warning that there is a real danger that the next few years could see the status quo shattered, bringing a new era of open mob warfare. After all, not only are *mafiya*-related crimes again on the rise, there are a number of very specific factors at work to undermine the current order.

First of all, it is in many ways threatened by its own success. The status quo has been kindest to groupings based in Moscow and St Petersburg. However, with the underworlds of the main cities now essentially divided between clearly-marked and strongly-defended turfs, it is difficult to find new areas for expansion, not least to reward and distract up-and-coming gangsters who might otherwise pose a threat to the established leaders. These networks have already incorporated many provincial groupings into themselves, but this is a loose affiliation more than anything else. There is a temptation instead to turn affiliation into subordination and 'conquer' poorer regions. Many of these local gangs are happy being large fish in small pools and thus resist closer integration into the major networks (sometimes called 'metropolitans' by the regional criminals, although in the Far East the term 'Varangian' is still used for gangs from the European west of the country). Furthermore, in some cases 'metropolitans' have set out to take over or supplant provincial gangs which are either independent or, more dangerous still, linked to other networks. The former risks triggering a 'scramble for Russia' reminiscent of the colonial 'scramble for Africa' in which imperial powers sought to snap up territories, often with little regard for more than simply denying it to their rivals. The latter carries with it the danger of 'proxy wars' between networks fought out in the provinces, which could yet spread back to the major cities.

A second threat to the status quo comes from the growing trade in and profits from narcotics. According to Cherkesov, 'the number of organized criminal groupings specialising in selling and transporting drugs has grown by 85% recently' [14]. By creating new opportunities for second-rank criminal gangs and networks to enrich themselves (the annual turnover of the domestic narcotics market is estimated by most sources to have reached $5 billion, although the GKN puts it at $8–10 billion [15]), it could form a new generation of outsiders with no stake in the current order and yet too powerful to suppress or ignore. Indeed, for many such gangs drug revenue is the only counter-weight at their disposal to prevent their conquest by the 'metropolitans'. In the Russian Far East, for example, Afghan, Pakistani and Iranian drugs gangs are beginning to take on and drive out existing Chinese and North Korean groups in an often violent struggle for regional criminal power. The indigenous Russian gangs, while secure in their own strongholds, have proven surprisingly unwilling to jeopardise their supplies of narcotics by intervening in these conflicts. By remaining neutral and dealing with all sides, they have avoided direct confrontations but also lost considerable face. Many of these drugs gangs are therefore now looking to find and support new local gangs as their contacts and representatives. This risks provoking a new round of turf wars as these hungry new gangs take on the established gangs. The latter will have political contacts and arrays of existing alliances, but the former will be likely to be more violent and unpredictable. If the drug smugglers are prepared to back them wholeheartedly, they may also have formidable resources. There is also the danger that existing first-rank groups might be prepared to abandon the current truce in order to expand their narcotics operations.

However, the omens are not all gloomy. The Russian state is not powerless. Its problems in fighting organised crime in the 1990s were largely threefold: corruption within the élite, a lack of resources, a lack of political will. Corruption is still a very serious problem, but it is one which is beginning to be addressed. Cabinet chief of staff Dmitri Kozak launched in 2004 a reform programme for the bureaucracy, which for the first time explicitly addresses the need to combat an entrenched culture of *kormlenie* ('feeding'—supplementing inadequate salaries with habitual bribe-taking). The Russian police and judiciary are still under-funded and thus under-trained and vulnerable to corruption, but this too is beginning to be addressed. In many ways, the opening salvo of this campaign was fired in June 2003, when almost the entire staff of MUR, the Moscow police Criminal Investigations Directorate, were suspended following allegations of widespread bribe-taking [16]. Finally, there is little reason to doubt Putin's political will. After the resounding success of his supporters in the December 2003 parliamentary elections, he is unassailable, and whereas he began his first term in office seemingly not regarding organised crime to be a threat to his vision of a strong Russian state, he will start his new term in 2004 having shed that delusion. Instead, he has come to realise that the spread and seeming invulnerability of the *mafiya* is weakening central authority in Russia, diluting the state's monopoly of coercion, discrediting the market economy and in the final analysis, usurping and distorting the very functions of the state. Especially if organised crime once again explodes into open internal warfare, Putin is likely to deploy the resources of the State to control it. Furthermore, judging by his campaigns against Chechen rebels and unruly big business 'oligarchs' alike, he is unlikely to be too fastidious in the methods employed.

Ultimately, though, coercion is more likely to drive organised crime underground than actually break it. Genuine victory against the *mafiya* will be a long-term process based as much as anything else on winning back the ground surrendered to organised crime. Businesses do not pay protection money or hire criminals as debt collectors, for example, because they want to, but because they regard it as their least-worst option when the police and the courts are inefficient, corrupt and powerless. Slowly, Russia's contradictory and loophole-ridden legal system is being reformed, and a new generation of police officers, magistrates and judges rising. One of the strengths of Russian organised crime has been its close, incestuous relationship with Russian business, but there are also signs that many successful Russian firms and entrepreneurs are beginning to consider abandoning their old 'robber baron' ways (or at least put those aspects of their businesses at arm's length), either because they appreciate the long-term dangers or, more likely, because they wish to be accepted fully into the international business community.

The same drift towards respectability is to be found amongst some (though by no means all) of the successful criminals who, after all, are generally also businessmen. Leoluca Orlando, mayor of Palermo and one who well understands the Sicilian mafia, has drawn parallels between the Italian and Russian experiences. In his view, 'Russian gangsters will allow the state to combat organised crime only once they are very, very rich' [17]. This generation of criminal is, indeed, 'very, very rich' and their tendency to seek a degree of security and stability for themselves and their heirs means that they themselves also have much to lose from a new era of *bespredel*, 'disorder'.

Notes

[1] Parts of this article are drawn from columns published in *Jane's Intelligence Review*, specifically the March 2000, June 2001, October 2002 and March 2003 issues.

[2] 'Russian mafia', *'mafiya'*, 'Russian-speaking organised crime', 'East European organised crime'—it is more than just a matter of choice what to call this phenomenon. 'East European organised crime' is blandly uncontroversial, but unhelpful in describing a phenomenon rooted as much in Vladivostok as Moscow. 'Russian-speaking organised crime' is similarly clumsy, not least as many of these gangs actually speak Ukrainian, Georgian or any one of a whole range of other tongues. While the criminal phenomenon shares some features with its Sicilian counterpart, it is also different in many key ways, so while 'Russian Mafia' is punchy, it is also misleading. Hence the transliteration of the Russian loan-word *mafiya* has real advantages, underlining both the similarities and also the distinctiveness of this form of organised crime. After all, it is defined primarily by origin, style and mode of organisation.

[3] See Glazov, Y. (1976), '"Thieves" in the USSR', *Survey* 22; Serio, J. and Razinkin, V. (1995), 'Thieves professing the code', *Low Intensity Conflict & Law Enforcement* 4—these last two articles are also reprinted in Galeotti, M. (2002) (ed.), *Russian and Post-Soviet Organized Crime* (Ashgate)—and Varese, F. (2001), *The Russian Mafia* (Oxford University Press).

[4] See Galeotti, M. (2000), 'Chechen crime alive and well', *Jane's Intelligence Review*, March.

[5] The Interior Ministry's claims that organised crime controls 40% of the Russian economy must be treated with considerable caution. Not only has it remained suspiciously static since 1993, but the 40% figure also seems interchangeably applied to proportion of firms under criminal control, proportion of GDP and proportion of the economy operating in the 'shadow sector'.

[6] Volkov, V. (2002), *Violent Entrepreneurs* (Cornell University Press).

[7] *Solntsevo or Solntsevskaya* is Russia's most powerful and most international organised criminal grouping. It first emerged during the 1980s, in the Moscow suburb whose name it bears, out of the remnants of the gang of a powerful criminal known as 'the Great Mongol'. It has since spread to over 30 countries, from the USA to China. It is a perfect example of the network-based nature of Russian crime, with powerful figures within it, but no clear hierarchy or chain of command. While never giving up the protection racketeering and black-marketeering of its early days, it has also moved into increasingly sophisticated operations, from financial crime on Wall Street to cybercrime. It is obviously a major client of the global money-laundering economy. One Swiss investigation has suggested it had placed up to $5 billion in that country's banks alone. At home, it has been linked with major politicians, banks and businesses in Russia. As far back as 1995, the Menatep bank was named in a CIA report as a possible *Solntsevo* front, and this bank—which failed in 1999—proved a major player in the multi-billion Bank of New York case.

[8] US Congressional Hearings, 'The Threat from International Organized Crime and Global Terrorism', *Committee on International Relations of the House of Representatives*, 1 October 1997.

[9] *Pravda.ru*, 22 May 2003.

[10] Although the US State Department's latest estimate is that 'Wild cannabis is estimated to cover some 1.5 million hectares in the eastern part of the country'. US State Department, *International Narcotics Control Strategy Report 2003* (released 2004).

[11] See Xhudo, G. (1996), 'Men of Purpose: the growth of Albanian criminal activity', *Transnational Organized Crime* 2; Galeotti, M. (1999), 'Albanian organised crime', *Cross Border Control International* 12.

[12] The majority of forces operating in Chechnya are actually from the Ministry of Internal Affairs, both paramilitary Interior Troops and also SWAT-type special police units drawn from across the Russian Federation. This has not only drained local police commands of many of the specialist officers they would need to combat organised crime, it has also further paramilitarised the Russian police, something which has done little to improve its links with, and legitimacy in the eyes of, the wider public.

[13] *St Petersburg Times*, 27 March 2001.

[14] *Mosnews*, 27 July 2003.

[15] *Pravda.ru*, 17 April 2003; *Pravda.ru*, 26 June 2003; *Mosnews*, 24 June 2004.

[16] See Galeotti, M. (2003), 'Russia tackles corrupt police', *Jane's Intelligence Review* August.

[17] *Izvestiya*, 1 March 1997.

References

Galeotti, M. (1999) 'Albanian organised crime', *Cross Border Control International*.

Galeotti, M. (2000) 'Chechen crime alive and well', *Jane's Intelligence Review*, March.

Glazov, Y. (1976) '"Thieves" in the USSR', *Survey* 22, reprinted in Galeotti, M. (ed.) (2002), *Russian and Post-Soviet Organized Crime* (Ashgate).

Jane's Intelligence Review, March 2000, June 2001, October 2002, March 2003.

Mosnews, 27 July 2003; 24 June 2004.

Pravda.ru, 17 April 2003; 22 May 2003; 26 June 2003.

St Petersburg Times, 27 March 2001.

Serio, J. & Razinkin, V. (1995) 'Thieves professing the code', *Low Intensity Conflict & Law Enforcement*, reprinted in Galeotti, M. (ed.) (2002), *Russian and Post-Soviet Organized Crime* (Ashgate).

US Congressional Hearings (1997) 'The Threat from International Organized Crime and Global Terrorism', in *Committee on International Relations of the House of Representatives*, 1 October.

US State Department, *International Narcotics Control Strategy Report 2003* (released 2004).

Varese, F. (2001) *The Russian Mafia*, Oxford University Press.

Volkov, V. (2002) *Violent Entrepreneurs*, Cornell University Press.

Xhudo, G. (1996) 'Men of Purpose: the growth of Albanian criminal activity', *Transnational Organized Crime*.

Organised Crime in East Central Europe: The Czech Republic, Hungary and Poland

Kelly Hignett

Since the revolutions of 1989 the Czech Republic, Hungary and Poland have largely succeeded in their quest for western-style political stabilisation and economic development. Developments in the region have made these countries increasingly attractive to organised crime however, and all of the East Central European (ECE) countries have seen levels of organised crime increase, both within and across national borders. According to a recent Interpol report, most of the well-known organised criminal networks have already established operations in ECE [1]. The growth of

Kelly Hignett is a researcher in the School of Politics, International Relations and Environment at Keele University, UK.

organised crime in the region is seen as a significant problem, confined not only to these countries themselves, or even within the European continent, but on a global scale, meaning that the countries of ECE now stand on the front line of the international fight against organised crime.

The Development of Organised Crime in East Central Europe

International concern about organised crime in ECE began to be voiced in the early 1990s. The roots of organised crime in the region however, can be traced much further back. Throughout the socialist period, systemic and professional organised crime in ECE was concealed within the 'criminal-political nexus' of state and society [2], described as an environment of 'institutionalised illegality' [3]. Constant economic shortages led to general acceptance of and reliance on the black market. Bribery was necessary to secure even the most basic goods and services and corruption was generally considered to be the rule rather than the exception when dealing with anyone in an official capacity.

This environment led to the development of a criminal subculture within society. Unable to rely on the state to provide adequately for their needs, people increasingly turned to the black market and relied on social networks, based around friends and family, to get things done [4]. Many of these social connections also formed the basis for the first professional criminal networks however, while the extensive informal economy provided the ideal environment to make large illegal profits. The roots of organised crime in ECE can be traced back as far as the 1970s when gangs of underground entrepreneurs controlled the illegal production and supply networks of black market goods and services on an extensive scale [5]. Some gangs specialised in property crime, particularly in burglary, with separate networks established for the sale of the stolen goods [6].

The countries of ECE were regarded as ideally situated for incorporation into European smuggling routes, despite the restrictions on travel and trade that existed within the Eastern bloc prior to 1989. Networks were established with Soviet criminals to smuggle goods into ECE [7], and from the other side of the iron curtain, electronic goods were regularly smuggled into ECE from western Germany [8]. Other gangs were already involved in the smuggling and supply of drugs [9]. Police reports from this period indicate that ECE countries blamed much of these activities on criminals from outside their own national borders, but the most likely scenario is that many of these operations required cross-border cooperation with gangs based elsewhere in ECE, in the Soviet Union and in Western Europe [10].

Admittedly many of these early criminal networks were rather primitive, often built around small, closed groups, and rudimentary in terms of their structure, level of development and the scope of their operations. However, these preliminary criminal networks did demonstrate many elements of organised crime in terms of both the personal relations between gang members and of their modus operandi [11]. Most maintained internal order through some kind of hierarchy and a division of labour;

their activities were profit orientated and their crimes were professionally and systematically carried out. What is particularly significant is that even at this embryonic stage, many gangs were already demonstrating some level of international criminal connections outside of their country of origin.

It was the collapse of socialism in 1989 and the subsequent transition process to democracy and market economics that provided organised crime with the opportunities to gain a real foothold in ECE. After the events of 1989, chaotic economic conditions, weak law enforcement, a permissive legal framework, unprotected borders and porous financial systems all combined to provide an environment highly favourable to the development of organised crime in the region [12]. The countries of ECE were engaged in a rapid and simultaneous 'triple transition' [13]. With all of the post-socialist governments keen to implement the necessary reform programme as quickly and as broadly as possible, official monitoring of the transition process was limited and mistakes were made. Criminal gangs were able to exploit legal loopholes in much of the new government legislation to find new sources of illegal income. For example, the introduction of a dual pricing system for different types of oil in Hungary in the early 1990s allowed a number of criminal groups collectively dubbed as the 'oil mafia' to import massive quantities of oil cheaply, which they then sold at a much higher profit [14]. It has been claimed that the oil mafia defrauded the Hungarian government of an estimated 400 million US dollars through these operations [15].

Post-socialist economic reform also provided the opportunity for criminal growth through investment in the legal economic sector of ECE. The privatisation process in each of the ECE states was dogged with allegations of corruption. The speed and scale of privatisation enabled criminal gangs to invest their illegal profits in businesses and real estate, which often served as a front for further illicit activities, or for laundering money. This led to the investment of a great deal of 'dirty money' in the ECE economies [16].

This favourable climate was also realised by criminal gangs based outside of the ECE region, and there was an influx of foreign mobsters in the early 1990s who viewed the region as a potential criminal haven [17]. The ECE countries were attractive to gangs of numerous nationalities due to their position in the heart of Europe, perfect for illegal transit operations involving both goods and people. The establishment of criminal operations in ECE was made easier with the opening of borders to encourage greater freedom of trade and travel after 1989. Criminal interest in ECE was raised further by the outbreak of war in the former Yugoslavia. Instability in the Balkan region meant that establishing new smuggling routes into Western Europe was necessary.

Today there is evidence that criminal gangs from Arab countries, Africa, Asia, the Balkan region, Turkey and Western Europe (including Italy) are all active in ECE [18]. Perhaps most noticeable however, was the influx of criminal organisations based in the Former Soviet Union (FSU) across ECE. By the mid-1990s intelligence reports were linking the powerful Moscow-based Solntsevskaya mafia, the St Petersburg

Tambovskaya organisation [19] and various Chechen gangs to operations across the region [20] and in 1998 the Russian Minister of Interior stated that ECE was acting as a 'headquarter' for organised crime originating from FSU territories [21].

In most instances incoming gangs tried to seize control of territory or markets by force, leading to a series of 'turf wars' between rival criminal gangs across ECE during the mid-1990s [22]. Most of these gangs were already heavily armed, while ongoing instability in the Balkans provided them with a constant source of weaponry and explosives [23]. Thus the turf wars were bloody and brutal, often spilling out of the underworld and into wider society. By the close of the 1990s the key battles had been fought and won. Weaker gangs had been decimated, or else incorporated into the structure of their stronger rivals. Compromises were reached and gangs established working relations. In many cases foreign-based gangs began 'subcontracting' to local criminal groups across the ECE territories [24].

East Central Europe: A Criminal Melting Pot

The turf wars triggered a fundamental reshaping of the underworld order in ECE, that resulted in the emergence of organised crime that was predominantly international in character. Today, ECE is a criminal melting pot. No single ethnic group has achieved dominance in ECE and even domestic criminal groups operating in the region rarely confine their operations within national borders. Evidence suggests that while certain ethnic groups may have specialised knowledge and control over certain markets or territories within ECE, the transnational scope of many operations requires a high level of collusion between different gangs. This is true even of gangs that have traditionally been considered to be ethnically closed, insular and largely self-sufficient (for example Albanian, Chinese and Turkish networks), at least at a regional level [25]. The level of cooperation should not be overstated however; as ties between criminal groups are primarily strategic alliances, formed in the interests of the gangs involved [26]. Such agreements are volatile and can often break down over the longer term; however, the situation in ECE demonstrates the increasing willingness of most criminal organisations to work together.

Organised crime across the region is also marked by the immense variation both in gang structure and in activities undertaken. Levels of organised crime penetration also vary to some degree both within and between countries in the ECE region. It does appear as though the increasing scope for international organised crime in the region has seen the traditional model of large monolithic criminal organisations with a strong, centralised pyramidal structure (as in the model of the Italian Cosa Nostra) replaced by smaller, more flexible and inter-connected networks [27]. The latest intelligence reports suggest that gangs operating in ECE are displaying increasing fluidity, are less compact and more fractionalised. Rather, organised crime today largely functions as a greater number of looser syndicates whose organisational style is altogether more entrepreneurial, embracing a particularly harmful blend of crime, politics and business, with activities carried out according to a risk-benefit analysis [28].

Most gangs remain based around some kind of loose structure and division of responsibility however, and the majority of criminal networks uncovered have been of medium size, (averaging 10–20 members) [29], although cases of gangs with over 100 members operating in ECE have been documented [30]. Most gangs retain some kind of internal discipline based on violence. Violence also remains infrequently directed outside of the gang hierarchy: at rival organisations and at individuals involved in the settling of scores. There has been no repeat of the widespread and systemic turf wars of the mid-1990s, but occasional incidents linked to organised crime demonstrate that these gangs have retained their capacity for violence. In addition, there is increasing evidence of criminals seeking to conceal or facilitate their activities through the corruption of law enforcement and politicians in all ECE countries [31].

The ECE underworld is in a constant state of flux. In the early 1990s criminal organisations from the FSU were seen as the principal threat to the region, but today Albanian gangs are one of the primary causes for concern [32]. It is highly probable that there will be further evolution in terms of gang structure and market control. While some of the strategic alliances currently in force in ECE will survive in the long term, others are likely to disintegrate and new alliances will be formed.

Criminal Operations in East Central Europe

Organised gangs working in the region rarely confine their scope to a single area of criminal activity. Indeed recent reports have stressed the 'multi criminal character' of East European organised crime [33]. It is believed that many gangs mix their involvement in 'high risk' criminal activities with lower risk enterprises. For example, it has been estimated that 20 percent of all Class-A drug smugglers also smuggle cigarettes [34]. Whichever activities various organised gangs are involved in however, they all channel their illegal capital through investment and money laundering and thus ECE also remains considered as a centre for economic crime.

The favourable geographical location of ECE means that countries of the region form a natural transit route through Europe and there is evidence of international smuggling operations carried out in the region by land, sea and air [35]. The smuggling of various commodities including alcohol, cigarettes, artwork, antiques, jewellery and fuel through the 'green borders' of ECE provides a growing market for organised crime [36].

During the early 1990s many gangs operating in the area began to specialise in the organised theft and smuggling of vehicles. EU member states recorded a general increase in the figures for vehicle theft from 1989–93 [37], and it is believed that many of these cars were smuggled on to Serbia, Ukraine, Russia and Central Asia [38]. Many stolen vehicles had already been transported out of the country before their theft was even registered, making them difficult to trace [39]. It is estimated that around 80 percent of vehicles smuggled through the ECE region are stolen, while others are simply imported illegally, without payment of the relevant import duties [40]. The criminals involved in this trade demonstrated considerable organisation, professionalism and specialisation.

In many cases cars were stolen 'to order' and often required some alterations to documentation and license plates before delivery, which generally occurred in the countries of ECE, en route to their ultimate destination [41]. Recent statistics suggest that from the mid-1990s the market in stolen vehicles has been in decline, largely because western vehicle manufacturers have developed more sophisticated anti-theft devices. It has also been noted, however, that in cases where organised vehicle theft does occur, gangs are resorting to more violent methods and the practice of carjacking is increasing in ECE [42].

The disintegration of the Warsaw Pact and ongoing conflicts in the Balkans provided a ready market for criminal organisations trafficking in arms in the 1990s. Weaponry, ammunition, explosives and even nuclear and radioactive materials from the Former Soviet Union have been smuggled through ECE. In 1998 Polish police exposed a gang involved in the smuggling of light weapons and ammunition worth almost $6 million, through the Polish post of Gdansk and on to countries that were under UN weapons embargoes [43]. Between 1998–2000 a series of seizures of arms and explosives in Hungary uncovered a clear link between Hungarian and Slovakian gangs involved in the arms trade [44], and as recently as 2000 the Czech customs authorities detected a total of 46 cases of illegal trading in weapons, explosives and radioactive materials [45].

Drug trafficking remains one of the most profitable markets for organised crime to develop operations in ECE. Heroin from Afghanistan, cocaine from Columbia and cannabis from Morocco all enter ECE en route to supplying markets in Western Europe and the USA. Operations in this area are believed to be controlled by a mixture of gangs including Albanian, Columbian, Nigerian, North African and Turkish members, however, many are believed to 'subcontract' operations to indigenous criminal organisations in ECE who act as couriers [46]. This not only enables the organisers to benefit from the local knowledge and connections of these criminals, but also makes their operations less visible to the authorities in many cases.

The Balkan routes remain perhaps the most significant transit routes for drugs into Europe (and for heroin in particular—it is estimated that 80 percent of heroin entering Western Europe does so via the Balkan routes) [47], The various routes usually encompass ECE territories. There has also been a recent resurgence in use of the old 'silk route' passing from Central Asia through the Former Soviet Union and into ECE [48]. In recent years there has also been an increase in synthetic drugs, such as ecstasy being smuggled out of western Europe: from countries such as Germany, the Netherlands and the UK [49]. In 1997 a joint operation between Austrian and Hungarian police led to the arrest of 25 gang members who were trafficking amphetamines into ECE [50].

Many gangs today use fractional transport to conceal their operations. Heroin enters ECE under the control of Turkish and Albanian organisations, where it is stored and then delivered into western Europe in smaller amounts by domestic criminal gangs [51]. Similarly, shipments of cocaine have been delivered by boat to Polish ports and then transported into the Czech Republic and Hungary by land [52]. It is believed that the Colombian Cali Cartel has links with Polish gangs who act as 'couriers' to smuggle cocaine across the Polish-German border [53]. Other gangs utilise the Danube–Rhine canal system, which enables barges from the Black Sea to enter Hungary [54]. Airports in ECE are also increasingly used to transport drugs into the region. Evidence suggests that airports in the Czech Republic, Hungary and Poland are used as key entrance points for cocaine from Africa and South America [55].

While initial interest in ECE was largely down to its value as a drug transit route, as ECE develops economically, and citizens develop greater purchasing power, the region is becoming increasingly viewed as valuable as a target as well as a transit region [56]. Of particular note is the rapid increase in levels of synthetic drugs produced in ECE, particularly in Poland (now reported to be the third largest producer of amphetamines in Europe) [57], and the Czech Republic where several professionally equipped laboratories have been discovered [58]. In addition there is evidence of a continuing trend towards cocktail-style drug trafficking with many individual gangs now dealing in more than one type of illegal substance [59].

Illegal immigration remains one of the most worrying aspects of organised crime in ECE and is recognised as a serious problem for EU member states. Again this is a trade often controlled by groups based outside of the region; with Albanian, Chinese, Russian and Turkish organised gangs believed to dominate the market. Many gangs have ethnic representatives based in the ECE transit countries, while others subcontract the transit of the migrants to gangs based on the domestic territories [60]. Organisers often make arrangements for the methods of transit, border crossings, accommodation and residence of the illegal immigrants for the full length of their journey however [61], and as some illegal immigrants (for example, those travelling from China) may pass through several countries en route to their destination, this also requires collaboration between criminal organisations of various ethnic and national backgrounds. The trade in illegal immigration generates high profits for the organisers but often with tragic results for their cargo. In one case, the bodies of 18 illegal immigrants from Sri Lanka were discovered hidden in a lorry in Hungary, which had been left just a few miles from the Austrian border [62].

Gangs involved in organising illegal immigration often employ highly specialised and professional methods to carry out transportation. Many use forged passports and documents to enable their cargo to gain entry to countries in Europe. In 1997 alone German police confiscated 1,700 false passports at the German–Polish border [63]. While the countries of ECE were initially seen as transit points along the route into western Europe, they are increasingly becoming destination countries themselves, as applications for either temporary or permanent residence in ECE have doubled in recent years [64]. Some illegal immigrants claim temporary residence in ECE and use this as a basis to move on (generally illegally) into Western Europe a few months later.

Despite a series of measures taken to improve border controls in the ECE countries in anticipation of EU membership, several border areas remain as cause for concern. The Czech-German border is one such example; in 1998 Czech police reported the existence of a 'human smuggling pipeline' running through the former Czechoslovakia and into Germany [65]. The borders between Poland and the FSU, and between Hungary and Ukraine also pose a problem. Significant advances have been made in border controls since the ECE states first applied for EU membership, but corruption amongst the border guard does still exist, and their eastern neighbours have often yet to benefit from the same level of technological and financial assistance given to the ECE states by the EU. There have even been reports of illegal immigrants simply walking through the Hungarian–Ukrainian border in wintertime, and of Ukrainian border guards following them, kicking snow over their footprints to hide the evidence! [66].

In a related market, some criminal gangs are involved in the illegal trafficking of human beings. It is estimated that this trade earns organised crime groups up to five billion US dollars per year [67]. The trafficking of women in particular has intensified since the early 1990s. On arrival at their destination they are forced into illegal employment and many become involved in the sex trade, also largely controlled by organised crime. Women are generally lured overseas with the promise of employment, and the criminals often use physical violence to force them into prostitution and take their passports to prevent them returning to their homeland [68]. Many ECE women are discovered each year working as prostitutes in Western Europe, with one report suggesting this figure may be as high as 10,000 [69].

Again, the organisers are often believed to operate outside of ECE with Albanian, Russian and Turkish groups all linked to this trade [70]. Two recent cases highlight the involvement of ECE criminals in this activity however; in 2000 a network organising the trafficking of young women for prostitution involving criminals from FSU, Poland, Bulgaria and Germany was uncovered. The women were transported from the FSU into Poland, where they were supplied with false passports and then sold on to work in brothels in Germany [71]. Also in 2000, ECE police uncovered a network organising the illegal transportation of young girls from Hungary and the Czech Republic into Austria where they were held against their will and forced to work as prostitutes in nightclubs owned by one particular criminal syndicate [72].

Despite the enormous range of activities that different criminal organisations are involved in, all are involved to some extent in economic crime and money laundering. Therefore ECE has also become a centre for economic crime. By 1992, Hungary was already considered to have become the third largest money launderer in Europe [73]. The lack of sufficient financial regulation coupled with mass privatisation across ECE in the 1990s enabled many criminals to purchase real estate and invest in legal businesses. Often though, these businesses simply serve as front companies to facilitate illegal activities and launder illicit profits. Italian-based organised crime, and criminal syndicates from the FSU are believed to use ECE as a major base for investment and money laundering [74]. Criminals also target banks in ECE: in 1999 the Central European International Bank in Budapest was linked to a financial scandal in Russia, involving Kremlin officials [75]. Since 1991 the increased use of credit cards and electronic money transfer techniques in ECE have also provided new opportunities for organised crime to exploit [76].

Fighting Organised Crime in East Central Europe

Negotiations for accession to the European Union began with the Czech Republic, Hungary and Poland in 1998. The criteria necessary for membership included meeting certain standards in Justice and Home Affairs, and ensuring effective border security. Particular concern has been voiced regarding the policing of the Eastern borders of the ECE countries, as these became external borders of the EU in 2004 [77].

Significant progress in combating organised crime has been made in ECE in recent years. All three countries have publicly launched programmes aimed at reducing and preventing organised crime. Changes in domestic law has recognised the existence of new forms of criminality and specific measures have been adopted in the fields of illegal immigration, drug trafficking and serious economic crime [78], (particularly money laundering, with banks now required to report suspicious transactions to police authorities). Specialised law-enforcement units, trained to combat organised crime have been formed in each of the ECE countries and have been granted extensive powers to aid in undercover work, such as the use of wire tapping and full access to the financial records of suspects under investigation [79]. Officers working undercover have managed to infiltrate a number of criminal organisations and a number of arrests have been made in connection with organised crime.

Greater commitment to border security has also been demonstrated. The countries of ECE have developed good working relations and cross-border cooperation along their western borders. For example, regular meetings are now held between the border authorities from the Czech Republic, Germany and Poland to enhance communication [80]. The countries of ECE are working together in their fight against organised crime, in recognition that cross-border crime in the region is a common threat. Since 1999 there have been bi-annual meetings between the Ministers of Interior of the Czech Republic, Hungary and Poland (including representatives from Austria and Slovakia) with the aim of coordinating procedures against organised crime and strengthening border controls [81].

Despite these advances in law enforcement and border security across ECE, organised crime continues to pose a problem for the countries of the region, and as a result significant intelligence gaps exist in regard to organised crime operating in ECE [82]. Police and border guards continue to complain of a lack of funding, technology and expertise [83]. Although the governments of ECE have committed themselves to fighting organised crime, there is often no corresponding financial commitment to tackle the problem. Police and border guards remain underpaid and corruption is a major problem. The competition for the limited resources available means that in some cases cross-border networks are actually more developed than communications between local police departments. They are often unwilling to share intelligence with their perceived 'rivals', which is vital considering the scope of organised crime throughout the region. Thus police work on organised crime often lacks the flexibility and specialist knowledge to be sufficiently effective [84].

The cost of improving border security by investing in modernised technology, increasing the number of border guards and ensuring they receive adequate training is high, although the ECE countries have received both strategic and financial assistance from their western European neighbours, and from the EU's PHARE fund [85]. Relations with their eastern neighbours have not progressed so well however; the situation at Poland's eastern borders was recently described by one German newspaper as 'chaos and corruption' [86].

The ECE countries have made agreements on fighting organised crime and information sharing with other countries on both a bilateral and a multilateral basis. Given the international nature of organised crime in the region, and the scope of criminal activities in terms of type and territory, there is a need for increased international cooperation if attempts to prevent organised crime are to be successful. International efforts to prevent organised crime require the speedy exchange of both strategic and operational information between foreign partners. In many cases a delay in exchanging this information is a limiting factor for those conducting operations against criminal organisations [87].

The level of criminal investigation needs to match the level of operation reached by organised gangs in ECE. It is impossible to combat criminals operating internationally with anything less than a truly international response. An effective programme to diminish the threats posed by organised crime can only be sustained through improved cooperation, collaboration and information exchange both within and across national borders [88]. In most cases, the exchange of information occurs on a bilateral basis only, and greater exchange of information through the international forum (for example, Interpol) would increase knowledge and understanding of organised crime in the ECE region and therefore benefit those trying to combat it.

Drug trafficking, Illegal immigration and Trafficking in human beings are some of the most significant problems facing the ECE countries. In each of these markets ECE remains primarily a region of transit at present. However, its attractiveness as a target destination is already increasing and this is likely to increase since these countries gain full EU membership. Criminal organisations will continue to target ECE as a lucrative market for their operations. The countries of ECE have already made significant advances in the fight against organised crime; now they must use their recent accession to the EU as the basis for preventing the further spread of organised crime on their territories. The recent inclusion of the Czech Republic, Hungary and Poland into the EU in May 2004, will provide a clear indication of how successful attempts to combat organised crime in the region have been to date.

Notes

[1] Calabresi, 'The Dons of the East', 20.
[2] This model, used by Professor Louise Shelley to demonstrate the extent of organised crime in Russia is equally applicable to the satellite states of Eastern Europe 1945–89. See Shelley, *The criminal-political nexus: A Russian case study*, 1–47.
[3] Galeotti, *Cross-Border Crime and the Former Soviet Union*, 1.
[4] Irk, *Organised Crime: special danger for new democracies*.

[5] Los, *The Second Economy in Marxist States*, 38.

[6] *Crime and Corruption after Communism.*

[7] Lefebvre, 'Crime and Society in Hungary: a survey', 98.

[8] *Crime and Corruption after Communism*, op. cit.

[9] 'Escalation of Drug Abuse Admitted', 37.

[10] 'Policemen Inadequately Educated, While Organised Crime Rises', 38.

[11] For one of the best and most recent criteria of what constitutes 'organised crime'; see the definition appended to the Ad Hoc Group on Organised Crime, *Report on the situation of organised crime in the European Union 1993.*

[12] Savona & Adamoli, *The Impact of Organised Crime in Central and Eastern Europe.*

[13] The simultaneous transformation of political systems, economic systems and boundaries and identities. See Offe, 'Capitalism by design? Democratic Theory facing the Triple Transition in Eastern Europe', 3–13.

[14] Kosztolanyi, *Greasing the Wheels: the parliamentary enquiry into the Hungarian oil scandals.*

[15] 'Hungary eyes police after scam'.

[16] 'Privatisation Scandal', *BBC Summary of World Broadcasts, East Europe.*

[17] *Remarks of US Ambassador to Hungary, Peter Tufo, at the signing of the letter of agreement for cooperation on organised crime.*

[18] *2000 EU Organised Crime Situation Report*, 5.

[19] Dunn, 'Major Mafia Gangs in Russia', 82–4.

[20] Bort, 'Illegal migration and cross-border crime', 200.

[21] *European Union situation report on East European organised crime*, 15.

[22] Salgo, *Challenge of Organised Crime.*

[23] 'Crime unstoppable, 1996 is a year of bombing', *BBC Summary of World Broadcasts, East Europe*, 2748/C3, 21 October 1996.

[24] *NCIS Threat Assessment*, 46.

[25] *2000 EU Organised Crime Situation Report*, op. cit., 4.

[26] Adamoli et al., *Organised Crime Around The World*, 49.

[27] *European Union situation report on east European organised crime*, op. cit. 2001.

[28] *Joint project Against Corruption in the Republic of Hungary*, 8.

[29] *2000 EU Organised Crime Situation Report*, op. cit., 5.

[30] *Answers to the questions of the Council of Europe Committee of Experts on the Criminological and Legal aspect of Organised Crime (PC-S-CO) for 2001*, Hungarian Ministry of Interior, 2002: 6.

[31] *2000 EU Organised Crime Situation Report*, op. cit., 9.

[32] *Seminar for Criminal Justice practitioners on the Implementation of the UN Convention against Transnational Organised Crime, Ministry of Interior*, Czech Republic, 15–17 July 2003.

[33] *2000 EU Organised Crime Situation Report*, op. cit., 10.

[34] *Seminar for Criminal Justice practitioners on the Implementation of the UN Convention against Transnational Organised Crime, Ministry of Interior*, Czech Republic, 15–17 July 2003.

[35] *Report on Organised Crime in the Czech Republic in 1998*, Czech Republic Ministry of Interior, 1999:13.

[36] *2000 EU Organised Crime Situation Report*, op. cit., 5.

[37] *European Union situation report on east European organised crime*, op. cit., 49.

[38] Liukkonen, *Motor Vehicle Theft in Europe*, 16.

[39] Orszang-Land, 'On the right track', 13.

[40] *International cooperation in the field of battling organised crime*, Polish Interior Ministry, 2002

[41] Stefancic, *Car Thieves.*

[42] *International cooperation in the field of battling organised crime*, op. cit.

[43] Dragsdahl, 'Polish Arms Smugglers Violated UN Embargoes'.

[44] 'Link between Hungarian, Slovak underworld believed to have been found', *BBC Summary of World Broadcasts, East Europe*, 3562/C4, 16 June 1999.

[45] *Report on the Security Situation in the Czech Republic in 2000*, Czech Ministry of Interior, 2001.

[46] *EU Organised Crime Situation Report*, (2000), op. cit.

[47] Calabresi, op. cit., 20.

[48] *Corruption and Organised Crime in States in Transition (OCTOPUS)*, Joint project between the Commission of the European Communities and the Council of Europe, Multilateral Conference in Sofia, Bulgaria, (December 1996), Meeting Report, 1997: 16.

[49] *EU Organised Crime Situation Report*, (2000), EUROPOL, The Hague, 31 October 2001.

[50] 'Hungarian, Austrian police raid drug ring', *BBC Summary of World Broadcasts East Europe*, 3060/C9 27 October 1997.

[51] *Answers to the questions of the Council of Europe Committee of Experts on the Criminological and Legal aspect of Organised Crime (PC-S-CO) for 2001*, Hungarian Ministry of Interior, 2002: 8.

[52] *Report on Organised Crime in the Czech Republic in 1998*, op. cit., 16.

[53] Adamoli et al. (eds), op. cit., 50.

[54] Savona & Adamoli, op. cit.

[55] Csoty, *Organized crime, drug related crime and illegal migration in the central and east European region*.

[56] Engelbrekt, 'Sharp rise in Drug Trafficking and Abuse in Former East Bloc', 48.

[57] Smart, 'Europol warning on Eastern Mafias'.

[58] *The Report on Organised Crime in the Czech Republic in 1998*, Czech Ministry of Interior, 1999: 24.

[59] *2000 EU Organised Crime Stuation report*, op. cit., 11.

[60] Ibid.

[61] *International cooperation in the field of battling organised crime*, op. cit.

[62] 'Police find 18 dead Sri Lankans in Bulgarian Lorry', *BBC Summary of World Broadcasts, East Europe*, 2357/A5, 15 July 1995.

[63] Bort, op. cit., 201.

[64] *European Union situation report on east European organised crime*, EUROPOL (2001).

[65] Connelly, 'Hundreds Held in Border Logjam' *The Guardian*, 9 October 1998

[66] *Seminar for Criminal Justice practitioners on the Implementation of the UN Convention against Transnational Organised Crime*, Ministry of Interior, Czech Republic, 15–17 July 2003

[67] Bort, op. cit., 201.

[68] *Country Report to the 11th OSCE Economic Forum: the Republic of Poland*, 19 May 2003: 3.

[69] *Factbook on Global Sexual Exploitation*.

[70] *The Report on organised crime in the Czech Republic in 1998*, Czech Ministry of Interior, 1999: 35.

[71] *Country Report to the 11th OSCE Economic Forum: the Republic of Poland*, 19 May 2003.

[72] *Report on the Security Situation in the Czech Republic in 2000*, Czech Ministry of Interior, (2001).

[73] Wright, 'Organised crime in Hungary: the transition from state to civil society', 71.

[74] *2000 EU Organised Crime Situation report*, op. cit.

[75] This allegation was denied by CEIB. 'Hungarian bank denies it laundered Russian money', *Russia Today*, 6 August 1999.

[76] *The Report on Organised Crime in the Czech Republic in 1998*, Czech Ministry of Interior, 1999: 5

[77] *Enlargement and EU External Frontier Controls*, Select Committee on the European Union, House of Lords, Paper 110, Session 1999–2000, 17th report, 24 October 2000.

[78] Savona & Adamoli, op. cit.

[79] Davis et al. (eds), *Organised crime, corruption and illicit arms trafficking in an enlarged EU*, Saferworld Arms and Security Programme, December 2001: 6.

[80] Bort, op. cit., 194.

[81]   *Country Report to the 11th OSCE Economic Forum: the Republic of Poland*, 19 May 2003
[82]   *Threat Assessment: The impact of east European organised crime on the EU*, EUROPOL, 2000.
[83]   Calabresi, op. cit., 22.
[84]   Davis et al. (eds), op. cit., 6.
[85]   For more information about PHARE, consult http://europa.eu.int/comm/enlargement/pas/ phare/
[86]   Bort, op. cit., 196.
[87]   *Threat Assessment: The impact of east European organised crime on the EU*, EUROPOL, 2000
[88]   Davis et al., (eds), op. cit.

References

Adamoli, S., et al. (1998) *Organised Crime Around The World*, HEUNI, p. 49.

Ad Hoc Group on Organised Crime, *Report on the situation of organised crime in the European Union 1993.*

Answers to the questions of the Council of Europe Committee of Experts on the Criminological and Legal aspect of Organised Crime (PC-S-CO) for 2001, Hungarian Ministry of Interior, 2002: 6

BBC Summary of World Broadcasts, East Europe, 'Privatisation Scandal', EE/2120, 7 October 1994.

BBC Summary of World Broadcasts, East Europe, 'Police find 18 dead Sri Lankans in Bulgarian Lorry', 2357/A5, 15 July 1995.

BBC Summary of World Broadcasts, East Europe, 'Crime unstoppable, 1996 is a year of bombing', 2748/C3, 21 October 1996.

BBC Summary of World Broadcasts East Europe, 'Hungarian, Austrian police raid drug ring', 3060/C9 27 October 1997.

BBC Summary of World Broadcasts, East Europe, 'Link between Hungarian, Slovak underworld believed to have been found', 3562/C4, 16 June 1999.

Bort, E. (2002) 'Illegal migration and cross-border crime', in *Europe Unbound*, ed. J. Zielonka, Routledge, p. 200.

Calabresi, M. (1998) 'The Dons of the East', *Time*, 30 November:20.

Connelly, K. (1998) 'Hundreds held in border Logjam', *The Guardian*, 9 October.

Corruption and Organised Crime in States in Transition (OCTOPUS), Joint project between the Commission of the European Communities and the Council of Europe, Multilateral Conference in Sofia, Bulgaria (December 1996), Meeting Report, 1997: 16.

Country Report to the 11th OSCE Economic Forum: the Republic of Poland, 19 May 2003.

Crime and Corruption after Communism, http://www.law.nyu.deu/eecr/vol6num4/feature/ interviewoncrime.html (accessed 27 January 2000).

Csoty, G. (1997) *Organized crime, drug related crime and illegal migration in the central and east European region*, http://www.vm.ee/nato/related/naa/docu/1997/ap84cc.htm (accessed 17 July 2000).

Czech Republic Ministry of Interior, 1999, *Report on Organised Crime in the Czech Republic in 1998.*

Czech Ministry of Interior, 2001, *Report on the Security Situation in the Czech Republic in 2000.*

Davis, I., et al. (eds)(2001) *Organised crime, corruption and illicit arms trafficking in an enlarged EU*, Saferworld Arms and Security Programme, December: 6.

Dragsdahl, J. (1998) 'Polish arms smugglers violated UN embargoes', *BASIC Reports*, no. 65, 14 August.

Dunn, G. (2000) 'Major Mafia gangs in Russia', in *Russian Organized Crime The New Threat?*, ed. P. Williams, 2nd edn., Frank Cass, pp. 82–84.

Engelbrekt, K. (1994) 'Sharp rise in drug trafficking and abuse in former East Bloc', *RFE/RL Research Report*, 4 March: 48.

EUROPOL (2000) *EU Organised Crime Situation Report*, The Hague, 31 October 2001.

EUROPOL (2000) *Threat Assessment: The impact of east European organised crime on the EU.*

Factbook on Global Sexual Exploitation, http://www.uri/edu/artsci/wms/hughes/catw/hungary.htm (accessed 27 January 2000).

Galeotti, M. (1995) *Cross-Border Crime and the Former Soviet Union*, Boundary and Territory Briefing 1:5:1

Irk, F. (1997) *Organised Crime: special danger for new democracies*, National Institute of Criminology, Hungary, http://www.okri.hu (accessed 9 July 2003).

Hungarian Ministry of Interior (2002) *Answers to the questions of the Council of Europe Committee of Experts on the Criminological and Legal aspect of Organised Crime (PC-S-CO) for 2001*: 8.

Joint project Against Corruption in the Republic of Hungary, Global Programme against Corruption Working Paper, UNODCCP, March 2003: 8.

Kosztolanyi, G. (2000) *Greasing the Wheels: the parliamentary enquiry into the Hungarian oil scandals*, Central Europe Review Ltd, UK.

Lefebvre, S. (1997) 'Crime and society in Hungary: a survey', *Low Intensity Conflict and Law Enforcement*, vol. 6, p. 98.

Liukkonen, M.(1997), *Motor Vehicle Theft in Europe*, HEUNI Paper no. 9:16

Los, M. (1990) *The Second Economy in Marxist States*, Macmillan, p. 38.

The Moscow Times, 'Hungary eyes police after scam', 28 March 2000.

NCIS Threat Assessment (UK National Criminal Intelligence Service, 2000), 46

Offe, C. (1996) 'Capitalism by design? Democratic theory facing the triple transition in Eastern Europe', *Social Research*, vol. 58, pp. 3–13.

Orszang-Land, T. (1998) 'On the right track', *International Police Review*, March/April:13.

Polish Interior Ministry (2002) *International cooperation in the field of battling organised crime.*

RFE/RL Research Report, 'Escalation of drug abuse admitted', 6 December 1985:37.

RFE/RL Research Report, 'Policemen inadequately educated, while organised crime rises', 31 July 1986: 38

Russia Today, 'Hungarian bank denies it laundered Russian money', 6 August 1999.

Salgo, L. (1999) *Challenge of Organised Crime*, speech given at conference, 'Organized crime: the national security dimensions', Germany, 31 July–2 August.

Savona, E. & Adamoli, S. (1996) *The Impact of Organised Crime in Central and Eastern Europe*, Transcrime Working paper no. 7, http://www.jus.unitn.it/transcrime/papers/Wp7.html (accessed 27 July 2003).

Select Committee on the European Union, House of Lords (2000) *Enlargement and EU External Frontier Controls*, Paper 110, Session 1999–2000, 17th report, 24 October.

Seminar for Criminal Justice practitioners on the Implementation of the UN Convention against Transnational Organised Crime, Ministry of Interior, Czech Republic, 15–17 July 2003.

Shelley, L. (1997) *The criminal-political nexus: A Russian case study*, NSIC conference, Mexico, March:1–47

Smart, V. (1995) 'Europol warning on Eastern Mafias', *The European*, 31 July.

Stefancic, M., *Car Thieves*, BANKA International, http://www.tel.hr/banka-mzb/96-07/6car.html (accessed 4 June 2000).

Wright, A. (1997) 'Organised crime in Hungary: the transition from state to civil society', *Transnational Organized Crime*, vol. 3, p. 71.

Chinese Organised Crime

Bertil Lintner

If Chinese restaurants are one feature of the world's Chinatowns, Chinese secret societies are another, wrote Shanghai-born author Lynn Pan in her excellent study of the Chinese diaspora, *Sons of the Yellow Emperor* [1]. Secret societies have always been endemic to Chinese overseas communities, where they have survived on fear and corruption and prospered through their involvement in a wide range of legal and illegal businesses. For many years, Hong Kong was seen as the 'capital' of this worldwide Chinese criminal fraternity and, in the 1980s, many outside observers and analysts thought the gangs which were based in the then British colony would leave for Canada, Australia and America once it reverted to Chinese rule in 1997.

Bertil Lintner is a senior writer for the *Far Eastern Economic Review* and the *Wall Street Journal* based in Thailand.

The Australian authorities, for instance, thought that 90,000 criminals with links to Chinese criminal gangs, or the Triads, would leave as soon as the five-star flag was hoisted over Hong Kong [2].

In the end, the reverse turned out to be the case. Not only did the Hong Kong Triads make arrangements with the territory's new overlords, but in Chinatowns all over the world, close links were also forged with mainland Chinese interests. In China itself, where cutthroat capitalism has replaced the old, austere socialist system, new secret societies, both Triad-linked criminal groups and various syncretic sects, are also expanding at a breathtaking pace. This—and the nature of the symbiotic but convoluted relationship that has always existed between organised crime and officialdom in Chinese societies—came under the scrutiny of many international law enforcement agencies when the biggest-ever corruption scandal broke in China in late 2000.

Lai Changxing, an influential local businessman in Fujian province on the mainland side of the Taiwan Strait, had used his connections with senior cadres in the ruling Communist Party of China (CPC) as well as generals in the People's Liberation Army (PLA) to build up a smuggling empire, based in the port city of Xiamen, that handled everything from crude oil to rubber, cars, tobacco and electrical appliances. Lai used local gangs and hoodlums to do the leg work while he managed to get on his payroll at least one of Xiamen's deputy party chiefs, Liu Feng, and the head of the city's police external liaison department, Wang Kexiang, and a top official in the Fujian Provincial Border Defence Force, Zhang Yongding. The manager of the Fuijian branch of the Bank of China and the chief of the Xiamen branch of Industry and Commerce Bank Corporation had also been bought off [3].

Lai was reported to have evaded $6 billion in taxes—before he, like to many other Chinese criminals, managed to escape to Canada [4]. Back home in Fujian, more than 300 people were arrested and tried. Fourteen death sentences (three of them suspended), 12 life sentences and 58 fixed-term prison sentences were handed down. Lai, for whom returning to China was out of the question, then began to talk about his business and high-level connections. He told the Canadian media that China has a network of businessmen in Canada and the United States who act as spies to steal industrial and military secrets. The network, he claimed, was run by the intelligence unit of the PLA and Beijing's Public Security Bureau [5].

Many felt that Lai was trying to show that he could be useful to the Canadian government in order to get political asylum in the country. But his revelations were strikingly similar to the findings of a top-secret study prepared for the Royal Canadian Mounted Police and the Canadian Security Intelligence Service as early as 1997. Known as 'Sidewinder', the report detailed an alleged pact between Chinese intelligence agencies, businessmen and criminal gangs operating in Canada. The report was subsequently rewritten and given a new code name, 'Project Echo'. The press accused the Canadian government of trying to water down the damning report so as not to upset relations between Canada and China [6].

Eventually, the original 'Sidewinder' report was leaked to the media and became extremely controversial. Some criticised it as being 'biased against China', and almost racist. But its basic findings received more credence when the Federal Bureau of Investigation, the FBI, in May 2001 arrested three Chinese-born scientists at the telecommunications giant Lucent Technologies and a smaller related enterprise in New Jersey. Accused of a 'complicated scheme of corporate espionage', the three men were brought in handcuffs before a federal magistrate in Newark and detained without bail. They had stolen voice and data software from Lucent to set up a joint venture with a Beijing company that would become the Chinese equivalent of the US data-networking powerhouse Cisco Systems.

The venture received $1.2 million in financing from Datang Telecom Technology, a Chinese-government-controlled maker of communications equipment based in Beijing [7]. Rick Fisher, a China expert with the Jamestown Foundation, who served on the Republican Policy Committee of the House of Representatives during a 1998 investigation of US technology transfers to China, described the arrests as 'a signal that the United States needs to "redouble" its efforts to find those persons working in this country for the benefit of the Chinese government' [8]. But was it just a joke that the China-financed New Jersey joint venture formed by the threesome was called ComTriad Technologies? Even if not part of a traditional Triad, the firm clearly saw itself as a high-tech version of China's age-old secret societies.

A string of revelations of Chinese industrial espionage in the United States had a severe impact on America's racial relations, and threatens to undermine the high level of acceptability that the Chinese-Americans have managed to achieve following decades of discrimination. Frank Ching, a Hong Kong-born Chinese-American wrote in 1999:

> ...virtually every Chinese is tarred—visitors, students, diplomats and business representatives. All are suspected of spying. Similarly, it is suggested that there are no legitimate Chinese companies—every one is considered to be a front for the Chinese military or some intelligence agency. It assumes that every member of every Chinese delegation is on an intelligence mission, as is every Chinese student [9].

The anti-Asian hysteria has echoes of World War Two, when every Japanese living in the United States was considered a spy, and nearly all of them were rounded up and interned in camps throughout the war. It is too often forgotten that it is the Asians themselves— the ordinary law-abiding Chinese in New York's Chinatown, the Vietnamese shopkeeper in the Indochinese-dominated suburb of Cabramatta in Sydney, Australia, the street vendor or minibus driver in Hong Kong, the student or scientist who comes under pressure to spy for Beijing—who suffer the most from ethnically-based organised crime, extortion, threats and clandestine operations within their respective communities. They are trapped in an evil social order, from which few have any recourse.

Street Gangs

A clearer understanding of the nexus between crime, business and officialdom can be gained by looking at some of its component parts: first, street gangs. Any country has its share of waifs, strays and juvenile delinquents who make a living by pick-pocketing, drug peddling in the streets, whoring and pimping. Many are drug addicts, willing to carry out any assignment, no matter how brutal, for financial reward. Triad 'snakeheads', or enforcers, recruit their foot soldiers from this milieu. An especially promising juvenile delinquent is brought to a secret place, where he meets others who have also been recruited. Incense is burned and an oath is taken whereby the new recruits are made to swear lifelong allegiance to the Triad society:

> I shall suffer death by five hundred thunderbolts if I do not keep this oath...I will always acknowledge my Hung [Triad] brothers when they identify themselves. If I ignore them I shall be killed by a myriad of swords... If I am arrested after committing an offence, I must accept my punishment and never try to implicate any of my sworn brothers. If I do, I will be killed by five hundred thunderbolts [10].

This oath has been passed on unchanged from generation to generation of Triad brothers, but, in modern times, fear of catching AIDS has forced new recruits to slit their own fingertips simultaneously and suck only their own blood rather than following the age-old initiation rite of drinking mingled blood of new recruits from a communal tumbler [11]. But regardless of how the oath is taken, the mystique of the secret initiation ritual is meant to discipline the otherwise unruly juvenile delinquents, and to give them a sense of belonging to something very special. They are then given perhaps a fancy suit, a pair of expensive sunglasses, or a mobile telephone, which make them feel important—and popular with the girls. The leader of each such gang of young recruits is usually a somewhat older enforcer who once went through the same ritual, survived warfare in the streets, and thus gained promotion from his superiors.

The Triads

There are many different, rival Triad societies, and the very first in Chinese history may have been the White Lotus Society, which was founded by monks and scholars in the twelfth century and played an important role in the struggle of the Mongol occupation in the thirteenth and fourteenth centuries. Most 'modern' Triads trace their origin to the *Tiandihui*, 'the Heaven and Earth Society', which many believe was set up in the seventeenth century to overthrow the Manchu Qing Dynasty, and to restore the more indigenous Mings. The nationalist-Chinese Kuomintang capitalised on this belief when its leader, Dr Sun Yat-sen, began his struggle against the Manchu Emperors in the late nineteenth century, although he wanted to turn China into a republic. Using the name of the *Tiandihui*, Dr Sun managed to solicit support for his cause among overseas Chinese communities in the Asia-Pacific region as well as in the Ming heartland in southern China, where most Chinese migrants came from anyway. However, more recent research, primarily by American professor Dian Murray, show that the *Tiandihui* was actually set up in the late eighteenth century—more than a hundred years after the fall of the Ming Dynasty—and then not as a political movement but as a mutual aid organisation in a volatile frontier area. People, especially outcasts and vagrants, needed protection both against bandits and the Emperor's mandarins, and grouped together in secret societies [12]. The name 'Triad', which was coined much later, refers to the magic number 'three'. Three multiplied by three equals nine and any number whose digits add up to nine is divisible by nine. In Chinese numerology, three was also the mystical number denoting the balance between Heaven, Earth and Man. Originally, the secret ritual was meant to bind these tightly-knit brotherhoods closely together in order to avoid betrayal by fellow members of the group.

In the same way, Chinese labourers in Singapore, Penang, Honolulu and San Francisco also needed protection in an often hostile environment, and the secret societies were able to fulfill that role. It was much later that the *Tiandihui* claimed patriotic credentials, and it is also clear that Dr Sun and other Chinese nationalists played up that aspect of the Triad in order to make use of their muscle to further their political goals. As a result, after the overthrow of the Manchu Dynasty in the 1911 revolution, ties between the Triads and the new, Kuomintang government were also very close. Chiang Kai-shek used the Green Gang, led by the notorious gangster Du Yuesheng, nicknamed 'Big-Eared Du', to control the trade unions and the communists in Shanghai in the 1930s. In the 1940s, new Triads were set up by Kuomintang officers and the nationalist government's secret police to fight the communists more effectively. The best known was the 14K Society, founded in 1947 by a Kuomintang general, Kot Sio Wong. The gang's name came from its first headquarters, which had been located at No 14, Po Wah Road in Guangzhou. When the communists emerged victorious from the civil war against the nationalists in 1949, General Kot fled to Hong Kong with hundreds of his followers. Many of them settled in Rennie's Mill, a run-down village on Junk Bay east of the old Kai Tai airport, where flags of the Republic of China (Taiwan) flew over the shabby-looking houses until the entire neighbourhood was 'sanitised' in time for the Chinese takeover of Hong Kong in 1997. But 14K remains one of the territory's most important Triads, with offshoots all over the world.

Big Business and Officialdom

Most of the mobsters are less flamboyant than those whom the public are used to seeing in Hong Kong and Taiwan action movies, and they may not be as patriotic as Dr Sun and others claimed, but they nevertheless perform an important function in Chinese societies: there are certain things that big business—and governments—just cannot do. A big businessman may, for instance contact a Triad snakehead and have him mobilise his foot soldiers to make life difficult for a business rival. A typical example was when in early 2000, young men dressed in black T-shirts, with their chests and biceps adorned with tattoos of dragons and phoenixes, suddenly appeared in the quiet village of Pak Tin in Hong Kong's New Territories. They would swear and kick doors as they demanded exorbitant rents from local residents. A car was parked in the village, with a sign on its dashboard clearly indicating that its owner belonged to the well-connected Sun Yee On Triad. When that message was not clear enough, a funeral van, an obvious sign of bad luck, was parked in Pak Tin.

The problem was that the local villagers, who had lived in Pak Tin for generations, had refused to give up their homes to a Hong Kong 'developer' who wanted to turn the rural area into a complex of 600 flats in four high-rise towers. Thanks to the brave efforts of Law Yuk-kai, a local human-rights activist and law graduate, the villagers resisted both the initially formal request from the 'developer'—and the more forceful methods of the hired hoodlums, when 'normal' means did not seem to work. Law had the courage to assist his fellow villagers to prepare to fight for their homes [13].

Given the Sun Yee On's well-placed connections, which go way up in the army and party hierarchy in China, Law's chances of success were almost nil—and it is those connections that enable the Sun Yee On, and other Triads, to run prostitution, illegal gambling rackets, and 'protection' of street hawking, minibus services, and the film industry, which often idealises the 'secret societies' and their mythical origin.

The Triads are also used by governments in the region. When the Taiwanese security services in 1984 wanted to get rid of a dissident, troublesome journalist in exile, Henry Liu, they delegated the task to hitmen from the island's most powerful crime syndicate, the United Bamboo Gang [14]. The Triad was more than willing to carry out the assassination, not because they had anything against Liu, but because in exchange for killing them him they would also get unofficial protection for their own businesses: gambling, prostitution and loan sharking.

A big businessman in Hong Kong or Singapore may need to transport a large load of cash to an offshore 'financial centre' to evade taxes. The Triads can mobilise their people for such duties. No one would dare to run off with the cash: death by a 'myriad of swords' would then follow. A businessman may also be in financial trouble and need some fast cash to cover his debts. He may decide to invest in a heroin deal, which gives enormous returns for a small outlay. A senior Triad snakehead would then be contacted. He, in turn, would mobilise junior snakeheads who would use their Triad foot soldiers as well as unorganised street thugs to carry out the deal. And, needless to say, it would be almost impossible to trace the deal back to the main investor. If anyone got caught, it would inevitably be a few expendable street thugs.

Illegal-alien smuggling, gun-running and similar activities are carried out along very much the same lines. Not all street gangsters are Triad members, and using the Triads to carry out assignments does not make big businessmen, or police officers, Triad members either. The Triads are in the middle; they are used by top echelons of society, and they employ thugs who may or may not be members to carry out the job. Yiu Kong Chu, a professor in the Department of Sociology at the University of Hong Kong, argues that the Triads are an integral, rather than a merely predatory, element of many sectors of the local economy [15].

Chinese organised crime is not, as some foreign observers presume, a cross between the Freemasons and IBM, well-organised corporate structures shrouded in Masonic ritual. While the criminals live outside the law, they have never been outside society. Apart from being useful for big business and government agencies, organised crime also helps the authorities police more unpredictable, disorganised crime. The Triads may run their extortion rackets, gambling dens and prostitution rings. But the streets that they control are largely free from pickpockets, bag-snatchers and other petty criminals. Even the Chinatowns of New York and San Francisco are in many ways the safest parts of those cities, thanks to the Triads. Shopkeepers and restaurant owners pay protection money to local gangs. In turn, New York's Chinatown may appear, at least superficially, much more orderly and peaceful than Harlem or the Bronx. But if a shopkeeper is unwise enough to refuse to pay, his life would be in danger.

At the same time, it would be incorrect to describe the Triads as Crime International Inc. The fact that many of the Triads use the same name in Macao, Hong Kong, London, Amsterdam, Shanghai or San Francisco—'14K', 'Wo On Lok', 'Big Circle Boys' and so on—does not mean that they are part of a worldwide network. A certain member of, for instance, the 14K may have been sent, or gone on his own initiative, to Kunming in Yunnan to trade in drugs from the Golden Triangle. There, he would gather some local thugs, tell them that 'we're all 14K', perform some rites, and then do his business. Using a name like the '14K' is meant to discipline the local thugs and to instil fear in local unorganised criminal rivals as well as local law-enforcement agencies. Most Triads are in fact very loosely organised, and shoot-outs and assassinations between rival factions of several gangs using the same name are not uncommon [16].

The New China

Nevertheless, China's new, post-Mao Zedong rulers began to discover the usefulness of the Triads as soon as they embarked on their bold capitalist ventures in the early 1980s. But it first became obvious to the public when on 8 April 1993, just as the people of the then still British Hong Kong were starting to get used to the idea of a return to the 'motherland', Tao Siju, the then chief of China's Public Security Bureau, gave an informal press conference to a group of television reporters from the colony. After making it clear that the 'counterrevolutionaries' who had demonstrated for democracy in Beijing's Tiananmen Square in 1989 would not have their long prison terms reduced, he began talking about the Triads: 'As for organisations like the Triads in Hong Kong, as long as these people are patriotic, as long as they are concerned with Hong Kong's prosperity and stability, we should unite with them' [17]. Tao also invited them to come to China to set up businesses there.

The statement sent shockwaves through Hong Kong and there was uproar in the media. Since 1845, Triad membership had been a crime in the territory, and the rule of law was considered one of the pillars that made it an international city. Claiming to be 'patriotic' was no excuse for breaking the law. But the people of Hong Kong should not have been surprised. Deng Xiaoping, the father of China's economic reforms, had over the years hinted at the existence of connections between China's security services and some Triads in Hong Kong. In a speech in the Great Hall of the People in October 1984, Deng pointed out that not all Triads were bad. Some of them were 'good' and 'patriotic' [18].

While Deng was making those cryptic remarks in Beijing, secret meetings were held between certain Triad leaders and Wong Man-fong, the deputy director of Xinhua, the New China News Agency, China's unofficial 'embassy' in Hong Kong when it was a British colony. Wong told them that the Chinese authorities 'did not regard them the same as the Hong Kong police did'. He urged them not to 'destabilise Hong Kong' and to refrain from robbing China-owned enterprises. But they could continue their money-making activities [19].

In the years leading up to the 1997 handover, and especially when the British on Hong Kong's behalf argued for more democratic rights to be included in its mini-constitution, or when the Hong Kong people themselves demonstrated their support for the pro-democracy movement in China, rather than fleeing the scene, certain 'patriotic' Triads were there as Beijing's eyes and ears. They infiltrated trade unions, and even the media. Hong Kong—and increasingly even China—experienced a paradoxical throwback to Shanghai of the 1930s, when the former rulers of the country, the Kuomindang, had enlisted gangsters to control political movements and run rackets to enrich themselves and government officials alike.

A few days before security chief Tao made his stunning public statement to the reporters from Hong Kong, a new, glitzy nightclub called Top Ten had opened in Beijing. One of the co-owners was Charles Heung of the Sun Yee On, one of Hong Kong's most notorious Triad societies—and another was Tao himself [20]. Sun Yee On, of all the Hong Kong Triads, seems to have established a very special relationship with the Chinese authorities. It is also the only Triad that has computerised membership records, and what appears to be a centrally-controlled structure. That cannot be said of the first 'mainland' Triad in modern times, the Dai Huen Jai, or the Big Circle Boys, which has got much more attention from the sensational media mainly because it was founded in the 1970s by former Maoist Red Guards who had failed to reintegrate into society once the Cultural Revolution was over [21]. The name 'Big Circle Boys', has cropped up in Hong Kong, Macao, Canada and even the United States, but, like the 14K, it is a name used by many different groups of mainland hoodlums with no central leadership. Some members of the Big Circle Boys may have their personal contacts with people within China's security services, but these are not on the same level as the relationship between the Sun Yee On and the Chinese authorities.

The interrelationship between criminals and powerful people in China is even more blurred when it comes to maritime piracy. According to numerous reports, many ships on the high seas were boarded by personnel from military gunboats bearing the markings of the Chinese navy, and the 'pirates' were dressed in genuine Chinese naval uniforms. The same reports suggest that while piracy may not be condoned by the Chinese navy as such, the temptation to participate in attacks on foreign ships, or to turn a blind eye to sea-robbery in exchange for bribes or part of the loot appears to be very strong [22].

This new relationship between organised crime and Chinese officialdom - coupled with new, enormous business opportunities in China—has spurred Chinese 'lodges' and 'clan associations' in America's Chinatowns to forge closer links with the mainland. In the past, most of these 'community groups'—which were heavily Triad-related—looked at Taiwan as their 'spiritual homeland'. Now, many Chinese businessmen and others in the Chinatowns of New York, San Francisco and Toronto have begun to fly the flag of the People's Republic, and its national day, October 1, is celebrated with more fanfare than 'Double 10'—10 October, the day that commemorates Dr Sun's uprising in China in 1911 that led to the end of the Qing Dynasty and the establishment of the Republic of China on 1 January 1912.

This shift in allegiances also coincides with the democratisation of Taiwan, which has forced many of the island's Triads to relocate to the mainland - and Southeast Asia. In 1997, Taiwan's popular, US-educated then minister of state and later justice minister, Ma Ying-jeou, stated: 'Yes, secret societies have been part of Chinese history. They have their own justice. But that type of justice is part of an agricultural society. We are an industrial, commercial society today. You can't take justice into your own hands. The days of Robin Hood are over' [23]. Organised crime is far from gone from Taiwan, but even the once-powerful United Bamboo Gang seem to have more business in Shanghai these days than in Taipei [24].

The United Bamboo Gang, including its 'spiritual leader', Chen 'Dry Duck' Chi-li, has also set up a new base in Cambodia, where they are active 'controlling' ethnic Chinese investment in the country's garment industry. In Vietnam, on the other hand, new local gangs, steeped in the same criminal culture as in China, have emerged to run that country's booming heroin business and prostitution rackets. Links to Indochinese refugee communities in Australia, especially Cabramatta, has led to a massive flood of drugs into local communities. Much less is known about connections between Vietnam's new gangs and the authorities than the more obvious such links in China, but the fact that they manage to thrive and prosper despite 'crackdowns' by the authorities, including numerous executions of known criminals, show that many of them are well-connected and protected [25].

The New Frontier

The new 'crime frontier' in the Asia-Pacific region, however, appears to be the Russian Far East rather than Southeast Asia. Organised crime has been a problem in the area's main port city of Vladivostok since the collapse of the Soviet Union in 1991, but the last few years have seen a dramatic increase in the number of Chinese Triad groups operating in the region. Large amounts of 'black money' from China have been invested in illegal logging and fishing deals, with timber and fish being smuggled to China, Japan and South Korea; costing the government millions of roubles every year in lost revenue [26].

Russia's Minister for Internal Affairs, Boris Gryzlov, has admitted that the Far Eastern region has the worst per-person crime rate in the country. However, the streets of Vladivostok appear to be safer and much more orderly today than they were a decade ago, when they were under the control of local crime bosses. Then, smuggling rackets, gambling dens and prostitution rings were rife, and kidnappings, drive-by shootings and car bombings were regular occurrences. The difference now is that most of the old, flamboyant Russian 'godfathers' are gone—and the Chinese Triads have arrived. They are better organised, more discreet, and they view civil disorder as a threat to their criminal enterprises.

Chinese gangs control many of the casinos in the region (there are more than a dozen gaming establishments in the Vladivostok area), many Chinese restaurants, and even some Russian hotels and eateries. Many small-time Russian gangsters now work for the Chinese syndicates, either as contacts for local business deals or as security guards at the casinos. The nature of the relationship between local Russian criminals and the Chinese crime bosses is not clear, but it seems that the Chinese are far better organised, and therefore have the upper hand [27].

The only area the Chinese do not dominate is the local drug trade, which is still in the hands of Tajik, Kazakh, Chechen and other Central Asian criminals, who bring in heroin from Afghanistan. According to the local police, only ephedrine and small quantities of Southeast Asian heroin are smuggled in from China and North Korea. Many of the leaders of the indigenous Russian organised crime groups that previously dominated the region have been killed in turf wars, while others have gone out of business or died in mysterious circumstances. The last of the city's big Russian crime bosses, Yevgeny Petrovich Vasin, nicknamed 'Dzhem' ('Jam') died of a heart attack in October 2001. Somewhat ironically, it was Vasin who first brought mainland Chinese Triads to Vladivostok to counter competitors from European Russia and Central Asia, who had flocked to the area after the collapse of the Soviet Union in 1991. In the mid-1990s, Vasin paid several visits to Shenyang in China's northeastern Liaoning province. His first partner in crime, who later rose to become the main organised crime figure in Vladivostok, was a Chinese known as 'Lao Da', or 'Elder Brother'. Lao Da already controlled a large part of Vasin's businesses and after his death, he is believed to have discreetly taken over what remained.

Large-scale Chinese migration to Russia's Far East has made it easier for the Triads to prosper in the region. As a result of Stalin's ethnic purges in the 1930s, Vladivostok—once a predominantly Chinese city—was until recently the only major port city in the Pacific Rim without a Chinese community. Now, Chinese merchants from across the border sell clothes, tools, toys, watches and other cheap consumer goods in a sprawling new market in one of the city's eastern suburbs. There is still no Chinatown as such there. The new immigrants live scattered in the suburbs—or they are concentrated in other far eastern towns such as Ussuriisk and Blagoveshchensk and in the smaller township of Pogranichnyi, where they outnumber the European population. Facing racial prejudice and the threat of deportation, many choose—or are forced—to work for ethnic Chinese groups linked to the Triads.

The problem of cross-border crime and illegal migration was deemed important enough to be highlighted in a joint declaration by Russian president Vladimir Putin and his Chinese counterpart Hu Jintao, that was signed on 27 May 2003. Russia and China agreed to create a joint working group to curb the uncontrolled movement of people across the common border.

The rise in Chinese organised crime and illegal migration has fuelled racist attitudes towards all Chinese, even ordinary businessmen who are actually victimised by the Triads through their protection rackets. Some sources, however, argue that the prevailing perception that Chinese migrants are coming like a 'tidal wave' is grossly exaggerated. But threat perceptions are important for local attitudes. After all, there are some 100 million people in China's northeastern region, while the population of Russia's Far Eastern Federal District—an area two-thirds of the size of the USA—is not more than seven million. Even if the number of newly arrived migrants from China did not exceed 200,000, or a mere 3 percent of the total population—a figure often mentioned in the local press—many locals see it as a trend, and believe that in another decade or two, the numbers could be much higher. Russia's Far East may be too poor to attract huge numbers of migrant workers, who are better off at home in China. But there is plenty of land, and thousands of Chinese farmers have settled in the border areas, where they grow vegetables and other crops. More importantly, business opportunities abound, especially in the booming underground economy.

How well connected in high places the Triads are is difficult to determine, but enforcing the law, and curbing corruption within the police and local government, has never been easy in this remote corner of Russia. Gryzlov noted that out of 151 bribery cases filed in 2001 and 2002, only 20 made it to court—and, in the end, only one of the suspects received a prison sentence [28]. Late last year, the police actually arrested Lao Da and about a dozen of his associates, but the case collapsed, and not one of them was brought to court. The local police are tight-lipped about Lao Da and are even unwilling to discuss his existence—which goes a long way to show how influential he has become, and how much central control has been undermined by the arrival of Chinese organised crime in the Far East.

The new face of Chinese organised crime in Asia is bound to have a profound impact on security in the region. Gone are indeed the days of the 'Robin Hoods'—the flamboyant gangsters from Hong Kong and Taiwan with their meat cleavers and scarred faces. An entirely new breed of entrepreneurs is emerging on the fringes of China. The businesslike and well-connected, pinstriped suit-wearing managers of the Sun Yee On have shown where the future lies. And gangsters such as Lao Da are breaking new ground, which could have far-reaching consequences for the stability of the entire region.

Notes

[1] Pan, *Sons of the Yellow Emperor: A History of the Chinese Diaspora*, 338.
[2] *Asiaweek*, 11 November 1989.
[3] Lawrence, 'A city ruled by crime', 14–18.
[4] *Asiaweek*, 22 December 2000.
[5] *The Sunday Province* (Vancouver), 22 April 2001.
[6] Mitrovica, 'PM's trip to China behind delay in spy report'. A copy of the original 'Sidewinder' report is in the author's possession.
[7] Romero, 'Technology Espionage Charges Add to China Tension', and Coughlin & Perone, 'Espionage at Lucent: Three Accused of Slipping Software to Firm in China'.

[8] Seger, 'FBI Arrests Two Lucent Scientists, Trio Charged With Sending High-Tech Gear to Beijing'.

[9] Ching, 'China Maligned'.

[10] For a complete list of the 36 Oaths of China's Triad Societies, see Lintner, *Blood Brothers: the Criminal Underworld of Asia*, 388–91.

[11] From a source close to the Macao Triads; Macao, 28 July 2001.

[12] See Murray, *The Origins of the Tiandihui: The Chinese Triads in Legend and History*.

[13] Schloss, 'Village Law'.

[14] For a detailed account of the murder of Henry Liu, see Kaplan, *The Fires of the Dragon: Politics, Murder, and the Kuomintang*.

[15] Chu, *The Triads as Business*.

[16] Lintner, 'Organised Crime: A Worldwide Web?' This is based on numerous interviews and conversations with local people close to organised crime in Hong Kong and Macao.

[17] Dannen, 'Partners in Crime'.

[18] Ibid.

[19] 'A social contract with territory's underworld', *South China Morning Post*, 14 May 1997.

[20] *The New Republic*, 14 & 21 July 14 1997.

[21] This information is based on numerous interviews and conversations with local people close to organised crime in Hong Kong and Macao over many years in the 1990s, when I was researching my book *Blood Brothers*.

[22] Dillon, *Piracy in Asia: A Growing Barrier to Maritime Trade*, 3.

[23] Cheng, 'Taiwan's Dirty Business'.

[24] Malhotra, 'Shanghai's Dark Side'.

[25] For an account of Vietnamese organised crime in Vietnam and Australia, see *Blood Brothers*, 308–12, 331–5.

[26] Interview with Vitaly Nomokonov, director of the Centre for the Study of Organised Crime at the Far Eastern State Univerisity, Vladivostok, 21 May 2003.

[27] See Lintner, 'Triads tighten grip on Russia's far east'. The article is based on interviews with academics, law enforcement agencies and local businesspeople during a visit to the Russian Far East in May 2003.

[28] Ibid.

References

Asiaweek, 11 November 1989; 22 December 2000.

Cheng, A. T. (1997) 'Taiwan's dirty business', *Asia Inc.*, April.

Ching, F. (1999) 'China maligned', *Far Eastern Economic Review*, 29 July.

Chu, Y. K. (2000) *The Triads as Business*, Routledge.

Dannen, F. (1997) 'Partners in crime', *The New Republic*, 14 & 21 July.

Dillon, D.R. (2000), *Piracy in Asia: A Growing Barrier to Maritime Trade*, Paper produced by the Asian Studies Centre and published by the Heritage Foundation, Washington, 22 June.

Kaplan, D. (1992) *The Fires of the Dragon: Politics, Murder, and the Kuomintang*, Atheneum.

Lawrence, S. V. (2000) 'A city ruled by crime', *Far Eastern Economic Review*, vol. 30, November: 14–18.

Lintner, B. (1999) 'Organised crime: A worldwide web?', *Global Dialogue*, (Cyprus) vol. 1/1, (Summer).

Lintner, B. (2003) *Blood Brothers: the Criminal Underworld of Asia*, Palgrave.

Lintner, B. (2003) 'Triads tighten grip on Russia's far east', *Jane's Intelligence Review*, September.

Malhotra, A. (1994) 'Shanghai's dark side', *Asia Inc.*, February.

Mitrovica, A. (2000) 'PM's trip to China behind delay in spy report', *The Globe and Mail*, 30 August. A copy of the original 'Sidewinder' report is in the author's possession.

Murray, D. H. (1994) *The Origins of the Tiandihui: The Chinese Triads in Legend and History*, Stanford University Press.

The New Republic, 14 & 21 July 14 1997.

Pan, L. (1990) *Sons of the Yellow Emperor: A History of the Chinese Diaspora*, Little, Brown.

Romero, S. (2001), 'Technology espionage charges add to China tension', *Sydney Morning Herald*, 5 May, and Coughlin, K. & Perone, J.R. (2001), 'Espionage at Lucent: Three Accused of Slipping Software to Firm in China', *The Star-Ledger* (Newark), 4 May.

Schloss, G. (2000) 'Village law', *South China Morning Post*, 29 June.

Seger, J. (2001) 'FBI arrests two lucent scientists, trio charged with sending high-tech gear to Beijing', *The Washington Times*, 4 May.

South China Morning Post, 'A social contract with territory's underworld', 14 May 1997.

The Sunday Province (Vancouver), 22 April 2001.

The Changing Face of the Yakuza

Peter Hill

The modern yakuza are derived from two distinct antecedents, gamblers (*bakuto*) and itinerant peddlers (*tekiya*) though the etymology of the generic term yakuza referring to a losing hand (*ya ku sa*—eight, nine, three) in a Japanese card game has an obvious gambling derivation. During the Tokugawa period (1600–1867) these groups suffered periodic bouts of persecution though more typically the authorities adopted a pragmatic attitude, seeing them as useful agents of social control and sources of intelligence. Gambling bosses frequently also operated as labour brokers to the central government's ambitious construction projects while local *tekiya* bosses were responsible for the organisation of stall-holders at festivals within their territory [1].

Dr Peter Hill is a British Academy Postdoctoral Fellow at the department of Sociology, University of Oxford.

With the gradual withering away of the power of the Tokugawa state and the emergence of a rich merchant class with money to waste, gambling groups enjoyed a period of dynamic growth and in the military and political turmoil surrounding the Meiji restoration, gambling bosses were able to deploy significant numbers of fighting men in support of either new or old regimes. For example, Shimizu Jirōchō with nearly five hundred armed gamblers captured a provincial city for the Meiji cause [2].

With the re-establishment of strong central government following the Meiji restoration, gambling groups once more experienced a period of government repression and their numbers declined temporarily. However, with the development of modern industry in the early 20th century, the Russian Revolution of 1917 and Japanese Rice Riots in 1918, industrialists and political leaders attempted to utilise these groups to counter labour unrest and the threat of political radicalism. In 1919 the Interior Minister set up the Dai-Nippon Kokusui-kai, a pan-Japan organisation comprising yakuza groups, to break strikes and left wing protests. Ultimately this alliance broke up due to internal squabbles and did not effectively meet its creator's aspirations [3].

Although many yakuza played an active role in extreme right-wing movements during the 1930s, once strong authoritarian government had been established, these groups were again subjected to renewed crackdowns. Following Japan's defeat in 1945, there was a near-total collapse in the formal economy, a discredited and disempowered police force and a large pool of unemployed and desperate men trained in the effective use of violence and brutalized by war. There consequently arose a flourishing black-market run under the auspices of neighbourhood bosses and their demobbed followers [4]. Black-market groups were typically referred to as *gurentai* (racketeer or hoodlum). Although they were not necessarily traditional yakuza groups, the more powerful *gurentai* groups either absorbed yakuza gangs or adopted many of their cultural symbols and norms (such as distinctive full body tattoos and the use of finger amputation, either as a punishment or a show of contrition). At the same time, due to the lack of economic alternatives, many gambling groups were forced to adopt (hitherto disparaged) *gurentai* business activities.

As Japan's economy recovered, the prime economic focus of these groups changed. The growing hospitality business, encompassing bars, clubs, restaurants and sexual service establishments, provided a new source of protection money. At the same time, many yakuza groups operated as labour brokers (*tehaishi*) providing day-labourers to the construction and docking industries, giving gangs considerable power over these sectors. Attempts to control these expanding and lucrative market opportunities led to widespread inter-gang conflict during what the police chronology refers to as the 'gang-war period' (1950–1963).

Although laws were enacted to more effectively counter this gang violence, the yakuza were broadly tolerated during this period, due to the combined effects of police weakness, links between politicians and yakuza at both local and national levels, a widespread fear of left-wing, student and labour agitation amongst elite groups and a belief that yakuza groups were an effective tool in the fight against radicalism.

Gangs also assisted the police by providing them intelligence and, once a territorial monopoly had been established, keeping their patches quiet.

In 1963, in response to widespread public criticism of yakuza violence and the ineffectiveness of police countermeasures, the authorities launched the first 'summit strategy' involving the mass arrests of yakuza members, in particular the top personnel. This operation was facilitated by a change in the gambling laws whereby individuals could be prosecuted merely on the basis of witness testimony. While this was effective in reducing the number of identified gang members from the 1963 peak of roughly 180,000 to 120,000 at the end of the decade, and led to the disbandment of various prominent gangs, it had the unintended consequence of consolidating the position of the larger, more sophisticated, syndicates with their diversified business interests, at the expense of the small, locally-based traditional gambling groups.

During the early 1970s, many of the yakuza members arrested under the summit strategy were released from prison and re-established their organisations. In order to insulate their leadership cadres from criminal prosecution, a system of tribute payments (*jōnōkin*) was introduced whereby lower ranking members paid membership fees to their boss every month. During the 1970s, the yakuza also developed new sources of income in response to increased police pressure on gambling. These included an expansion in amphetamine dealing and the creation of groups spuriously advocating right wing political views (*ese uyoku*) or social issues—most usually *burakumin* [5] emancipation (*ese Dōwa*).

During this period the yakuza also became systematically involved in *sōkaiya* activities. The *sōkaiya* are effectively either corporate blackmailers who receive payoffs for not asking embarrassing questions at company annual general meetings (a practice which in other countries might be considered normal shareholder behaviour) or protective *sōkaiya* who protect companies from the activities of such predatory *sōkaiya* [6]. While not all *sōkaiya* were themselves yakuza (police estimates for the early 1980s suggest a figure of about one third), most of the rest were reliant on yakuza protection. If they lacked such protection, *sōkaiya* would be easily countered; the intended victim could simply employ yakuza to deter unprotected *sōkaiya*. We can see clearly the way in which yakuza operate as providers of protection or, as defined by Gambetta [7], a *mafia*.

In 1982, the commercial code was reformed to combat rampant *sōkaiya* activity, resulting in a decline of *sōkaiya* identified by the police from 6,738 in 1982 to 1,682 the following year. The decline was largely an accounting effect (the new law created a stockholding threshold below which shareholders were shorn of full shareholders' rights (crucially that of attending annual general meetings) and many lower level *sōkaiya* continued as corporate extortionists but as rogue journalists (*shinbun goro*) or 'company ruffians' (*kaisha goro*).

The 1982 reforms also resulted in an increase in corporate extortion from spurious right-wing and *dōwa* activists seeking contributions or purchases of their publications. Failure to comply would result in either right-wing armoured loudspeaker cars parked outside the company's offices and broadcasting old military songs and propaganda at high volume or denunciation by angry and violent *burakumin*.

A further consequence of the anti-*sōkaiya* provisions was the increase in *minbō*. *Minbō*, literally the violent intervention in civil affairs (*minji kainyū bōryoku*), refers to the set of activities engaged in by yakuza in which they make use of their group's reputation for violence to gain some financial advantage usually in civil disputes. A frequently cited example of *minbō* is yakuza involvement in traffic dispute settlements. Because the legal machinery for the resolution of civil dispute (such as traffic accidents) is slow and expensive in Japan, injured parties might find it expedient to engage yakuza to negotiate a settlement out of court. Of course, any settlement thus reached would reflect less the merits of the case than who had employed yakuza (and in cases where both parties had done so, who had employed the stronger). Other types of *minbō* include debt collection, financial and corporate racketeering, and 'crisis management' [8]. While in many cases the yakuza are providing a genuine service for which there is consumer demand, inevitably there are also cases in which the yakuza engineer a pretext for claiming compensation. Examples include yakuza deliberately crashing cars and then claiming damages from the other driver (in one case a sex worker was hired by yakuza to engage the victim in distracting activities while driving in order to reduce his ability to claim innocence) and yakuza claiming that expensive suits have been ruined by a laundry. Even when *minbō* is a genuine protection, it is highly likely to be protection afforded to 'the wrong people'[9].

For the authorities, *minbō* is problematic for two key reasons. Firstly it directly impinges on members of the public in ways that more traditional yakuza business does not. When organized criminal activity is restricted to governance of illegal markets and involvement in what are perceived as 'victimless crimes', tolerance of such groups is politically acceptable. Although this is not a strictly accurate reflection of all traditional yakuza activities, groups hitherto victimized by them had generally been politically marginal or antithetical to business and political elites. With the yakuza now adversely impinging directly on the lives of ordinary members of the public, there was an increasing perception of them not so much as romantic rough diamonds with their own moral code and fierce loyalty, but *bōryokudan* (violent pathological groups), resulting in increased pressure on the authorities to take more proactive steps against them.

At the same time, *minbō* is a difficult category of yakuza activity for the authorities to deal with under criminal law (given that yakuza membership is not itself a criminal offence) because typically the perpetrators deliberately steer clear of criminal intimidation as defined by law. Because the shared identifiers of yakuza membership, such as amputated fingers, tattoos, particular patterns of speech and dress, are readily understood by ordinary Japanese, and yakuza name-cards and lapel-badges baldly demonstrate gang membership, explicit intimidation is not necessary; the intimidation is implicit in yakuza/*bōryokudan* membership and their universally recognized reputation for violence. Therefore, when a driver is handed a name-card bearing a yakuza crest and the suggestion made that he pay compensation for the damage caused by his reckless driving, there is no doubt what is going on, but no direct threat has been made. During the 1980s a significant proportion of yakuza income was therefore derived from activities that, though clearly intimidatory, were not easily dealt with by the existing legal framework.

Keizai Yakuza

Perhaps the most lucrative type of *minbō* for the yakuza over the 1980s was *jiage* (land sharking). Japan's land laws impose a number of barriers to a free market in real estate. In particular it is extremely difficult to evict tenants, which can present major time- and financial costs to real-estate development. To circumvent these costs, real estate firms would engage yakuza to encourage tenants to relinquish their leases and/or small landholders to sell their property. *Jiage* operations would typically earn a 3% commission for the yakuza although on a particularly large or expensive site this might be less. Given the real estate bubble during the 1980s, the amount of money involved was massive. With the wealth generated from *jiage* operations, yakuza joined the rest of Japan in speculative investment in Japan's supposedly ever-rising real estate and equities markets. This was the heyday of the *keizai* (economic) yakuza.

The most notable of these were Ishii Susumu, the underboss (*wakagashira*) and then Boss of the Inagawa-kai syndicate, and Takumi Masaru, *wakagashira* of the Yamaguchi-gumi. Ishii, released from prison in 1985, set up a number of real-estate businesses just one of which, Hokushō Sangyō, increased its turnover from $1.48 million in 1986 to $84.1 million the following year. Ishii was also active in stock market speculation though as one of the country's most influential yakuza, he enjoyed advantages unavailable to other investors; a close relationship with two of the Japan's largest brokerages enabled him to have the value of his shares ramped as the brokers advised other clients to invest too. During this period yakuza frequently demanded to engage in speculation on credit or demand compensation when their shares underperformed [10].

During the mid 1980s, the yakuza attracted nationwide attention (and considerable opprobrium) when the Yamaguchi-gumi, the country's largest syndicate, split in two following a dispute over the leadership succession following the death of the third generation boss, Taoka Kazuo. The subsequent five-year conflict resulted in twenty-five deaths, seventy injuries (four of whom were ordinary members of the public), and over five hundred arrests [11]. By the standards of gang wars in more trigger-happy jurisdictions this may be slight but in Japan this was a major event. Ishii Susumu of the Tokyo-based Sumiyoshi-kai, recognising the negative repercussions this event would have on the yakuza collectively, urged the warring parties to find a peaceful solution as the police were considering new anti-yakuza laws [12].

The Bōtaihō

This was indeed the case. However, there were a number of reasons for the changed police position other than the Yamaguchi-gumi's civil war: pressure from the United States at both political and law-enforcement levels; public disgust at the corruption-ridden ruling Liberal Democratic Party (LDP), a number of yakuza conflicts involving the deaths of police officers and innocent members of the public; the inadequacy of the criminal law to deal with *minbō* style activities directly victimizing ordinary members of the public; all these played a part in forcing the authorities to draft a new anti-yakuza law [13]. In 1991 the *bōryokudan* countermeasures law (*bōryokudan taisaku hō* or, more simply, *bōtaihō*) was passed unanimously by the Diet and came into effect the following year.

It is by no means clear that the political elite's support for this law was anything other than a piece of window dressing. Although the scandal was yet to break, during the late 1980s, Liberal Democrat Party (LDP) godfather Kanemaru Shin called upon Ishii Susumu to silence a group of right-wing extremists who were trying to sabotage Takeshita Noboru's attempt to become Prime Minister. In 1988, Kanemaru personally thanked and praised Ishii at a traditional restaurant; they both offered the other the seat of honour [14]. Two years later, Kanemaru also made use of Ishii to silence extremist criticism of his trip to North Korea. As more recent events suggest [15], LDP/yakuza links are neither confined to Kanemaru nor have they been ended following the introduction of the *bōtaihō*.

By the standards of the US RICO statutes or European anti-organised crime laws, the *bōtaihō* adopts a mild regulatory approach concentrating on closing the legal loophole abused by yakuza *minbō*. Under the provisions of the *bōtaihō*, the regional Public Safety Commissions [16] are empowered to designate a group as a 'designated *bōryokudan*' provided that (a) over a certain proportion of its members have a criminal record, (b) the group is organized hierarchically and (c) the organisation's members make use of the group's reputation to make money. Once a group has been designated, its members are prohibited from making 'violent demands', which the law defines as demand or request made while exploiting the yakuza's reputation for violence (*Bōtaihō*, article 9). This effectively covers the gamut of *minbō* activities [17].

A party subject to such a yakuza demand is then able under the provisions of the *bōtaihō* to appeal the police or the Public Safety Commission (PSC) which then issues an administrative order to the perpetrator ordering them to desist. Should this injunction be broken, the perpetrator in question is then liable to a fine of up to a million yen (almost $10,000), up to a year's imprisonment, or a combination of both.

The law also empowers PSCs to order the closure of gang offices at times of inter-gang (and following revision in 1997, intra-gang) conflict for up to three months, an order that can be extended for a further three months. PSCs can also issue injunctions prohibiting the public display of gang insignia on gang offices and behaviour in the vicinity of gang offices which the PSC judges likely to cause anxiety to the general public.

In addition the *bōtaihō* provides for the establishment of regional centres for 'promoting the eradication of *bōryokudan*'. The duties of these centres include running public awareness campaigns, training individuals at risk from yakuza predation in ways to deal with 'violent demands' and encouraging yakuza members to secede from their gangs and return to mainstream society. As these centres are set up under the aegis of the Public Safety Commissions, it should come as no surprise that they are closely linked to the prefectural police forces and many of their staff are retired police officers.

It is difficult to gauge accurately the impact on the yakuza of this new law as its introduction coincided with another event of colossal significance for the yakuza: the collapse in 1999 of speculative bubble in Japan's real estate and equities markets. The yakuza themselves refer to these two events as a 'double punch'.

It is however clear that the law has not been neutral. Even before the law came into effect the leaders of the top syndicates were meeting to discuss ways in which they could limit inter-gang conflict and there was a noticeable increase in brotherhood ceremonies between senior personnel in the big syndicates which came to be known as *sakazuke* diplomacy referring to the traditional sake-drinking rites cementing such relationships. Following the establishment of such bonds, subgroup members would be firmly instructed to avoid conflict with subgroups belonging to the boss's new brother.

The Yamaguchi-gumi, which accurately saw that it was the main target of the *bōtaihō*, took particularly active steps to avoid the new law's effects. Subgroups were ordered to remove gang insignia from outside gang offices; set up groups to study the law's provisions; establish better relations with neighbouring groups; establish a front company. Groups were also instructed to cease all cooperation with the police, and to deny them access to gang offices without a warrant. Although the Yamaguchi-gumi has traditionally had far worse relations with the police than the big Tokyo groups, there had been a degree of behind-the-scenes give and take, which now dramatically declined.

Once the law came into effect and the major groups had been designated, a number of groups, including the Yamaguchi-gumi and the Kyōto-based Aizu-kotetsu launched legal suits against the new law arguing, inter alia, that it violated their constitutionally guaranteed freedom of association and undermined the principle of equality before the law. These appeals were all rejected.

The *bōtaihō* has been effective in various respects. In particular, it has plugged the legal loophole of *minbō* activities. Naturally, the fact that a law exists does not *ipso facto* prevent yakuza participation in activities that the law prohibits. In a 2003 nationwide postal survey of 3,000 companies [18], just under 30% of respondents (response rate 63%) had received demands for money or contracts from yakuza or front groups in the last year. Most (83.8%) respondents that had been targeted in the past claimed that they had refused such demands outright while 8.7% confessed they had acceded in some way to these demands (and one assumes the remaining 7.5% had too). The dark figures for the non-respondents (37% of the total) and the veracity of respondents are open to question.

However, individuals who are subjected to purely predatory yakuza demands now have the option of seeking an injunction. Of course this is an option denied individuals who are themselves operating at the margins of or outside the law, such as illegal immigrants, prostitutes, companies cutting legal corners in some area of their business or other (though in this latter case, it seems that many such firms are willing consumers of yakuza protection).

Like the earlier legal changes, the *bōtaihō* has had unintended consequence for the authorities. Not only have the yakuza largely ceased whatever cooperation they formerly extended to the police, they have also become harder to identify. In order to evade the provisions of the law, many groups formally expelled some of their members. These individuals then set up as political groups or businessmen but operating with the muscle of their former groups still backing them up. At the same time, many members who were not pulling their weight under the harsh post-double punch environment either fled or were expelled. Given the dearth of alternative sources of legitimate employment, these individuals still remained within the criminal sphere but free from any restraining influence their groups might earlier have had.

The increase in criminal activities not traditionally associated with the yakuza (such as organized theft of automobiles and construction equipment for export), or crimes formally forbidden by the large yakuza syndicates (most notably dealing in amphetamines), is not entirely a yakuza affair. Ex-yakuza are also involved. Yakuza interviewees often complain that they are unfairly blamed for these trends but such assertions are not entirely supported by arrest data.

Economic Downturn

Japan's economic troubles have obviously had a major impact on the yakuza in a number of ways. The most obvious of these is that those yakuza who had acquired extensive real-estate and equity portfolios using overvalued assets as collateral to finance these investments were left with massive debts. Of course many other Japanese were in the same position but for banks recovering debts from yakuza presented particular problems. Some of the financial institutions that were most proactive in their recovery efforts (sometimes making use of yakuza to do so) found their executives subjects to attack [19].

The area of Japanese bad-debt crisis that attracted most public attention was the *jūsen* [20] debacle in which Ministry of Finance (MOF) officials left a loophole in their restrictions on lending to real-estate speculators. According to MOF officials, at least $50 billion of this unregulated lending made after the bursting of the bubble went to front companies of yakuza [21]. Estimates of the total of extent of Japan's bad debt range from $420 billion (Financial Services Agency) to $2.37 trillion (Goldman Sachs) [22]. Miyawaki Raisuke, a widely cited authority on yakuza affairs, suggests that 10% of this is directly related to the yakuza and a further 30% has some indirect yakuza link [23].

This does not of course mean that the yakuza have profited by (using the lower range of estimates) $4.2 billion; the value of the assets they hold is now a fraction of what it was when they were purchased. To this extent they are losers like the rest of Japan's eager investors of the bubble years. However, clever yakuza have managed to find ways of making money from the recession.

As providers of private protection, the yakuza are in a position to protect debtors from creditors (and as debtors themselves they protected themselves in this way too) and creditors from debtors. When both parties were protected by yakuza groups, the result could be violent conflict but more typically the groups would negotiate a deal reflecting the relative strengths of the protective groups.

Another area in which the yakuza could extract profit was by obstructing the disposal of property held as collateral. This would typically take the form of auction obstruction (*kyōbai bōgai*), usually achieved by occupying part of the building in question (usually legally through a sublet) and then making sure that potential purchasers would realize that they were yakuza (by displaying gang signs from windows, parking right-wing propaganda trucks outside and so on). By deterring other potential investors from purchasing, yakuza could then either purchase the building cheaply themselves or extract money from the owner to vacate the property and relinquish their leaseholder's rights. While legal machinery exists to resolve problems of this kind, they are typically slow and uncertain so paying off yakuza in this way is frequently a more cost-effective strategy.

Those yakuza that did have money were also able to consolidate their position by lending it to those who had found themselves financially embarrassed. Although Japan currently has a large number of legitimate firms offering easy loans to people, those that end up in a trap of debt and with no alternative sources of credit, find themselves relying on yakuza or yakuza-related sources of funds. In cases where rich yakuza are lending to poor ones this can cause all sorts of problems and in the interests of intra-group harmony, the main syndicates have instructed their sub-group members not to lend to fellow syndicate members. When a yakuza member defaults on his debts then his boss can be held responsible for them so bosses also have a financial interest in the borrowing patterns of their members as well as a desire to reduce the likelihood of conflict with creditor groups.

Most of the lower-ranking yakuza are weathering the recession badly. Many have switched to amphetamine dealing though this is an activity formally prohibited by the larger syndicates. Members of large syndicates found to be involved in amphetamine dealing are typically expelled. While some observers, most notably the widely cited Miyawaki, identify Japan's decade-long slump as a 'yakuza recession', this is an overstatement. The existence of the yakuza has exacerbated a bad situation but the origins and persistence of Japan's economic woes are to be found in the short-sighted arrogance and entrenched vested interests of its business, bureaucratic and political elites (and ultimately the preparedness of the Japanese electorate to put up with them).

The Death of Takumi

An event of considerable significance in the yakuza world of the late 1990s was the killing of Takumi Masaru in 1997. Takumi was the Yamaguchi-gumi *waka-gashira* (number two), and arguably its most important figure. He was killed by members of one of the same syndicate's biggest groups, the Nakano-kai. After some hesitation, the Nakano-kai was formally expelled from the syndicate.

Despite orders from the syndicate's leadership forbidding Takumi-gumi members from making revenge attacks against the Nakano-kai, such activity continued. Police action in the aftermath of this event resulted in three top executives either in custody or on the run, and the leadership core of the Yamaguchi-gumi was left in a state of paralysis. As of September 2003, the leadership crisis continues with the important *waka-gashira* post vacant and police contacts suggest informally that the current boss is ill-equipped to provide clear direction without an able *waka-gashira* [24].

When the ban on admitting Nakano-kai members into other Yamaguchi-gumi sub-groups was lifted in October 1997, most of the Nakano-kai fled and joined the biggest Yamaguchi-gumi sub-group, the Yamaken-gumi. As of 2002, only a rump of 170 members remains of the once formidable Nakano-kai.

The Takumi killing and its aftermath demonstrate a number of problems within the Yamaguchi-gumi: strict orders were issued by the senior executive group, which were promptly broken; supposedly sacrosanct *oyabun-kobun* ('father-son') loyalty was ignored by the Nakano-kai subgroups deserting their boss for the security of the Yamakeni-gumi; syndicate leadership has been seriously weakened and has vacillated over the appropriate punishment of Nakano; intra-group harmony is fragile. All these bode ill for a supposedly imposing organisation.

21st-Century Yakuza

According to the police statistics for 2002, the number of *bōryokudan* members in Japan stood at 84,400. Of these roughly half (43,100) were seen as full members (*kōsei-in*) and the remainder associate members (*junkōsei-in*). Slightly over 90% are members of designated *bōryokudan* groups under the provisions of the *bōtaihō*. Although the yakuza population is now considerably below its 1963 peak of over 184,000, it has been growing slowly from its 1995 low of 79,300 [25]. Until the introduction of the *bōtaihō*, it was fairly straightforward for the police to compile these statistics as gang offices would have membership details displayed on the walls of gang offices. After 1992, this became much harder due to the steady increase in hidden members and the restricted access to gang offices.

To compound problems there seems to be a discrepancy in the ways in which individual police forces collect their data. For example between 2001 and 2002 the Okayama prefectural police recorded a 33% rise in the number of *bōryokudan* members while the number of gangs more than doubled. This was purely due to a change in accounting practices to account for 'hidden' yakuza such as political front groups and individuals who were resident elsewhere but came back to staff gang offices. Okayama police assert that other prefectures would also show a similar shift if they were to apply the same recording practices [26]. If we confine ourselves to the designated *bōryokudan* groups, these vary in size from the 17,900-man Yamaguchi-gumi to the Shinwa-kai, which comprises just 70. Three-quarters of yakuza are members of the large national syndicates the Yamaguchi-gumi, the Inagawa-kai and the Sumiyoshi-kai [27].

Organisational Structure

Yakuza syndicates are composed of groups tiered in a pyramidal structure. In the case of the Yamaguchi-gumi, the head family is comprised of men who are themselves bosses of second-level groups. The senior executives of second-level groups will in turn be bosses of third-level groups and so on. The Sumiyoshi-kai has traditionally had a flatter federal organisational structure (and consequently lower membership dues) but has recently moved towards a centralised pyramidal hierarchy.

The hierarchical relationships within these groups are cemented by the creation of father-son (*oyabun-kobun*) and brother (*kyōdaibun*) relationships at ceremonies centred on the ritual exchange of sake. It is unusual for these to be based on actual family ties [28]. The boss of a group will have an *oyabun-kobun* relationship with all but the most senior executives of his group who will be his 'younger brothers'. If the gang is a syndicate subgroup then the boss will, in turn, be *kobun* of the superior group's boss.

Important ceremonies, such as those marking a group's leadership succession are ornate affairs. The ceremony marking the transfer of power from Ishii Susumu to Inagawa Yūko, the video of which I have been shown, went on for several hours (reminiscent of a Japanese wedding and about as boring to anyone without a direct interest). Those in attendance included the leaders of all Japan's main yakuza groups, dressed up in traditional Japanese *hakama*, and the officiating Shintō priest.

As mentioned above, gang members typically pay a monthly membership fee. Due to the recent financial problems facing many yakuza this has been declining in recent years. Members are also expected to periodically staff the gang office, three times a month in the case of one interviewee, as well as attend various yakuza ceremonies (*girikake*) at which presents of money are expected. Membership therefore imposes very real financial costs on yakuza.

In addition gang members are subject to a code of discipline imposed both by the senior leadership cadre of the head family and their immediate boss, backed up by a punishments ranging from fines and confinement to the office to beatings, finger amputation, expulsion and, in extreme cases, death. Finger amputation, perhaps one of the most famous aspect of yakuza life, still exists though is more common in western Japan than in Tokyo. To avoid embarrassment while videoing his children's school sports day, one yakuza I know has an artificial finger while others keep their hands out of view when possible.

The benefits are of course that membership grants one the right to engage in certain (but not all) criminal activities with an established support network and brand image to protect the member and his clients from the criminal predation of others. The question remains: do the benefits outweigh the costs? It seems that many lower-ranking yakuza make a very precarious living often supplemented by the earnings of their wives and girlfriends. We might hypothesize therefore that these individuals are staying in the yakuza in the hope that they may reap future benefits as a boss with a number of *kobun* bringing in monthly tribute payments. An alternative explanation may be that the barriers to exit compounded by the lack of attractive alternatives in the legitimate labour market for ex-yakuza keep them locked in. This merits future research.

Recruitment and Training

Traditionally the key pool of yakuza recruits comprised juvenile delinquent groups and *bōsōzku* youth biker gangs. However, at least within Tokyo, it is not uncommon to find graduates of Tokyo's less illustrious universities (Kokushikan and Takushoku being notable in this respect). In the Tokyo group with which I am most familiar there are also a significant proportion of boxers and martial artists. I do not know of any cases of forcible recruitment (although these are reported in police data) and in one case the aspiring member was so keen to join that he actually chopped off his finger beforehand to demonstrate his strength of commitment.

Yakuza training typically lasts for a period of six months to two years. Trainees are expected to 'see with their eyes, hear with their ears and keep their mouth shut'. When they make a mistake, they are hit. By avoiding acts or omissions that incur beatings they gradually learn appropriate yakuza behaviour. Because it is now easier for trainees to flee and get by as drifters (*freeter*) doing odd jobs, beatings have become less severe and yakuza now complain that trainees are now becoming full members without their physical and mental toughness sufficiently proven.

Sources of Income

As the historical section hopefully shows, yakuza business activities change rapidly to reflect developments both in market opportunity and, more importantly, levels of law enforcement. Although many of the businesses outlined above have suffered as a consequence of legal and economic changes, they still exist. A good example of this is the traditional outdoor stall business of the *tekiya*. Due to the current ubiquity of convenience stores selling beer, ice cream, snacks and so on, these stalls are seriously undercut. At the same time, efforts by some prefectural police forces to drive yakuza out of the festival stall market has marginalized the *tekiya* further. However *tekiya* manage to retain a foothold within shrine precincts where the police seem more reluctant to exercise control [29].

Japan's vast hospitality industry (including its highly developed sexual services industry) is highly regulated by the police, who continually pressure bars, clubs and soapland (massage baths) establishments to sever all links with the yakuza, a pressure that has become particularly intense following the revision of the public morals law (*fūeihō*) in 1997. Whereas twenty years ago yakuza protection would be the norm for such establishments, this is no longer the case. One of my research sites in Kabukichō, a large hostess club, receives several phone calls a week from yakuza enquiring who 'looks after them'. Although the club does not pay protection money to anyone (police officers drink at a discount), the club is able to firmly refuse such advances as the manager is well connected to both yakuza and police [30].

The experience of less well-connected places which do try and sever links with yakuza is not always happy. In one recent case in Kitakyūshū, a club that was playing a prominent role in an anti-yakuza campaign was subject to a succession of retaliatory actions including the stabbing of the manager, glue in the locks, excrement smeared on the walls and most recently, in August 2003, a grenade attack that injured seven (the damage would have been more had the grenade not bounced off the head of a hostess and back towards the yakuza assailant) [31].

Other yakuza sources of income include illegal disposal of industrial waste, construction, bankruptcy management, real estate, money-lending, amphetamine dealing (disparaged by all yakuza I have discussed this with), 'crisis management' (typically resolving disputes out of court) and protecting companies involved in these various industries [32]. Recently some yakuza have attempted to ride the dot.com wave thorough involvement in Osaka's NASDAQ Japan and Tokyo's Mothers (venture capital) markets [33]. Though it is naïve to assume that such activities have ceased completely, these markets are now more tightly regulated and the dot.com mania has subsided. Another hi-tech innovation is yakuza involvement in internet scams imposing spurious or excessive charges on visitors to pornographic and other sites. It seems that in these cases, yakuza are not directly operating the sites themselves but protecting those that do [34].

Any estimates as to the scale of yakuza income must be treated with extreme caution. During the peak bubble year of 1989, the police estimated total gang income at 1.3 trillion yen. Mizoguchi, a highly respected journalist, suggests a figure of seven trillion gross annual income during the mid 1980s, of which just over five trillion would be profit [35]. More recent estimates for the early 21st century suggest a figure of one trillion yen, though it is by no means clear how this figure is derived. What is clear is that the majority of yakuza are currently suffering financially.

Conflict and Conflict Resolution

By the standards of organised crime in other jurisdictions, in recent decades yakuza inter-gang warfare has been remarkably limited; between 1992 and 2001 the average number of fatalities and injuries due to yakuza inter-gang conflict were 3.1 and 11.5 respectively. Over the same period, gang conflicts averaged 8.6 [36]. Typically a few shots will be fired at a rival group's office door or a stolen dump-truck crashed into the office, the rivals will retaliate in kind. This will be repeated several times before the combatants are pushed into some sort of peaceful settlement (usually involving the payment of money) by their superior groups. Settlement is much harder if members have been killed but in most cases conflict is resolved within one week [37].

This comparative pacificity is due to a number of factors: the mature state of Japanese organised crime; the low background levels of violence in Japanese society; and recently, more robust legal measures and judicial interpretation concerning such activities.

The vast majority of yakuza are now members of large syndicates with a reasonably well-established equilibrium. They act as a restraining influence on these groups as the leadership elites have more to lose than gain from the open display of violence (which may not be the case for a young gangster who has yet to establish his reputation). The Tokyo yakuza have long been aware of the costs of inter-group violence and since 1972 have run a pan-Tokyo association, the Kantō Hatsuka-kai comprising all of the *bakuto* groups in the capital. The purpose of this organisation is to provide a mechanism for the speedy resolution of conflict and the prevention of misunderstanding. The members of all groups are prohibited from using firearms against each other. As a consequence of the *bōtaihō* and its provisions for the closure of gang offices during periods of conflict, the traditionally more combative western syndicates (such as the Yamaguchi-gumi) have also increased their efforts to minimise warfare.

For example, in a conflict centred on Tochigi prefecture (April-June 2003) involving the Kōdō-kai (a Yamaguchi-gumi sub-group) and the Shinwa-kai (a Sumiyoshi-kai sub-group), both parent organisations supported peaceful resolution and publicly distanced themselves from the conflict stressing that it was problem between the two subgroups alone. The main reason for their distancing was that they did not want gang-office closure orders extended to their headquarters.

In addition, gang bosses are also aware that currently they now run the risk of being sued personally. In recent years there have been a number of cases of civil litigation against bosses for employer responsibility (*shiyōsha sekinin*) when a subordinate has mistakenly killed a member of the public or police during inter-gang conflict. [38] This not only encourages parent groups to impose stricter control on subgroups and, when this is not possible, to wash their hands of involvement, thereby undermining one advantage in belonging to a large syndicate: the military back-up it implies in times of trouble.

Attempts at conflict minimisation, however, ultimately come up against the brute fact that the central prop supporting these groups is their ability to deploy violence. Given that many sources of their income are under greater pressure due to a more hostile economic and law-enforcement environment, yakuza are continually striving to find new ways of making money and this, almost inevitably, brings them into conflict with other yakuza. Because there is less money in circulation there is also less room for compromise and for mutually beneficial outcomes for these disputants.

This has even affected the supposedly amicable Kantō Hatsuka-kai. During an internal conflict between factions of the Kokusui-kai in 2001, offers of intercession from the Kantō Hatsuka-kai were rejected by both sides. The same year, the two most powerful groups in the organisation, the Sumiyoshi-kai and the Inagawa-kai, also came to blows following the fatal shooting of two Sumiyoshi-kai members by Inagawa-kai at a Sumiyoshi-kai funeral. The inability of the Kanto Hatsuka-kai to deal with either of these problems suggests it is insufficiently robust to deal with problems in the harsher yakuza environment of recent years. One mid-ranking Sumiyoshi-kai executive, interviewed by me in 2003, dismissed the KHK as a talking shop for old men that no longer functions.

Although yakuza all possess handguns, they rarely carry them and usually they are hidden in a third party's house or an apartment rented by a non-yakuza. Even bodyguards are typically unarmed except in times of conflict and then the bodyguard will maintain a discreet distance from their boss, because recent legal interpretation of the law means that bosses can also be prosecuted for violation of the relevant firearms law if their guards are armed. Due to Japan's strict prohibition of weapons, firearms are expensive. A cheap Chinese Tokarev copy currently costs around $3,000 while a more exotic US machine pistol might fetch $10,000.

Yamaguchi-gumi

Perhaps the most significant recent development of recent years is the increased expansion of the Yamaguchi-gumi to the Tokyo area. Although the Yamaguchi-gumi has had a long-standing agreement with the Inagawa-kai not to establish gang offices in the capital, the agreement has become blurred with Yamaguchi-gumi members establishing front companies or operating without official gang offices. During the bubble period the syndicate was involved in real estate, loan sharking and construction in Tokyo with an estimated 200–300 members in the capital by 1990. Since then, their presence has increased at an accelerating rate and by 2002 police estimates put the total at 35 sub-groups totalling 750 members, though other sources put the figure at 3,000–4,000 [39]. Because some members shuttle back and forth between western Japan and the capital, and the fact that they do not have official offices, it is hard to say what the real figure is. The consensus is that yakuza raised in the rougher more aggressive Kansai area find it relatively easy to make money in the softer, and more wealthy, Tokyo.

In Kabukicho, the entertainment area of Tokyo where I am currently conducting most of my fieldwork, Yamaguchi-gumi members are particularly active in money-lending which can now be conducted using little more than a mobile phone. Although this might be expected to result in a backlash from incumbent groups, this does not seem to be the case. One Tokyo gang boss I know tells me that as long as they pay him a cut for the right to conduct business on his territory, he is happy. Another lower-ranking Tokyo gang member expressed the situation this way:

'I don't know how the guys at the top feel about it, but I think that we get along fine. I suppose that there are times when incidents lead to conflict but in those cases it can eat into our own rice as well. Live and let live guys, eh?' [40].

Globalisation?

Another development that has attracted much media and political attention over recent years is the spectre of foreign organised crime groups (OCGs) penetrating Japan. This of course makes a good story for all concerned: xenophobic demagogues, such as Tokyo Governor Ishihara Shintarō, the media, the police, and the yakuza themselves all have something to gain by encouraging a moral panic. While the number of foreigners in Japan has increased dramatically in recent years, as far as Kabukicho goes (and this is the area supposedly most heavily infiltrated by Chinese gangs), foreigners tend to operate in conjunction, rather than in direct competition, with the incumbent yakuza groups. As will be discussed below, the presence of non-Japanese criminals in Japan is likely to become more significant in the future.

Foreign OCGs are in a precarious position as they are frequently in Japan illegally and have a disadvantage vis-à-vis the yakuza in terms of information/distribution channels and connections with the upper-world, a disadvantage that encourages mutually profitable co-operation rather than competition. Weapons and amphetamines are both commodities that are far more readily available abroad than in Japan. Due to significant wage differentials, there are also strong economic factors encouraging foreign participation in the Japanese sexual-services industry.

There is therefore the necessity for international links with those capable of supplying these goods and workers. Such links predate the current moral panic but have changed over time to reflect the political and economic conditions of the countries concerned. For example, amphetamines currently come from North Korea though formerly South Korea and, before that, Taiwan were the main sources of amphetamines. Firearms come predominantly from four main routes: the USA, the Philippines, China and Russia. Women come primarily from other Asian countries though South Americans and blonde East Europeans and Russians are now also much in evidence.

The other aspect of globalisation that is relevant here is whether or not the yakuza themselves are expanding overseas. While cases of yakuza activity have been uncovered abroad, we should be careful in interpreting these cases. Yakuza foreign activity can generally be broken into four distinct categories: firstly, yakuza groups shaking down Japanese firms abroad; secondly, yakuza involvement in foreign clubs, bars and sexual-services establishments catering to Japanese tourists; thirdly, yakuza conspiring with local groups to smuggle illegal workers, drugs and weapons into Japan; fourthly, yakuza investment in foreign real estate. Many 'yakuza' in places like the Philippines, are, in fact, ex-members who have been expelled from their gangs [41]. Recently it has become difficult for yakuza with criminal records (the vast majority) to legally enter the United States due to increased vigilance and better intelligence of US immigration officials [42].

Fashion and Self-presentation

The changing nature of the yakuza can also be seen in the way in which they present themselves. The traditional 'yakuza style' of permed hair, diamond rings and gold bracelets are now seen as slightly old-fashioned. Although lower-ranking yakuza on the streets of Osaka or Kabukichi-cho are still readily recognizable in their exaggerated sportswear, senior yakuza frequently look like ordinary executives. In the

Tokyo group with which I am most familiar, the boss typically wears a shell suit and golfing cap, though he dons a suit when conducting business with non-yakuza. His executives generally wear suits. His expelled subordinate wears jeans and sweatshirts and, until reinstated, will not wear anything that might look yakuza-like, a trend to more sober presentation can also be seen in the choice of yakuza cars. Although the Mercedes-Benz remains popular, it is no longer the yakuza cliché it once was; many non-yakuza now drive Mercedes while yakuza increasingly opt for high-class Japanese cars.

Whither Japanese Organised Crime?

The yakuza have changed considerably over the last half-century and no doubt will change in the decades to come. The main factors driving this change have been changes in the legal- and law-enforcement environment, and the emergence and disappearance of economic opportunities that can be exploited. Since the 1990s both of these areas have generally been unfavourable to the yakuza. Although Japan's economy may eventually recover to the advantage of the yakuza, the harsher legal regime and now widespread antipathy to the yakuza will remain for the foreseeable future. The yakuza are therefore likely to become progressively more isolated from mainstream Japanese society.

Increased use of formal legal procedures for dispute resolution (already apparent) will continue to reduce the role played by the yakuza as behind-the-scenes fixers, thereby further encourage the marginalisation of the yakuza. Yakuza members that do operate in close proximity to the upperworld will therefore become increasingly hard to identify.

Japan's comparative wealth will continue to make it a magnet for hungry and ambitious individuals from other Asian countries and further afield. Barring the ascendancy of the xenophobic right wing, Japan will increasingly have to admit such individuals to work (and to pay taxes) to compensate for Japan's rapidly ageing population. The flip side will be yet further penetration of Japan by foreign criminals, which will have profound implications for the yakuza; they will either have to co-opt these individuals to supplement their own ageing ranks, or face competition from younger, hungrier and more aggressive foreign groups who don't recognise the unwritten rules of the games played by police and by the various yakuza groups. Given that yakuza syndicates and sub-groups are led by people with widely divergent tastes, priorities and acumen, it is to be expected that both strategies will be adopted.

One certainty is that Japan's illegal markets will not disappear therefore guaranteeing the existence of organised crime [43]. While the yakuza will be profoundly changed by wider social, political and economic developments, it is unlikely that they will disappear any time soon. While recent legal developments have adversely affected the yakuza, continued evidence of links between senior political figures and yakuza members means we must be deeply sceptical as to the commitment of Japan's political elite to serious, proactive organised crime countermeasures.

Notes

[1] Iwai, *Byōri Shūdan no Kōzō*, 34; DeVos, *Socialisation for Achievement*, 283.

[2] Iwai, 42–5.

[3] Iwai, 46.

[4] These are ideal aetiological conditions for mafia-type organisations; see for example Gambetta, *The Sicilian Mafia: The Business of Private Protection*; Varese, *The Russian Mafia: Private Protection in a New Market Economy*. For a more detailed account of the postwar black market see Dower, *Embracing Defeat: Japan in the Aftermath of World War II* or Whiting, *Tokyo Underworld: the Fast Times and Hard Life of an American Gangster in Japan*.

[5] *Burakumin* (or, to use the currently accepted euphemism, *dōwa*) refers to the descendents of Japan's outcaste communities. Although ethnically identical to mainstream Japanese society, *burakumin* have suffered consistently worse life chances than their compatriots and have disproportionately featured in the ranks of the yakuza.

[6] See Szymkowiak, 'Sōkaiya, An Examination of the Social and Legal Developments of Japan's Corporate Extremists', *International Journal of the Sociology of Law*; Szymkowiak, *Sōkaiya: Extortion, Protection and the Japanese Corporation*; West, 'Information, Institutions, and Extortion in Japan and the United States: Making Sense of Sōkaiya Racketeers'.

[7] See Gambetta.

[8] In which yakuza sort out problems behind the scenes for politicians, businessmen and ordinary members of the public.

[9] See Gambetta.

[10] Nakagawa, 'Sono Otoko wa Mihatenu Yume wo Otta', 234; Kyōdō *(Tsūshin)*, *Riken Yūchaku: Seizaibō - Kenryoku no Kōzu*, 194–215, 241–2. In English see Alletzhauser, *The House of Nomura*; Kaplan & Dubro, *Yakuza: Japan's Criminal Underworld; Tokyo Business Today*; Hill, *The Japanese Mafia: Yakuza, Law and the State*.

[11] Yamadaira, *Yakuza Daijiten 2*, 287–8.

[12] Mizoguchi, *Yamaguchi-gumi to Bōryokudan Shinpō*, 247–8.

[13] Hill, 138–46.

[14] *Kyōdō* op. cit., 118–29; Mizoguchi, *Gendai Yakuza no Ura-chishiki*, 114–25.

[15] Three examples from 2003: senior LDP member Kamei Shizuka was discovered to have received (fairly small) campaign contributions from a prominent loan shark very closely connected to the Goryō-kai, a yamaguchi-gumi sub-group; Kamei denied knowing the donor's background. New Conservative Party parliamentarian Matsunami Kensiro was discovered to be paying his aides' salaries partly with money from a yakuza front company, he did not resign (*Asahi Shinbun*, 22 April 2003). An interviewee working in a yakuza-related business assures me that political donations from yakuza and their front organisations are standard practice. The interviewee's boss and yakuza associates frequently attend political fund-raising parties (including those of well-known mainstream political figures) bearing substantial sums (interview, provincial city in Japan, 2003).

[16] Committees of local worthies charged with democratic oversight of the regional police forces. Despite their ostensible purpose, these groups have been captured by their respective forces and are effectively rubber stamps.

[17] Hill, 157–66 provides a more detailed coverage of this law.

[18] *Heisei 14 nendo kigyō taishō bōryoku ni kan suru ankeeto* (http://www.npa.go.jp/bouryokudan/boutai1/ketkagaiyou-2.pdf).

[19] *Tokyo Business Today*, December 1994; Hill, 184–90.

[20] Housing and Loans institutions.

[21] *South China Morning Post*, 1998.

[22] *Financial Times*, 15 October 2002 and *Bloomberg News*, 4 April 2002 respectively.
[23] Formerly an elite bureaucrat at the NPA and now a yakuza countermeasures consultant, Miyawaki is a well-known yakuza expert. His contact details are on file at the Foreign Press Centre in Tokyo. Foreign journalists doing their yakuza story invariably cite him. See for example Kaplan and Dubro, 201–2; *Financial Times*, 12 December 1995.
[24] Informal discussions, Tokyo, 2003.
[25] *Keisatsu Hakusho* (Police White Papers) (Ōkura-shō Insatsukyoku) passim.
[26] *Shūkan Jitsuwa*, 26 June 2003.
[27] Using figures for designated *bōryokudan* strength Keisatsu Hakusho 2002: 198.
[28] Although the Inagawa-kai seems to be adopting dynastic leadership with the grandson of first-generation boss Inagawa Kakuji apparently being groomed for leadership after a short interregnum following the retirement of current boss Inagawa Yūko.
[29] Interview, *tekiya* boss, Tokyo, 2003.
[30] Interviews, Kabukichō club staff, 2003.
[31] *Mainichi Shimbun*, 19 August 2003 and 20 August 2003.
[32] See Hill, chapters 4 and 6.
[33] *Financial Times*, 10 April 2001.
[34] Mizoguchi interview, Tokyo, January 2003.
[35] Mizoguchi, 'Urashakai no Seiji-keizaigaku', 182.
[36] *Keisatsu Hakusho* (2002), 196.
[37] Keiji-kyoku (Keisatsu-chō Keiji-kyoku Bōryokudan Taisaku-bu) *Bōtaihō Shikō Jū-nen* (2002), 15.
[38] Hill, 268.
[39] *Jitsuwa Jidai*, August 2003.
[40] *Jitsuwa Jidai*, August 2003.
[41] Interview, Kabukichō insider, 2003.
[42] Interviews, Tokyo, 2003.
[43] While it is interesting to speculate on the demand for sexual services, amphetamines and gambling in a predominantly elderly society, the probability is that Japan will be forced to import significant amounts of foreign labour. These foreigners will in turn have implications for these markets, due to their different preferences.

References

Alletzhauser, A. (1990) *The House of Nomura*, Bloomsbury.
Bloomberg News, 4 April 2002.
DeVos, G. (1973) *Socialisation for Achievement*, University of California Press, p. 283.
Dower, J. (1999) *Embracing Defeat: Japan in the Aftermath of World War II*, Penguin.
Financial Times, 15 October 2002; 12 December 1995; 10 April 2001.
Gambetta, D. (1993) *The Sicilian Mafia: The Business of Private Protection*, Harvard University Press.
Heisei 14 nendo kigyō taishō bōryoku ni kan suru ankeeto (http://www.npa.go.jp/bouryokudan/boutai1/ketkagaiyou-2.pdf).
Hill, P. (2003) *The Japanese Mafia: Yakuza, Law and the State*, Oxford University Press.
Iwai, H. (1963) *Byōri Shūdan no Kōzō*, (Seishin-Shobō), p. 34.
Jitsuwa Jidai, August 2003.
Kaplan, D. & Dubro, A. (2003) *Yakuza: Japan's Criminal Underworld*, University of California Press.
Keiji-kyoku (Keisatsu-chō Keiji-kyoku Bōryokudan Taisaku-bu) (2002) *Bōtaihō Shikō Jū-nen*, p. 15.
Keisatsu Hakusho (Police White Papers) (Ōkura-shō Insatsukyoku) passim.

Kyōdō (Tsūshin), Riken Yūchaku: Seizaibō—Kenryoku no Kōzu (Kyōdō News Service, 1993), 194–215, 241–2.

Mainichi Shimbun, 19 August 2003 and 20 August 2003.

Mizoguchi, A. (1986), 'Urashakai no Seiji-keizaigaku', in *Bessatsu Takarajima* 56, *Yakuza to Iu Ikikata* (Takarajima), 182.

Mizoguchi, A. (1992), *Yamaguchi-gumi to Bōryokudan Shinpō*, in *Bessatsu Takarajima* 157, *Yakuza to Iu Ikikata: Kore Ga Shinogiya!* (Takarajima), 247–8.

Mizoguchi, A. (1997) *Gendai Yakuza no Ura-chishiki* (Takarajima), 114–125.

Nakagawa, H. (1992), "Sono Otoko wa Mihatenu Yume wo Otta", in *Bessatsu Takarajima* 157, *Yakuza to Iu Ikikata: Kore Ga Shinogiya!* (Takarajima), 234.

Shūkan Jitsuwa, 26 June 2003.

South China Morning Post, 31 May 1998.

Szymkowiak, K. (1994) 'Sōkaiya, An Examination of the Social and Legal Developments of Japan's Corporate Extremists', *International Journal of the Sociology of Law*, vol. 22.

Szymkowiak, K. (2002) *Sōkaiya: Extortion, Protection and the Japanese Corporation*, M. E. Sharpe.

Tokyo Business Today, December 1994.

Varese, F. (2001) *The Russian Mafia: Private Protection in a New Market Economy*, Oxford University Press.

West, M. (1999) 'Information, Institutions, and Extortion in Japan and the United States: Making Sense of *Sōkaiya* Racketeers', *Northwestern University Law Review*, vol. 93.

Whiting, R. (1999) *Tokyo Underworld: the Fast Times and Hard Life of an American Gangster in Japan*, Vintage.

Yamadaira, S. (1993) *Yakuza Daijiten*, vol. 2 (Futabasha), pp. 287–288.

State Crime: The North Korean Drug Trade

Raphael F. Perl[1]

At least 50 documented incidents in more than 20 countries around the world, many involving the arrest or detention of North Korean diplomats, link North Korea to drug trafficking. Such events, in the context of ongoing, credible, but unproven, allegations of large-scale state sponsorship of drug production and trafficking, raise important issues for the global community in combating international drug trafficking. Reports that North Korea may be limiting some of its food crop production in favour of drug crop production are particularly disturbing, though the acreage in question is comparatively small. Another issue of rising concern is the degree to which profits from any North Korean drug trafficking, counterfeiting, and other crime-for-profit enterprises may be used to underwrite the costs of maintaining or expanding North

Raphael Perl is a Specialist in International Affairs at the Foreign Affairs, Defense, and Trade Division of the US Congressional Research Service.

Korean nuclear programs. As the DPRK's drug trade becomes increasingly entrenched, and arguably decentralised, analysts question whether the Pyongyang regime (or any subsequent government) would have the ability to restrain such activity, should it so desire.

Background

Allegations of North Korean drug production, trafficking, and crime-for-profit activity have become the focus of rising attention in the US Congress, the international press, and diplomatic and public policy fora. As early as 28 October 1997, Senators Charles Grassley and Jessie Helms sent a letter to US Secretary of State, Madeleine Albright, questioning why North Korea was not included in the State Department's 1997 annual International Narcotics Control Strategy Report (henceforth INCSR) as a country involved in illicit drug production and trafficking. The Senators noted that according to press reports, North Korea's opium production in 1995 was 40 metric tons, roughly comparable to Mexico's, and that they believed that this figure 'clearly represents a figure of over 1,000 hectares'—the threshold cropland figure for inclusion in the report and designation as a major drug producing country [2]. The Department of State's response cited an inability to obtain data to substantiate North Korean production levels. Subsequently, in October 1998, the conferees for the Fiscal Year 1999 Omnibus Appropriations Act directed the President to include in the next INCSR '...information regarding the cultivation, production, and transhipment of opium by North Korea. The report shall be based upon all available information' [3]. Senate Bill No. 5, Section 1209 of the Drug Free Century Act, introduced in January 1999, proposed a statement of congressional concern that the Department of State has 'evaded its obligations with respect to North Korea' under the Foreign Assistance Act and encourages the President to submit any required reports.

In what can be described as an ongoing 'cat and mouse' game between the Executive Branch of the US government and the Congress, the Department of State has consistently been cautious not to pin a label of 'state sponsorship' on North Korean drug trafficking activity. To do so would arguably require the imposition of foreign aid sanctions on the Pyongyang regime, a move seen by many as (1) over prioritising drugs vis-à-vis more pressing issues (primarily nuclear proliferation) and (2) unwisely restricting the portfolio of Administration options for dealing with the rogue state. Moreover, if the amount of North Korean illicit poppy cultivation cannot be verified, the 1,000-hectare threshold triggering foreign aid cut-off under the Foreign Assistance Act of 1961 will not be met. Consistent with such policy concerns, the Department of State steadfastly maintains that although allegations of illicit drug activity 'remain profoundly troubling... the United States has not been able to determine the extent to which the North Korean Government is involved in manufacturing and trafficking in illegal drugs' [4].

With aid from the United State and other donors extremely limited (US foreign aid to North Korea has been severely restricted because of North Korea's designation by the US Secretary of State as a country that has 'repeatedly provided support for acts of international terrorism' [5]), Pyongyang has been forced to look to alternative revenue. In the year 2000, North Korea's legal exports amounted to $708 million in goods—most of which were to its neighbours China, Japan and South Korea [6]. During the same period, imports (mostly from the same three nations) totalled $1.686 billion, leaving a shortfall of $978 million [7]. Both export and import figures are expected to grow dramatically, in the absence of unforeseen events, with no indication at this point of a narrowing trade gap in the immediate future. For example, North/South Korea trade increased by about 50 percent in 2002 over 2001 levels [8]. Moreover, North Korea's need for hard currency is exacerbated by worsening economic conditions; an estimated per capita gross domestic product of $1000, and an ongoing nuclear program that according to a 1998 informal interagency consolidated estimate exceeded well over $200 million per year in 1998, and which North Korea accelerated from 1999 onwards [9].

Allegations of Drug Trafficking

President George W. Bush, in his annual determination for 2004 of major illicit drug trafficking and transit countries, registered his growing concern over heroin and methamphetamine trafficking linked to North Korea, and expressed his intent for the United States to intensify its efforts to stop North Korean involvement in narcotics production and trafficking. In the words of his memorandum for the Secretary of State:

> We are deeply concerned about heroin and methamphetamine linked to North Korea being trafficked to East Asian countries, and are increasingly convinced that state agents and enterprises in the DPRK are involved in the narcotics trade. While we suspect opium poppy is cultivated in the DPRK, reliable information confirming the extent of opium production is currently lacking. There are also clear indications that North Koreans traffic in, and probably manufacture, methamphetamine. In recent years, authorities in the region have routinely seized shipments of methamphetamine and/or heroin that had been transferred to traffickers ships from North Korean vessels. The April 2003 seizure of 125 kilograms of heroin smuggled to Australia aboard the North Korean-owned vessel 'Pong Su' is the latest and largest seizure of heroin pointing to North Korean complicity in the drug trade. Although there is no evidence that narcotics originating in or transiting North Korea reach the United States, the United States is intensifying its efforts to stop North Korean involvement in illicit narcotics production and trafficking and to enhance law-enforcement cooperation with affected countries in the region to achieve that objective [10].

President Bush's concern over the probable scale of North Korean drug trafficking activity reflects the hardening view expressed in the Department of State's 2003 INCSR, which also notes longstanding DPRK links to drug trafficking:

> For years during the 1970s and 1980s and into the 1990s, citizens of the Democratic People's Republic of (North) Korea (DPRK), many of them diplomatic employees of

the government, were apprehended abroad while trafficking in narcotics and breaking other laws. More recently, police investigation of suspects apprehended while making large illicit shipments of heroin and methamphetamine to Taiwan and Japan have revealed a North Korean connection to the drugs. Police interrogation of suspects apprehended while trafficking in illicit drugs developed credible reports of North Korean boats engaged in transporting heroin and uniformed North Korean personnel transferring drugs from North Korean vessels to traffickers' boats. These reports raise the question whether the North Korean government cultivates opium illicitly, refines opium into heroin, and manufactures methamphetamine drugs in North Korea as a state-organised and directed activity, with the objective of trafficking in these drugs to earn foreign exchange [11].

The 2003 INCSR includes little information on North Korea in its money laundering section, but notes reports that Pyongyang has used Macao to launder counterfeit $100 bills and used Macao's banks as a repository for the proceeds of North Korea's growing trade in illegal drugs [12]. More detail on DPRK criminal activity is included in the 1998 INCSR's money laundering section, which reads in part as follows:

> The most profitable lines of state-supported illegal businesses remain drug trafficking, gold smuggling, illegal sale and distribution of endangered species, trafficking of counterfeit US currency, and rare earth metals... North Korean officials appear to be increasing their involvement in financial crimes as a means to generate operational funds and support their country's anaemic economy [13].

Concerns over North Korean drug production and trafficking have also been expressed in the regular Reports of the United Nations International Narcotics Control Board [INCB]. The 1997 Report, for example, in the circumspect language common to such UN documents, notes that 'The Board has received disquieting reports on the drug control situation in the Democratic People's Republic of Korea. Therefore, the Board expresses its concern that the Government of the Democratic People's Republic of Korea has not yet accepted its proposal, originally made in 1995, to send a mission to that country to study and clarify drug control issues' [14]. In addition, US Drug Enforcement Administration (DEA) data and a plethora of domestic and foreign press reports portray an ongoing pattern of drug trafficking, trafficking of counterfeit US currency [15], and other smuggling-for-profit activities by North Korean diplomats over the past 24 years. Since 1976, North Korea has been linked to over 50 verifiable incidents involving drug seizures in at least 20 countries. A significant number of these cases involved arrest or detention of North Korean diplomats or officials. All but four of these incidents have transpired since the early 1990s [16].

Press reports citing North Korean defectors and South Korean intelligence sources, as well as US Government investigative agency source material, paint a grim picture of a failing economy in North Korea, held back by disproportionate military spending, dysfunctional economic policies and the consequences of a broad economic and trade embargo led by the United States since the Korean War. The criminal activities taking place do not seem solely or even mainly the private enterprise of particular corrupt individuals [17]. Instead, pressed for cash, and perceiving its vital national security at stake, the regime reportedly created an office to bring in foreign currency,

Bureau No. 39, under the ruling North Korean Communist Party which is headed by North Korean Leader Kim Jong Il. This office is reported to be in charge of drug trafficking and according to some reports all crime-for-profit activity, including:

(1) opium production and trafficking;
(2) methamphetamine production and trafficking;
(3) counterfeiting; and
(4) smuggling.

Drugs are reportedly exported through China and Russia to Asia and Europe via government trading companies, diplomatic pouches, and concealed in legitimate commercial cargo. Foreign exchange earned by Bureau 39 is reportedly used to:

(1) buy loyalty from Party elites and military leaders to Leader Kim Jong Il;
(2) fund costs of overseas diplomatic missions;
(3) finance national security activity—especially technology and electronic purchases for the intelligence and military services, and
(4) procure overseas components for North Korea's weapons-of-mass-destruction programs [18].

Bureau 39 activities, according to interviews conducted by the *Wall Street Journal* with Asian intelligence officials, have generated a cash hoard, of which an amount in the range of $5 billion is currently stashed away by the Pyongyang regime [19].

Farmers in certain areas reportedly are ordered to grow opium poppies, with cultivation estimates of 4,000 hectares for the early 1990s and 7,000 hectares for 1995. Current production, however, is believed to be below 1995 figures because of heavy rains and the broad decline of agricultural output as a consequence of poor policies, and insufficient fertiliser and insecticides. Looking at all available estimates, a cultivation estimate of 3,000–4,000 hectares for 1998 would appear reasonable, but nevertheless based on indirect and fragmented information. US Government investigative agency sources estimate North Korean raw opium production capacity at 50 tons annually, with 40 tons reportedly produced in 1995. North Korean Government pharmaceutical labs reportedly have the capacity to process 100 tons of raw opium per year [20]. Current production figures, to the extent that they may be available, remain classified, but clearly would not be expected to be below 1998 levels as the DPRK's need for foreign exchange has grown more pressing to accelerate foreign purchases of components of North Korea's secret uranium enrichment program.

Methamphetamine production in North Korea is reported to have started in 1996 after heavy rains decreased income from poppy production. This coincides with a time when markets for methamphetamine are dramatically expanding in Asia, especially in Thailand, Japan, and the Philippines [21]. For example, in 2002, North Korea was the source of approximately one third of the methamphetamine smuggled into Japan [22]. North Korea's maximum methamphetamine production capacity is estimated to be

10–15 tons of the highest quality product for export. According to the INCB, North Korean legitimate pharmaceutical needs for ephedrine (a traditional precursor for methamphetamine) are 2.5 tons per year, one ton higher than US investigative agency source estimates. INCB officials confirm receipt of reports of North Korean involvement in an alleged diversion of 20 tons of ephedrine [23]. Moreover, US investigative agency personnel have in the past noted concerns that North Korea may be bypassing the highly regulated market for ephedrine in favour of an alternate technology for a benzene-based product, raising speculation that US and allied petroleum assistance to North Korea may be used to sustain illicit drug production.

Conservative estimates suggest North Korean criminal activity, carefully targeted to meet specific needs, generated about $85 million in 1997: $71 million from drugs and $15 million from counterfeiting [24]. Recent estimates of drug income, however, are substantially higher with the *Wall Street Journal* citing US military estimates that North Korea's annual drug exports have risen to at least $500 million from about $100 million a few years ago [25]. Income from counterfeiting of US bills has reportedly remained more or less constant, with US military sources reportedly estimating such income at $15–20 million for the year 2001 [26].

If credence is to be given to UN, Department of State reporting, and DEA shared information, as well as press reports citing North Korean defectors and South Korean intelligence sources, a pattern of activity emerges which indicates that in the 1970s, North Korean officials bought and sold foreign-source illicit drugs and by the middle of the decade, North Korea was cultivating opium poppy as a matter of state policy. By the mid-1980s, North Korea was refining opium poppy for export and exporting refined opium products, so that by the mid-1990s, after heavy rains reduced opium production in 1995 and 1996, it had begun manufacturing and exporting methamphetamine to expanding markets in Southeast Asia. If this pattern reflects reality, an important question is the degree to which the Government of North Korea may respond to increased financial pressures and expanding methamphetamine markets by dramatically increasing currently reported levels of drug trafficking activity.

Some analysts, however, question the reliability of information reported in the press attributed to North Korean defectors and South Korean government sources in the past context of what was seen as a cold war propaganda battle between the two Koreas. They note that in a closed state such as North Korea 'hard' data is difficult to obtain, thus what is obtained is fragmentary and indirect at best. North Korea continues to dismiss media reports and speculation on government involvement in drug trafficking activities as anti-North Korean slander based on politically-motivated adversary propaganda sources. North Korean officials are known to stress privately that corruption, drug use, trafficking, and criminal activity in general are maladies to which individuals in all societies may fall prey, and that any involvement by North Korean individuals in such activity is in no way state-connected or state-sanctioned. Further, officials have stressed that in instances where such activity has come to the attention of authorities, individuals involved have been duly punished. Finally, North Korean officials maintain that issues such as drug trafficking and production are matters that should be handled, and are best handled, by their government as an internal matter. UN officials also point to the politically charged milieu of allegations of drug trafficking by North Korea and point out that drug smuggling by individuals in the diplomatic community is by no means limited to North Korea.

Issues for Decision-Makers

At least 50 documented drug trafficking incidents coupled with credible (if unproven) allegations of large-scale North Korean state sponsorship of opium poppy cultivation, and heroin and methamphetamine production and trafficking, raise significant issues for the United States and America's allies in combating international drug trafficking. The challenge to policy makers has been how to pursue sound counter-drug policy and comply with national and international law that may require cutting off aid to North Korea while effectively pursuing other high-priority foreign policy objectives, including limiting Pyongyang's possession and production of weapons of mass destruction, its willingness to produce and export ballistic missiles as well as its involvement in terrorism, counterfeiting and international crime, all the while addressing the humanitarian needs of ordinary North Koreans.

US aid to North Korea is currently limited to providing food and other humanitarian assistance, for example. Reports that North Korea may be limiting some of its food crop production in favour of drug crop production are particularly disturbing, though the acreage in question is comparatively small. Another issue of rising concern is the use of profits from any North Korean drug trafficking, counterfeiting, and other crime-for-profit enterprises to underwrite the costs of maintaining or expanding North Korean nuclear programs.

Central to the policy debate is the need for hard data such as satellite imagery to confirm the extent of reported opium poppy cultivation in North Korea, however, multiple tasking for such imagery and reportedly 'bad weather' have consistently defeated attempts to collect hard data [27].

Enhanced policy focus and law-enforcement intelligence cooperation on targeting, reporting, and tracking North Korean opium/heroin and methamphetamine trafficking and production in the late 1990s has made it significantly more difficult for North Korean entities to engage in illicit smuggling activities. The result, according to many intelligence analysts, has been a need for North Korean trafficking fronts to enter into joint-venture arrangements with criminal organisations in neighbouring nations, notably Russian, Chinese, and South Korean and Japanese criminal enterprises. As generally profits are shared (often as much as 50/50) in such ventures, the level of North Korean drug smuggling activity would presumably need to more-or-less double to keep income levels for DPRK illicit drug enterprises constant with levels achieved in 1998.

The interesting case of the *Pong Su*, arguably, is demonstrative of such joint venture activity. Traditionally, it was assumed that such joint ventures were established to facilitate the smuggling and distribution of DRPK-sourced drugs. In contrast, reported evidence in this case suggests that such joint-venture relationships have become a 'two-way street' with North Korean enterprises smuggling drugs for partner groups as well. After all, this North Korean merchant ship, intercepted by Australian commandos after a four-day sea chase in 2003, appears to have been involved in the large-scale smuggling of heroin from another Southeast Asian source.

Another question, yet unresolved, is the degree to which Pyongyang will be able to maintain its control over its reported drug smuggling activities as they become more decentralised, with more foreign criminal organisations and gangs participating. Deteriorating economic conditions and rising corruption among mid-level DPRK party functionaries threatened with declining lifestyles gives rise to speculation in the intelligence community that rogue operations constitute an increasing proportion of DPRK drug smuggling activity [28].

A final and daunting challenging facing policymakers, both in the DPRK and beyond, is the degree to which the North Korea regime would be able to curtail its reported illicit drug activity should it desire to do so. Policy analysts have repeatedly suggested that any North Korean drug trafficking activity has been carefully controlled and limited in the past to fill specific foreign-exchange shortfalls. Experience suggests, however, that those engaged in the drug trade often find themselves 'addicted' to the income generated and are unlikely to cease such activity, in the absence of draconian disincentives. Moreover, over time, such illicit activity is often seen as becoming 'institutionalised'—taking on a life of its own, a phenomenon that does not bode well for those who would seek to curb drug trafficking activity in North Korea.

Notes

[1] This chapter is based on the author's *Drug Trafficking and North Korea: issues for US policy*, Congressional Research Service Report, 5 December 2003.

[2] North Korea's climate and soil are relatively inhospitable to poppy cultivation and fertiliser is in short supply. Best-guess US government estimates are that such conditions would yield roughly the equivalent of 10 kg of opium gum per hectare with 40 metric tonnes of raw opium, indicative of 3,000 to 4,000 hectares of poppy cultivation. Note also that the DPRK produces some licit opium. According to the INCB, the DPRK reported cultivating 91 hectares of opium poppy in 1991 which produced 415 kg of opium.

[3] H.R. 4328, P.L. 105–277, 112 Stat. 2681, signed into law October 21, 1998. For conference report language see *Congressional Record*, 19 October 1998, H11365.

[4] US Department of State, *International Narcotics Control Strategy Report* March 2003, VIII–45

[5] See Congressional Research Service Report no. 10119, *Terrorism and National Security: the Future*, by Raphael Perl [updated regularly].

[6] Contrast this amount to $1.7 billion in exports in 1990 according to South Korea's central bank. Note also that according to Agence France Presse, 23 October 2003, since the mid-1980s, North Korea has exported some 400 Scud missiles along with missile-related parts to

the Middle East valued at approximately $110 million. Estimates by US Military Forces Command in Korea are substantially higher: $580 million from missile exports to the Middle East for the year 2001 alone. See *Yomiuri Shimbum*, 22 August 2003 and *Reuters*, 4 March 2003, dispatch from Seoul. *Chosen Soren* (ethnic North Korean) overseas remittances to the DPRK are estimated at some $200–$600 million annually, see *Yomiuri Shimbum*, 18 May 2003.

[7] Central Intelligence Agency, *The World Factbook, 2002*: North Korea. Note that 20 May 2003 Congressional testimony by Nicholas Eberstadt of the American Enterprise Institute places North Korea's overall merchandise trade deficit at about $1,200 million a year. See testimony to the Financial Management, Budget and International Security Subcommittee of the US Senate Government Affairs Committee, 20 May 2003.

[8] *New York Times*, 30 December 2002.

[9] The 1998 figure cited on cost of nuclear programs is relatively low because of minimal labour costs.

[10] *Presidential Determination No. 2003–38*, 15 September 2003, *Presidential Determination on Major Drug Transit or Major Illicit Drug Producing Countries for 2004*, 5.

[11] US Department of State, *International Narcotics Control Strategy Report 2003*, VIII–43.

[12] *Ibid*, XII–200.

[13] US Department of State, *International Narcotics Control Strategy Report 1998*, 623

[14] *INCB Report* for 1997, 17.

[15] For example, the *1998 INCSR*, 623, cites a February 1997 article in the Russian newspaper *Izvestiya* on the arrest of a third secretary of the North Korean Embassy, apprehended attempting to exchange counterfeit US dollars. Russian officials tied him to a smuggling operation designed to sell more than $100,000 in counterfeit US bills which they believe was his main function at the embassy.

[16] For example: May 1976, 400 kg of hashish seized from a North Korean diplomat in Egypt; July 1994, Chinese officials arrested a Chinese national on charges of smuggling 6 kg of North Korean-produced heroin through the DPRK Embassy in China; August 1994, DPRK intelligence agent arrested by Russian authorities for trying to sell heroin to Russian mafia group; January 1995, Chinese officials in Shanghai seize 6 kg of heroin and arrest two DPRK nationals, one with a diplomatic passport; July 1998, DPRK diplomat arrested in Egypt with 500,000 tablets of rohypnol (the so-called 'date rape' drug); January 1998, Russian officials arrest two DPRK diplomats in Moscow with 35 kg of cocaine smuggled through Mexico; October 1998, German officials arrested a DPRK diplomat in Berlin seizing heroin believed made in North Korea; February 1999, an employee of the DPRK consulate in Shenyang, China was caught attempting to illicitly sell 9 kg of opium; April 1999, Japanese police caught Yakuza gang members attempting to smuggle 100 kg of DPRK-sourced methamphetamine into Japan on a Chinese ship; April 1999, authorities at Prague airport detain a DPRK diplomat stationed in Bulgaria attempting to smuggle 55 kg of rohypnol from Bulgaria; May 1999, Taiwanese police apprehend four members of a Taiwanese drug organisation attempting to smuggle 157 kg of DPRK source methamphetamine; October 1999, Japanese authorities seize 564 kg of DPRK methamphetamine from the Taiwanese ship *Xin Sheng Ho*; February 2000, Japanese police seize 250 kg of DPRK-made methamphetamine, leading to arrests of members of a Japanese crime group and members of a *Chosen Soren*-run trading company; October through November 2001, Filipino authorities detain a ship twice in their territorial waters which had received first 500 kg and then 300 kg of methamphetamine from a North Korean ship; December 2001, Japanese patrol boats, in a skirmish, sink a North Korean vessel believed to be carrying drugs to Japan (the same vessel had been photographed in 1998 smuggling drugs into Japan); January 2002, Japanese authorities seize 150 kg of DPRK-source methamphetamine from a Chinese ship in Japanese territorial waters that had earlier rendezvoused with a DPRK

vessel for the drug transfer; July 2002, Taiwanese authorities confiscate 79 kg of heroin that a local crime group had received from a North Korean battleship; November and December 2002, packages containing 200 kg of methamphetamine believed to be of DPRK origin float ashore in Japan; April 2003, Australian police seised the DPRK ship *Pong Su*, which had attempted to smuggle 125 kg of heroin through Singapore into the territorial waters of Australia.

[17] See also Galeotti, 'Criminalisation of the DPRK'.

[18] For an excellent and well-researched exposé of DPRK crime for profit activity, see Solomon, 'Money trail'. See also *US News and World Report*, 15 February 1999; *Tokyo Sankei Shimbum*, 29 December 1998; *AP*, 24 May 1998; *Digital Chosun Ilbo WWW*, [South Korea] 12 November 1996; *Moscow-interfaks*, 22 June 1997; *Tong-A Ilbo* (Seoul), 14 February 1996; *Washington Times*, 26 February 1995; *Choson Ilbo* (Seoul), 7 August 1994. Note that Bureau directs the expenditure of North Korea's foreign exchange resources with two priorities: (1) procurement of luxury products from abroad that Kim Jong-il distributes to a broad swathe of North Korean military, party, and government officials to secure their loyalty—Mercedes Benz automobiles, food, wines, stereos, deluxe beds, Rolex watches, televisions, etc., estimated at $100 million annually by US military officials in Seoul, according to a Reuters report of March 4, 2003; and (2) procurement overseas of components and materials for North Korea's weapons of mass destruction and missiles. (See especially the *Wall Street Journal*, 14 July 2003. See also Niksch, *Korea:US Korean Relations—Issues for Congress*.)

[19] *Wall Street Journal*, 14 July 2003.

[20] *Kyodo News Service* (Japan), 13 December 1998. Total arable land in the DPRK is estimated to exceed 1.3 million hectares.

[21] In August 1998, Japanese authorities arrested members of a Japanese criminal organisation and seised 200 kg of a 300 kg shipment of methamphetamine believed manufactured in North Korea. Earlier, in April, 58.6 kg of the same drug, thought to have been manufactured in China, was seized by Japanese authorities in the cargo of a North Korean freighter. *Yomiuri Shimbun* (Japan), 8 January 1999.

[22] Between 1999 and 2001, Japanese authorities reportedly seized 1,113 kg of methamphetamine en route from North Korea—some 34 percent of Japanese seizures. For China during the same period the percentage reportedly constitutes 38 percent (over 2,000 kg). See *The Asian Wall Street Journal*, 23 April 2003.

[23] For example, in January, 1998 Thai police reportedly seized, but later released, 2.5 tons of ephedrine en route from India to North Korea. This was reportedly part of an 8-ton shipment North Korea had attempted to purchase which the INCB reportedly limited to two 2.5 ton shipments over a two year period. However, INCB officials staunchly deny that such an arrangement transpired.

[24] The $71 million for drugs breaks down as $59 million from opium/heroin and $12 million from amphetamines, although one, admittedly speculative, US law enforcement agency source estimate for world market price of heroin produced by the DPRK in 1995 is $600 million. For the $15 million figure on counterfeiting, see the *Korea Herald*, 16 November 1998. See also *Newsweek*, 10 June 1996. Note that according to some sources, income from counterfeiting is considerably higher, around $100 million. Note also that data on amounts of US dollars counterfeited is carefully guarded so as not to undermine confidence in the US dollar. North Korean counterfeit US $100 notes have been detected in at least 14 countries including the US. For data on other forms of DPRK criminal/smuggling activity, see Marcus Holland, *Avoiding the Apocalypse: The Future of the Two Koreas* (Institute for International Economics, 2000) p.119.

[25] *Wall Street Journal*, 14 July 2003.

[26] See *Seoul Yonhap* (English), 13 May 2003, citing Japanese *Yomiuri Shimbum* report of 12 May 2003. Media reports suggest that when Assistant Secretary of State James A. Kelly, visited North Korea in October 2002, he asked that printing of the counterfeit bills be suspended. Some of the bills are reportedly printed on machines stolen by the KGB from the US Mint after World War II and provided to North Korea by the USSR in the late 1980's—see *Foresight* (Tokyo; in Japanese) 15 March–18 April 2003. Others are believed to be printed on equipment purchased by the DPRK in Europe in the 1990s. Quality control is reportedly exercised by use of state-of-the-art equipment designed to detect counterfeiting, reportedly also purchased in Europe. Note that not only US currency is reportedly counterfeited. DPRK payment of a typical purchase of goods or technology from the Middle East may well include a percentage of top-quality Middle Eastern counterfeit bills.

[27] Some analysts have compared the alleged poppy cultivation situation in the DPRK with that of Colombia in the mid-1980s. Beginning about 1986, numerous reports were received from informants regarding poppy cultivation in Colombia. However, despite U-2 aircraft broad sweep imagery, it was not until the mid-1990s that such imagery was able to confirm cultivation, which at that time approximated the 4,000–5,000 hectare range.

[28] Note that DPRK defectors maintain that North Korea's underground economy is controlled by some 1000 'big dealers' who regularly give bribes in US dollars and valuable gifts to Kim Chong-il and party, administration and military elites, See *Seoul Chugan Chosen* 19 June 2003. Note also that Mr Kim's personal assets in foreign countries are widely estimated to be in $130 billion range, with as much as $4.3 billion reportedly in Swiss bank accounts. See *Shukan Posuto* (Tokyo), 16 June 2003, citing Chuck Dawns, a former Deputy Director, Far Eastern Affairs Division of the Pentagon in the Bush and Clinton Administrations. Press reports citing US military sources in Seoul state that Pyongyang spends about $100 million a year on imported luxury cars and liquor for its elite; see *Reuters* 4 March 2003 dispatch from Seoul. The South Korean Unification Ministry website estimates DPRK GNP at $706 per head in 2001, down from $751 in 2000.

References

AP, 24 May 1998.
The Asian Wall Street Journal, 23 April 2003.
Central Intelligence Agency, *The World Factbook, 2002*.
Choson Ilbo (Seoul), 7 August 1994.
Digital Chosun Ilbo WWW, [South Korea] 12 November 1996.
Galeotti, M. (2001) 'Criminalisation of the DPRK', *Jane's Intelligence Review*, vol. 13, no. 3 (March).
Holland, M. (2000) *Avoiding the Apocalypse: The Future of the Two Koreas*, Institute for International Economics.
Korea Herald, 16 November 1998.
Moscow-interfaks, 22 June 1997.
Newsweek, 10 June 1996.
Niksch, L.A., *Korea: US Korean Relations—Issues for Congress*, Congressional Research Service Report No. IB98045.
Perl, R. F. (2003) *Drug Trafficking and North Korea: issues for US policy*, Congressional Research Service Report, 5 December 2003.
Perl, Raphael, F., *Terrorism and National Security: the Future*, Congressional Research Service Report no. 10119 (updated regularly).
Solomon, J. (2003) 'Money trail', *Wall Street Journal*, 14 July 2003.
Tokyo Sankei Shimbum, 29 December 1998.

Tong-A Ilbo (Seoul), 14 February 1996.
US Department of State, *International Narcotics Control Strategy Report 1998.*
US Department of State, *International Narcotics Control Strategy Report 2003.*
US News & World Report, 15 February 1999.
Wall Street Journal, 14 July 2003.
Washington Times, 26 February 1995.

The Crime–Terror Continuum: Tracing the Interplay between Transnational Organised Crime and Terrorism

Tamara Makarenko

The September 11th 2001 terrorist attacks in New York and Washington DC unleashed unprecedented academic, corporate, and government interest in uncovering the contemporary dynamics of international terrorism. As a result, a plethora of post-9/11 literature has emerged, seeking to provide explanations of various issues related to the terrorist threat. In addition to specific accounts of Al Qaeda, the role of ideology, recruitment, state relations, group organisation, and target selection, have also elicited

Tamara Makarenko is a research fellow at the Centre for the Study of Terrorism and Political Violence at the University of St Andrews.

growing analytical attention. One topic, however, that has received comparatively limited analytical interest is the financing of terrorism. Although the immediate post-9/11 environment—with a concentrated focus on Al Qaeda—has provoked the need to understand hawala banking [1], the abuse of charities and donations from diaspora communities, and the use of legitimate business by terrorist groups, few comprehensive accounts of terrorist financing exist [2]. Furthermore, despite sporadic media coverage and official references to the use of criminal activities by terrorist groups, the relationship between organised crime and terrorism remains under-investigated in the public domain.

Increasingly since the end of the Cold War and the subsequent decline of state sponsorship for terrorism, organised criminal activities have become a major revenue source for terrorist groups worldwide. Building on the precedent set by narco-terrorism, as it emerged in Latin America in the 1980s, the use of crime has become an important factor in the evolution of terrorism. As such, the 1990s can be described as the decade in which the crime–terror nexus was consolidated. Generally referring to the relationship between organised crime and terrorism, the nexus most commonly applies to the straightforward use of crime by terrorist groups as a source of funding—such as taxing the drug trade, or engaging in credit-card fraud. The nexus has also been used to relate to the formation of alliances between criminal and terrorist organisations. These two types of relationship constitute the major components of the nexus, as it currently exists; however, the relationship between organised crime and terrorism has evolved into something more complex. Taking advantage of the immediate post-Cold War environment— which offered relatively unrestricted access to technological advancements, financial and global market structures, diaspora communities worldwide, weak states faced with civil war, and numerous geographical safe-havens—the distinction between political and criminal motivated violence is often blurred. In many respects, the rise of transnational organised crime in the 1990s, and the changing nature of terrorism, have produced two traditionally separate phenomena that have begun to reveal many operational and organisational similarities [3]. Security, as a result, should now be viewed as a cauldron of traditional and emerging threats that interact with one another, and at times, converge. It is in this context that the crime–terror continuum exists.

Outlining the Crime–Terror Continuum [4]

Relations that have developed between transnational organised crime and terrorism are not static, but have evolved over the past decade into a continuum that inherently seeks to trace how organisational dynamics and the operational nature of both phenomena changes over time. The crime–terror nexus is placed on a continuum (Figure 1) precisely because it illustrates the fact that a single group can slide up and down the scale—between what is traditionally referred to as organised crime and terrorism—depending on the environment in which it operates.

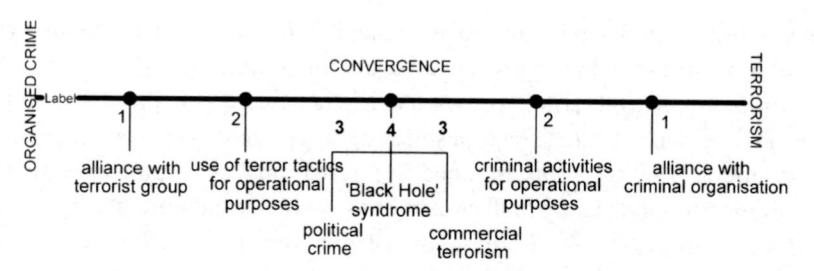

Figure 1 The Crime Terror Continuum

As depicted in Figure 1, organised crime and terrorism exist on the same plane, and thus are theoretically capable of converging at a central point. Organised crime is situated on the far left, with traditional terrorism situated on the far right—each holding distinct and separate positions. At the fulcrum of the continuum lies the point of 'convergence', where a single entity simultaneously exhibits criminal and terrorist characteristics. In assessing the various relationships that have developed between criminally and politically motivated groups, seven categories are discernible—each of which are illustrated as distinct points along the continuum. These seven points, however, can be divided into four general groups: alliances (1), operational motivations (2), convergence (3), and the 'black hole' (4).

Alliances [5]

The first level of relationship that exists between organised crime and terrorism is the alliance. Alliances exist at both ends of the continuum: criminal groups forming alliances with terrorist organisations, and terrorist groups seeking alliances with criminal organisations. The nature of alliances between groups varies, and can include one-off, short-term and long-term relationships. Furthermore, alliances include ties established for a variety of reasons such as seeking expert knowledge (i.e. money-laundering, counterfeiting, or bomb-making) or operational support (i.e. access to smuggling routes). In many respects alliance formations are akin to relationships that develop within legitimate business settings. As Louise Shelley succinctly notes with specific reference to organised crime, 'cooperation with terrorists may have significant benefits for organised criminals by destabilising the political structure, undermining law enforcement and limiting the possibilities for international cooperation.' [6]

The most commonly cited alliances exist in the realm of the international drug trade. For example, Colombian authorities have reported that the Medellin cocaine cartel hired the ELN to plant car bombs in 1993 because they did not have the capabilities to conduct terrorist acts themselves [7]. Furthermore, FARC has entered into alliances with criminal groups outside of Colombia, including Mexican drug-trafficking groups. Although FARC has denied this relationship, US government officials have reported that FARC sends cocaine to Mexico in return for arms shipments [8]. A similar relationship was established with Russian criminal groups who sent arms to Colombia in exchange for cocaine shipments [9].

In addition to relatively straightforward alliances based on the provision of specific services, more sophisticated relationships have emerged between criminal and terrorist groups. This is best exemplified in international smuggling operations that move various commodities from illicit narcotics, weapons and human cargo, between countries and continents. For example the Islamic Movement of Uzbekistan entered into a strategic relationship with the Afghan drug mafia and Central Asian criminal groups to ensure that shipments of heroin could be safely transported between Afghanistan and the Russian Federation and the Caucasus [10]. There are also numerous allegations suggesting that militants linked to Al Qaeda established connections with Bosnian criminal organisations to establish a route for trafficking Afghan heroin into Europe via the Balkans [11]. The Pakistan-based Indian criminal organisation, D-Company (led by Dawood Ibrahim) has established relations to numerous terrorist groups, including Al Qaeda, the LTTE, and Lashkar e-Tayyaba. Furthermore, it is also believed that criminal networks in southern Thailand have smuggled small arms into Sri Lanka and the Indonesian conflict zones of Aceh, Sulawesi and Maluku [12]—with the specific intent of arming terrorist groups.

The most illustrative nexus between a criminal and terrorist group—one in which a mutual relationship has proven integral to the operations of both entities—is the relationship between the Albanian mafia and the Kosovo Liberation Army (KLA) during the Kosovo conflict. After the fall of the Albanian government in 1997, the Albanian mafia secured its authority over heroin-trafficking routes through the Balkans. At approximately the same time, the KLA was established to seek an independent state from Serbia. As noted in a report published in the *Washington Times*, a very specific relationship developed between the political wing of the KLA—the Kosovo National Front (KLF)—and Albanian criminal groups to smuggle heroin. These ties thus 'provided a well-oiled arrangement: the profits from the Pristina cartel, estimated to be in the 'high tens of millions', were funnelled to the KLA, where they were used primarily to buy weapons, often in 'drugs-for-arms' arrangements' [13]. This relationship, however, is significantly more complex than the straightforward alliance discussed here, and in fact, both the Albanian mafia and KLA could be considered hybrid groups based on the nature of their activities throughout the 1990s.

As illustrated in the examples cited above, in most instances the ties that have developed between organised crime and terrorism have been isolated in specific geographic regions. This indicates that it is in the interest of criminal and terrorist groups—invariably within unstable regions—to form alliances to ensure that an environment conducive to both their needs is sustained. Instability is in the interest of terrorists because it diminishes the legitimacy of governments in the eyes of the mass populations—the very people terrorists seek to gain support from; and it is in the interest of criminal groups seeking to maximise criminal operations. This is especially true for groups engaged in wide-scale smuggling of licit or illicit commodities. For this reason, crime–terrorist alliances have been especially common in Latin America, Southeast Asia, the Middle East, and Eurasia.

Operational Motivations

Despite the existence of alliances between organised crime and terrorist groups, groups have increasingly sought to forgo creating alliances if they can. As the 1990s progressed, it became apparent that criminal and terrorist groups were seeking to 'mutate their own structure and organisation to take on a non-traditional, financial, or political role, rather than cooperate with groups who are already effective in those activities' [14]. The primary reason for acquiring in-house capabilities is to ensure organisational security, and to secure organisational operations. In doing so criminal and terrorist groups have sought to avoid the inherent problems present in all alliances, including: differences over priorities and strategies, distrust, the danger of defections, and the threat that alliances could create competitors [15]. Thus most criminal and terrorist groups operational in the 1990s and into the twenty-first century have developed the capacity to engage in both criminal and terrorist activities.

Criminal groups using terrorism as an operational tool, and terrorist groups taking part in criminal activities as an operational tool, constitute the second component of the crime–terror continuum. Although the use of terror tactics can be traced back into the history of organised crime [16], terrorist engagement in organised crime to secure profits for future operations did not emerge as a serious problem until the early 1990s. In both cases, however, the post-Cold War era exacerbated conditions and drove many criminal and terrorist groups to shift their operational focus. As a result, criminal groups have increasingly engaged in political activity in an effort to manipulate operational conditions present in the rising numbers of weak states; whereas terrorist groups have increasingly focused on criminal activities to replace lost financial support from state sponsors.

Organised criminal groups have regularly used terror tactics in order to fulfil specific operational aims. Although these groups have, at times, apparently engaged the political, it is important to clarify that their intention was not to change the status quo, but merely to secure their operational environment. As Dishman notes, criminal organisations use 'selective and calibrated violence to destroy competitors or threaten counternarcotic authorities. As such, a violent attack directed by a TCO [transnational criminal organisation] is intended for a specific 'anti-constituency' rather than a national or international audience, and it is not laced with political rhetoric' [17]. Despite utilising terror tactics, such as bombings and assassinations, the primary motivation of these groups often remains illicit profit-maximisation. For example, terror tactics were utilised by the Italian Mafia in the 1990s in response to a relatively successful government drive to counter the influence of the Italian Mafia in the country [18]. As early as 1990, the Italian government's Anti-Mafia Commission reported that because the Mafia controlled political, institutional and economic powers and had a monopoly over the use of violence, it was evident that the Mafia had moved from a strategy of cohabitation with the legal power to one of confrontation. Further illustrating this point, Alison Jamieson has argued that bombing against tourist attractions by the Italian Mafia in the early 1990s revealed a distinct deviation from the understanding that organised crime sought to remain unnoticed by the majority of the population. Instead:

> The traditional Mafia groups have learned to use the magnifying glass of symbolic violence to reach a wider audience: in 1993 the Sicilian Mafia carried out a series of car bomb attacks in the Italian mainland near historic sites such as the Uffizi Galleries in Florence and the church of St. John Lateran in Rome; plans were laid to blow up the Leaning Tower of Pisa. The aim was not to eliminate an enemy, but to intimidate public opinion and Parliament into abrogating recently passed antimafia legislation [19].

Terror tactics were thus used by the Mafia to 'subvert anti-Mafia actions and legislative moves, these bombings were meant to openly challenge the political elite and send a message to the 'powers-that-be' [20]. Comparable with any traditional terrorist group, the Mafia engaged in terrorism as a tactical tool to force the government into negotiation and compromise.

More recently, criminal groups in Brazil have also realised the potential effectiveness of using terror tactics to force political demands on the government, especially when their illicit operations are threatened by the state. Following the inauguration of a new Brazilian administration in April 2002, and the rising power of indigenous drug traffickers, authorities were immediately tasked with cracking down on criminal groups—especially those operating from Rio de Janeiro. Imposing tougher restrictions on group leaders in the prison system—including Comando Vermelho, Amigos dos Amigos, and Terceiro Comando—the government provoked these groups into 'launching a campaign of political violence' [21]. During this time members of the aforementioned groups bombed buses, fired shots at government buildings, and targeted police officers. This wave of violence dissipated only after the state appeared to grant the criminal group leaders immunity in order to continue conducting their criminal operations with limited obstacles.

Comparable to criminal groups engaging in terrorism; many terrorist groups have become well versed in the conduct of criminal operations. In response to the virtual elimination of state support after the end of the Cold War, criminality was the most pragmatic avenue to secure finances for future terrorist operations. Equally important to note is that terrorists who engage in criminal activities 'ostensibly retain paramount political objectives, and as such, ill-gotten monies serve only as a means to effectively reach their political ends' [22]. The most common criminal activity terrorist groups have been involved in is the illicit drug trade. Since the 1970s groups such as FARC, Basque Homeland and Freedom movement (ETA), the Kurdistan Workers Party (PKK), and Sendero Luminoso have all been linked to the drugs trade [23]. Taking advantage of its geographic co-location with the Balkan Route, which is used to smuggle heroin from Asia to Europe, the PKK has garnered the majority of its profits from illicit drug operations. Its position within the drug trade also 'links members of the PKK to high-ranking members of the Turkish government, and major organised crime groups in Istanbul' [24]. Since the early 1990s additional groups, including Hizbullah, have also realised the financial gains of participating in the illicit drugs trade. It is alleged that Hizbullah protects heroin and cocaine laboratories in the Bekaa Valley [25].

Although terrorist groups have commonly been associated with trafficking in illicit narcotics, they have also engaged in a wide variety of other crimes such as fraud, counterfeiting and human smuggling. According to Rohan Gunaratna, Al Qaeda's financial network in Europe, dominated by Algerians, is largely reliant on credit-card fraud [26]. Gunaratna quotes that nearly US$1 million a month has been raised from these alternative criminal avenues. Furthermore, European security agencies have admitted that prosecuting terrorists engaged in credit-card fraud has been a daunting task because 'al-Qaeda's cadres are continually learning new techniques to evade detection' [27]—illustrating the extent to which Al Qaeda has manipulated processes of globalisation and its networked organisation. Terrorist groups have similarly used the trade in counterfeit products as a source of profit. According to Ronald Noble, Secretary General of Interpol, paramilitary groups in Northern Ireland, and Albanian extremist groups are heavily engaged in moving counterfeit products, from cigarettes to computer software [28].

As the 1990s progressed and both criminal and terrorist groups incorporated economic and political capabilities into their remit, many groups lost sight of their original motivations and aims. Thus at the start of the twenty-first century a growing number of groups have simultaneously displayed characteristics of organised crime and terrorism. Furthermore, in assessing the development of these hybrid organisations, it is evident that the motivations, organisation, and operations of criminal and terrorist groups have also converged—thus making it analytically difficult to make a distinction between the two phenomena.

Convergence

The final point occupying the crime–terror continuum is the 'convergence thesis', which refers explicitly to the idea that criminal and terrorist organisations could converge into a single entity that initially displays characteristics of both groups simultaneously; but has the potential to transform itself into an entity situated at the opposite end of the continuum from which it began. Transformation thus occurs to such a degree 'that the ultimate aims and motivations of the organisation have actually changed. In these cases, the groups no longer retain the defining points that had hitherto made them a political or criminal group' [29].

In its most basic form, the convergence thesis includes two independent, yet related, components. First, it incorporates criminal groups that display political motivations; and second, it refers to terrorist groups who are equally interested in criminal profits, but ultimately begin to use their political rhetoric as a façade solely for perpetrating criminal activities. The first category can be further subdivided into two parts. First, it includes groups who have used terror tactics to gain political leverage beyond the disruption of judicial processes or attempts to block anti-crime legislation (which is a common tactic utilised by organised crime in order to secure their operations). Instead they are interested in attaining political control via direct involvement in the political processes and institutions of a state. Second, it includes criminal organisations that initially use terrorism to establish a monopoly over lucrative economic sectors of a state. In controlling economic sectors—including strategic natural resources—and financial institutions, these entities proceed to ultimately gain political control over the state itself. This is based on the premise that in a contemporary world dominated by the dynamics of the free market economy, economic strength is the obvious prerequisite for political power; and political power subsequently sustains both the life of the organisation and its activities—be they criminal and/or political. As Xavier Raufer notes, 'Grabbing control of financial institutions can both bring home the cash and advance political ambitions. Many groups, of course, will retain narrow portfolios of objectives, targets, and methods; others are becoming conglomerates of causes' [30].

Russian and Albanian criminal organisations provide such examples of 'conglomerates of causes' as both groups seek to produce an environment once only associated with terrorism: to 'break or ruin the sense of social and political calm in a country' [31]. In several regions of the Russian Federation—including the Maritime Province of the Russian Far East—and in Albania, organised criminals have found that 'in order to mobilise sufficient power to resist the state, they must move their organisations beyond pure criminalism with its limited appeal to most citizens and add elements of political protest' [32]. Commenting specifically on the rise of the Albanian Mafia, Ralf Mutschke of Interpol has called it a 'hybrid' group because its activities indicate that its 'political and criminal activities are deeply intertwined' [33]. Mutschke further notes that the Albanian mafia is intrinsically linked to 'Panalbanian ideals, politics, military activities and terrorism,' explaining why Albanian criminal organisations used their criminal profits to purchase arms and military equipment for the Kosovo Liberation Army from 1993 [34]. Contributing to the convergence between crime and politics in Albania is the fact that Albanian criminal and terrorist groups have an interchangeable membership and recruitment base—essentially posing as terrorists by day and criminals by night.

The second component of the convergence thesis addresses terrorist groups that become so engaged with their involvement in criminal activities (as discussed in the previous section) that they merely maintain their political rhetoric as a façade for perpetrating criminal activities on a wider scale. There is growing evidence indicating that despite increasingly focusing on criminal activities, terrorist groups 'maintain a public façade, supported by rhetoric and statements, but underneath, they have transformed into a different type of group with a different end game' [35]. No longer driven by a political agenda, but by the proceeds of crime, these formerly traditional terrorist groups continue to engage in the use of terror tactics for two primary reasons. First, to keep the government and law enforcement authorities focused on political issues and problems, as opposed to initiating criminal investigations. Second, terror tactics continue to be used as a tool for these groups to assert themselves amongst rival criminal groups. Added to this, by continuing to portray their political component to the public domain, these terrorist groups are able to manipulate the terrorist support network that had previously been put in place. For example, they continue to focus on political grievances (combined with financial rewards) to attract recruits—giving justification to what would normally be regarded as purely criminal acts. Thus by simultaneously focusing on criminal and political goals, these groups are able to use two sets of networks which allow them to 'shift focus from one application of terrorism to another, or to pursue multiple applications simultaneously' [36].

Groups that are illustrative of a terrorist entity evolving into a group primarily engaged in criminal activities include Abu Sayyaf, the Islamic Movement of Uzbekistan [37], and the Revolutionary Armed Forces of Colombia (FARC). For example, since 2000, Abu Sayyaf has been primarily engaged in criminal activities such as kidnapping operations, and most recently, operating marijuana plantations in the Philippines. It has been estimated that in 2000 alone, kidnapping deals garnered Abu Sayyaf $20 million [38]. In light of Abu Sayyaf's operations, which are focused on criminal activities, there is little indication that the group remains driven by its original political aim, which was to establish an independent Islamic republic in territory currently comprising Mindanao, surrounding islands, and the Sulu Archipelago.

By the mid-1990s, following the death of Jacobo Arenas—the ideological leader of FARC—FARC, as subsequently happened with Abu Sayyaf—deepened its involvement in criminal activities. More specifically, several FARC units shifted their involvement in the regional drugs trade from that of protector of crops and laboratories, to 'middlemen' between farmers and illicit drug cartels. This shift directly resulted in the group acquiring more profits from the drugs trade, and subsequently more power within Colombia. Thus, by 2000, it was believed that FARC controlled 40 percent of Colombian territory, and received revenues of $500 million annually from illicit narcotics [39]. Supplementing its bankroll from drugs, FARC also engages in other criminal activities, including kidnapping and extortion. Referring to both FARC and the ELN, Paul Wilkinson concludes that because of the level of their involvement in organised crime,

> ...it is clear that this has made them, both in reality and popular perception, little more than a branch of organised crime, decadent guerrillas rather than genuine revolutionaries, irredeemably corrupted by their intimate involvement with narco-traffickers and their cynical pursuits of huge profits from kidnapping and from their 'protection' of coca and opium production, processing and shipping facilities [40].

Thus, in the Colombian context groups such as FARC, once 'impassioned and ideological', have 'lost their old revolutionary "purity"' and turned their terrorism in a new direction—development as criminal cartels' [41].

Although the entire crime–terror continuum poses a threat to international security, arguably the single greatest threat emanating from the convergence of transnational organised crime and terrorism is that which is exhibited at the fulcrum point.

'Black Hole' Thesis

This section of the crime–terror continuum specifically refers to the situations in which weak or failed states foster the convergence between transnational organised crime and terrorism, and ultimately create a safe haven for the continued operations of convergent groups. The 'black hole' syndrome encompasses two situations: first, where the primary motivations of groups engaged in a civil war evolves from a focus on political aims to a focus on criminal aims; second, it refers to the emergence of a 'black hole' state—a state successfully taken over by a hybrid group as outlined in the previous section. What these two scenarios have in common, and the reason why they perfectly illustrate the most extreme point along the continuum, is that they reveal the ultimate danger of the convergence between these two threats: the creation or promotion of a condition of civil (or regional) war to secure economic and political power. States that fall within this category, as a result of current or past experiences, include Afghanistan, Angola, Myanmar, North Korea, Sierra Leone, and Tajikistan. Furthermore, areas in Pakistan (the Northwest Frontier Province), Indonesia and Thailand—where government control is extremely weak—are also in danger of succumbing to the 'black hole' syndrome.

To begin with, evidence suggests that the dynamics of civil wars, just like the dynamics of traditional organised crime and terrorism, have changed. They have evolved from wars fought for ideological or religious motivations to wars hijacked by criminal interests and secured by terror tactics. As David Keen comments, 'Increasingly, civil wars that appear to have begun with political aims have mutated into conflicts in which short-term economic benefits are paramount. While ideology and identity remain important in understanding conflict, they may not tell the whole story' [42]. The end of the Cold War, coupled with the decline of superpower support (proxy wars) indirectly caused a decline in the strength of revolutionary political ideologies in groups such as the Khmer Rouge and UNITA. All of these groups thus 'gravitated from a strong ideological agenda to one dominated by economic aims' [43]. Comparable to terrorist groups who lost sight of their political ideology as a result of having to depend on criminal activity for their survival, these groups also appear to have betrayed their ideological ideals in the interest of holding on to power at whatever cost [44]. Two examples that illustrate this aspect of the 'black hole' syndrome are Afghanistan and North Korea.

Afghanistan could be considered a 'black hole state' since the 1989 withdrawal of Soviet troops, for several reasons. First, although factions fighting in the Afghan civil war (notably the Northern Alliance) officially articulated ideological goals, their involvement in criminal activities, and frequent changes in group allegiances and alliances, indicate that group survival was their paramount concern. In the absence of any central authority capable of establishing widespread stability and order, warlords were able to divide the country into local fiefdoms to secure territorial control in order to sustain activities such as the production and trafficking of opiates and the smuggling of weapons and a variety of licit commodities (specificlally pharmaceuticals) across the border with Pakistan. Second, as a result of incessant instability sustained by rival warlord factions, Afghanistan became an important safe haven, congregation, and training point for a number of terrorist groups, and transnational criminal organisations. The cauldron of terrorist and criminal interests converging and cooperating in Afghanistan therefore illustrates the dangers inherent in the 'black hole' syndrome. Not only was Afghanistan destroyed by incessant domestic instability, its very essence as a 'black hole state' meant that it directly threatened the security of the wider region. Furthermore, Afghanistan proved to be a direct security threat to the United States, Southeast Asia, and the rest of the world, primarily because it fostered the rise and global reach of Al Qaeda.

While it exhibits some characteristics of a weak state, the Democratic People's Republic of Korea (DPRK) is most illustrative of a criminal state. Officials of the DPRK have allegedly been directly engaging in criminal activities since the 1970s. For example, in 1976 the Norwegian government expelled all the staff of the North Korean embassy, suggesting they were involved in the smuggling of narcotics and unlicensed goods [45]. The DPRK has intensified its criminal activities over the last decade—arguably because the leadership in North Korea has been replaced 'by a younger group, less committed to the dogma of socialism and seemingly more eager to experience the good life' [46]. An indication of this development is the government's establishment of 'Bureau 39', an official government department tasked with generating hard currency by any means, including drug trafficking, counterfeiting, money laundering and piracy [47].

The second scenario, on the other hand, refers to the situation where politically motivated criminal organisations or commercial terrorist groups perpetuate their existence and activities by promoting domestic and/or regional instability. Although political goals may have played a role in the initial emergence of instability, after a time it became evident that economic motivations took precedence. Terror tactics are utilised to sustain criminal activities, and it may be concluded that many ongoing civil wars are merely draped in ideological rhetoric to gain legitimacy and to ensure a steady supply of new recruits. There is growing evidence that these non-state actors are producing alternative economic and political structures in the absence of a strong state. In fact, criminal and terrorist groups in weak states have already constituted de facto governments who imitate the characteristics of formal state activities, despite perpetuating their involvement in activities considered illegal by formal state structures.

It may be suggested that this aspect of the 'black hole' syndrome is the natural progression of political criminal organisations or commercial terrorist groups gaining economic and political control over a parcel of territory or an entire state. In an effort to secure an environment conducive to their criminality, these entities may seek to wreak havoc and instability in the areas of their main operations. A successful criminal organisation with political interests or a commercial terrorist group, however, will effectively challenge the legitimacy of a state, and ultimately replace the state in many (if not all) of its functions. The basic characteristics of this predicament are evident in numerous examples, including ongoing instability in the Balkans [48], Caucasus [49], southern Thailand [50] and Sierra Leone.

Taking Sierra Leone as an illustrative example, the descent into state terrorism was not accompanied by an exclusive 'logic of political violence,' but it was intertwined with the 'logics of banditry, hedonism and brutality' and was intrinsically linked to the illicit trade in diamonds [51]. Crime was an integral component of the Revolutionary United Forces (RUF) that took precedence over any political aim. Any belief in the existence of a political component to the violence that penetrated Sierra Leone throughout the 1990s is amply eradicated once the following points are considered:

> The 'rebellion' has had no known spokesmen or political program; it does not seem to have the goal of gaining political power. It has no reason to appeal politically to the population in the areas in which it is active; its 'strategy' is marauding terror of the subject population and denying control to the government so that the government cannot suppress its lawlessness. The fact that government forces have been known to act as atrociously as the rebels does not improve matters [52].

In both contexts of the 'black hole' syndrome, it may be concluded that war has provided 'legitimation for various criminal forms of private aggrandisement while at the same time these are necessary sources of revenue in order to sustain the war. The warring parties need more or less permanent conflict both to reproduce their positions of power and for access to resources' [53]. Thus, regardless of whether these civil wars began with an ideological agenda and transformed into a criminal struggle, or emerged because of the successful operations of politically motivated criminal organisations or commercial terrorist groups, they share several common characteristics.

To begin with, conflict that besets the 'black hole' syndrome has no clear military objective and lacks political purpose. Instead, military units constitute 'little more than marauding bands acting quite independently of any order and showing no discipline whatsoever in the actions they were committing' [54]. Furthermore, where political motivations do follow the criminal activities of belligerents in violent conflicts, it is evident that the perpetuation of conflict, as opposed to victory, becomes a priority in order to create ideal conditions for transnational criminal activities to flourish [55]. Groups that thrive within 'black hole' environments are all equally motivated by the 'accumulation of wealth, control of territory and people, freedom of movement and action, and legitimacy. Together, these elements represent usable power—power to allocate values and resources in society' [56].

Future Dynamics

As outlined in this article, the relationship between transnational organised crime and terrorism encompasses several distinct facets—each of which may be placed along a continuum that traces the evolution of groups depending on the predominant operational environment. During the Cold War, concerns about a crime–terror nexus were relatively insignificant, as nexus was almost entirely precluded to the relationship between insurgent groups in Latin America and regional drug cartels. However, the international environment that emerged at the end of the Cold War, and subsequently as a result of the fall of the Soviet Union, created conditions that supported the development of criminal and terrorist organisations into increasingly sophisticated and international entities. The result being the emergence of transnational organised crime, and international networked terrorist groups as exemplified by Al Qaeda. Each of these groups created a state of heightened insecurity within the world as governments accustomed to military threats posed by state-actors were forced to react to the economic and societal destruction increasingly perpetrated by non-state actors.

Growing reliance on cross-border criminal activities—facilitated by open borders, weak states, immigration flows, financial technology, and a highly intricate and accessible global transportation infrastructure—and an associated interest in establishing political control in order to consolidate and secure future operations, have all contributed to the rise of the crime–terror nexus. As a result, non-state actors, in the guise of transnational organised crime and terrorism, are directly challenging the security of the state—arguably for the first time in history. The realisation that economic and political power enhance one another, suggests that more and more groups will become hybrid organisations by nature [57]. This is enhanced by the fact that criminal and terrorist groups appear to be learning from one another, and adapting to each other's successes and failures. Furthermore, given the unremitting existence of territory that is not adequately under state control—such as the Northwest Frontier Province of Pakistan, areas within Tajikistan, and the Triborder Region—environments that provoke and promote strengthened ties between organised crime and terrorism endure.

Considering the various components of the crime–terror continuum, one consistent and relatively easily identifiable factor is criminality. Regardless of where a group sits along the continuum (apart for each extreme end), every point necessitates some degree of involvement with criminal activities. As a result, the continuum inherently implies that focusing on criminal activity, as opposed to political aims and motivations, in formulating policy responses to—especially to terrorism—has been under-utilised. Thus, for example, although it is important to understand the political motivations of terrorist groups, on a practical level counter-terrorist policy and initiatives would likely meet with greater initial success in locating group weaknesses and vulnerabilities if they focused on criminal aspects. Furthermore, limiting access to lucrative profits from illicit activities simultaneously eliminates the operational capacity, and subsequent political influence, of both criminal and terrorist groups. Thus, it is essential that greater attention and resources are given to cutting off funds acquired through crime (in particular credit-card and insurance fraud, money laundering, smuggling), or on criminal services that terrorist groups depend on (such as document and identity fraud).

Understanding the crime–terror continuum expands the security tools that a state can employ in order to respond to the ever-evolving threats of transnational organised crime and terrorism. Acknowledging, and continuously tracing, the crime–terror continuum as it pertains to the evolving dynamics of transnational organised crime and terrorism will therefore have an explicit impact on the formation of counter-terrorist and anti-crime policies. The crime–terror continuum thus seeks to highlight the importance of overlapping counter-terrorist and anti-crime policies as a way of formulating an effective state response to both evolving, and periodically converging, threats.

Notes

[1] An informal transnational financial exchange system relying on informal contacts.
[2] A few surveys of terrorist financing have been published, including Ehrenfeld, *Funding Evil: how terrorism is financed and how to stop it* and Napoleoni, L., *Modern Jihad: Tracing the Dollars Behind the Terror Networks*.
[3] For example, both transnational organised crime and terrorism are often cell- and network-based, require safe havens and the support of diaspora communities, conduct intelligence and counter-intelligence operations, depend on similar deployment techniques (such as the use of counterfeit documentation), and conduct cross-border operations.
[4] This section is, in part, based on a similar section—albeit with different examples—published in Makarenko, 'The Ties That Bind: Uncovering the Relationship Between Organised Crime and Terrorism'.
[5] The view that a nexus exists between organised crime and terrorism has received some negative attention, primarily because of the persistent perception that organised crime and terrorist groups have no interest in cooperating because they are intrinsically different. For example, Phil Williams has argued that although terrorists use crime to finance themselves, and may work with organised crime, there is 'no nexus'. Williams, 'The Changed Landscape: from Slime Molds to Terrorism'.
[6] Shelley, 'Identifying, Counting and Categorizing Transnational Organised Crime'.
[7] Clawson & Lee, *The Andean Cocaine Industry* p. 53.
[8] 'Colombian Rebel Connections to Mexican Drug Cartel,' Statement by Richard Boucher, Spokesman for the US Department of State, (29 November 2000), http://www.fas.org/irp/news/2000/11/irp-001129-col.htm (Downloaded 3 November 2002); Gutierrez Esparza, 'La Mafia Rusa en Mexico'; and *Organized Crime and Terrorist Activity in Mexico, 1999–2002*, a report prepared under an Interagency Agreement by the Federal Research Division, Library of Congress.
[9] *The Washington Times* 20 August 2001; 'Peru: a spy story replete with arms, drugs-dealers and bears,' *CNN* 8 September 2000; and, 'Farclandia,' a discussion of narco-states cited in the transnational crime section of the Centre for the Study of International Security website (Washington, DC): http://www.csis.org
[10] This conclusion is based on confidential discussions conducted with analysts in European Customs & Excise departments, and with various European intelligence agents.
[11] *The New York Times*, 10 December 2001.
[12] Davis, 'The Complexities of Unrest in Southern Thailand'.
[13] *The Washington Times*, 4 June 1999.
[14] Dishman, 'Terrorism, Crime and Transformation'.

[15] Williams, 'Criminal Cooperation: trends and patterns'.

[16] For example, the rise of the Sicilian Mafia in the early twentieth century was completely intertwined with a political agenda that included attaining territorial control over much of the region of Sicily, and subsequently Neopolitana by the Camorra.

[17] Dishman, 'Terrorism, Crime and Transformation', 45.

[18] For an excellent account of Italy's fight against organised crime, see Jamieson, *The Antimafia*.

[19] Jamieson, 'Transnational Organised Crime: A European Perspective'.

[20] Gorka, 'The New Threat of Organised Crime and Terrorism'.

[21] Day, 'Crime Groups Turn to Terrorism in Rio de Janeiro'.

[22] Dishman, 'Terrorism, Crime and Transformation', 47.

[23] For a good overview of the pre-1991 involvement of terrorist groups in the drug trade see Steinitz, 'Insurgents, Terrorists and the Drug Trade'.

[24] Roule, 'The Terrorist Financial Network of the PKK'.

[25] *The Jerusalem Post*, 17 June 1997; and US State Department, *International Narcotics Control Strategy Report*, 1996.

[26] Gunaratna, *Inside al-Qaeda: Global Networks of Terror*. This is also discussed by Radu, 'Terrorism After the Cold War: Trends and Challenges'.

[27] Gunaratna (2002), 65.

[28] *The New York Times*, 16 July 2003.

[29] Dishman (2001), 48.

[30] Raufer, 'New World Disorder, New Terrorisms: New Threats for Europe and the Western World', 35. Raufer first introduced his thoughts about grey area threats in: 'Grey Areas: a New Security Threat'.

[31] Harmon, *Terrorism Today*, 54.

[32] Metz, *The Future of Insurgency*.

[33] Mutschke, Ralf, Assistant Director, Criminal Intelligence Directorate, International Criminal Police Organisation, 'The Threat Posed by Organised Crime, International Drug Trafficking and Terrorism'.

[34] Ibid.

[35] Dishman (1999), 48.

[36] Lesser et al. (eds) *Countering the New Terrorism*, 98.

[37] For a detailed account of the IMU as a terrorist group that exemplifies the convergence between organised crime and terrorism, see: Makarenko, 'Drugs in Central Asia: Security Implications and Political Manipulations,' and 'Crime, Terror and the Central Asian Drugs Trade'.

[38] Joyce, 'Terrorist Financing in Southeast Asia'.

[39] McDermott, 'Financing Insurgents in Colombia'.

[40] Wilkinson, *Terrorism Versus Democracy: The Liberal State Response*, 15.

[41] Harmon (2000), xvii.

[42] Keen, *The Economic Functions of Violence in Civil Wars*, 11.

[43] Keen (1998), 34.

[44] It is accepted that the betrayal of revolutionary ideals is not a new phenomenon in and of itself. The leaders of many revolutionary movements throughout history (French, Russian) had betrayed their ideals in order to hold on to the power they had acquired. What is being argued here, however, is that an apparently new dynamic has been added to the equation—one that sees ideological groups not only engage in state terrorism to hold on to power, but use the state monopoly over the legitimate use of violence in order to privately profit from illicit activities, such as drug trafficking and arms smuggling.

[45] Galeotti, 'Criminalisation of the DPRK', 10.

[46] Ibid.

[47] *The Washington Post*, reprinted in *Guardian Weekly*, 4 April 1999.

[48] Kaldor, *New and Old Wars* provides a detailed accounts of the criminal–political nexus in Sarajevo.
[49] On the political nature of organised crime in Chechnya, or conversely the criminal nature of Chechen politics, see: Lieven, *Chechnya: Tombstone of Russian Power* and Kulikov, 'Trouble in North Caucasus'.
[50] For an excellent analysis of the convergence of terrorism and organised crime in southern Thailand, see Davis, 'The Complexities of Unrest in Southern Thailand', 16–19.
[51] Bangura, 'Understanding the Political and Cultural Dynamics of the Sierra Leone War', 130–3.
[52] Snow, *Uncivil Wars*, 78.
[53] Kaldor (1999), 110.
[54] Snow (1999), 109–11.
[55] Berdal & Serrano (eds), *Transnational Organized Crime and International Security*, 199.
[56] Manwaring (ed), *Grey Area Phenomena*, 7–8.
[57] For an overview of over 70 terrorist groups plotted on the crime–terror continuum, see: Makarenko, 'A Model of Terrorist–Criminal Relations'.

References

Bangura, Y. (1997) 'Understanding the political and cultural dynamics of the sierra leone war', *Africa Development*, vol. 22, no. 3/4.
Berdal, M. & Serrano, M. (eds) (2002) *Transnational Organized Crime and International Security*, Lynne Rienner.
Boucher, R. (2000) 'Colombian rebel connections to Mexican drug cartel,' Statement for the US Department of State http://www.fas.org/irp/news/2000/11/irp-001129-col.htm (downloaded 3 November 2002).
Centre for the Study of International Security website (Washington, DC): http://www.csis.org., transnational crime section.
Clawson, P. & Rensselaer, L. (1996) *The Andean Cocaine Industry*, St Martin's Press.
Davis, A. (2002) 'The complexities of unrest in Southern Thailand', *Jane's Intelligence Review*, vol. 14, no. 9 (September 2002).
Day, M. (2003) 'Crime groups turn to terrorism in Rio de Janeiro', *Jane's Intelligence Review*, vol. 15, no. 7 (July 2003).
Dishman, C. (2001) 'Terrorism crime and transformation', *Studies in Conflict and Terrorism*, p. 24.
Ehrenfeld, R. (2003) *Funding Evil: how terrorism is financed and how to stop it* (Bonus Books).
Federal Research Division, Library of Congress (2003) *Organized Crime and Terrorist Activity in Mexico, 1999–2002* (February).
Galeotti, M. (2001) 'Criminalisation of the DPRK', *Jane's Intelligence Review*, vol. 13, no. 3 (March).
Gorka, S. (2000) 'The new threat of organised crime and terrorism', *Jane's Terrorism and Security Monitor*.
Gunaratna, R. (2002) *Inside al-Qaeda: Global Networks of Terror* (Hurst & Company).
Gutierrez Esparza, L. (2001) 'La Mafia Rusa en Mexico', *Memorando*, 29 July, http://latamcent.org.mx
Harmon, C. (2000) *Terrorism Today*, Frank Cass.
Jamieson, A. (2000) 'Transnational organised crime: A European perspective', *Studies in Conflict and Terrorism*, vol. 24, p. 379 (2001).
Jamieson, A. (2000) *The Antimafia*, Macmillan.
Joyce, B. (2002) 'Terrorist financing in Southeast Asia', *Jane's Intelligence Review*, vol. 14, no. 11 (November).
Kaldor, M. (1999) *New and Old Wars*, Stanford University Press.
Keen, D. (1998) *The Economic Functions of Violence in Civil Wars*, Adelphi Paper No. 320.

Kulikov, A. (1999) 'Trouble in North Caucasus', *Military Review* (July–August).

Lesser, H. et al. (eds) (1999) *Countering the New Terrorism* (RAND).

Lieven, A. (1998) *Chechnya: Tombstone of Russian Power*, Yale University Press.

Makarenko, T. (2003) 'A model of Terrorist–Criminal relations', *Jane's Intelligence Review*, vol. 15, no. 8 (August).

Makarenko, T. (2002) 'Crime, terror and the Central Asian drugs trade', *Harvard Asia Quarterly*, (Summer).

Makarenko, T. (2001) 'Drugs in Central Asia: security implications and political manipulations', *Cahiers d'études sur la Méditérranée Orientale et le Monde Turco-Iranien*, pp. 32, (July–December).

Makarenko, T. (2004) 'The ties that bind: uncovering the relationship between organised crime and terrorism', in *Global Organized Crime*, eds de Bunt, Siegel & Zaitch, Kluwer.

Manwaring, M. (ed.) (1993) *Grey Area Phenomena* Westview, pp. 7–8.

McDermott, J. (2003) 'Financing insurgents in Colombia', *Jane's Intelligence Review*, vol. 15, no. 2 (February).

Metz, S. (1993) *The Future of Insurgency*, US Army War College, 10 December.

Mutschke, R., (2000) 'The threat posed by organised crime, international drug trafficking and terrorism', written testimony to the *General Secretariat Hearing of the Committee on the Judiciary Subcommittee on Crime* (13 December).

Napoleoni, L. (2003) *Modern Jihad: Tracing the Dollars Behind the Terror Networks*, Pluto Press.

Radu, M. (2002) 'Terrorism after the cold war: trends and challenges', *Orbis* (Spring).

Raufer, X. (1992) 'Grey areas: a new security threat', *Political Warfare* (Spring).

Raufer, X. (1999) 'New World Disorder, New Terrorisms: New Threats for Europe and the Western World', *Terrorism and Political Violence*, vol. 11, no. 4 p. 35 (Winter).

Roule, T. (2002) 'The terrorist financial network of the PKK', *Jane's Intelligence Review*, vol. 14, no. 6 (June).

Shelley, L. (1999) 'Identifying, counting and categorizing transnational organised crime', *Transnational Organised Crime*, vol. 5, no. 1 (Spring).

Snow, D. (1996) *Uncivil Wars*, Lynne Reinner.

Steinitz, M. (1985) 'Insurgents, terrorists and the drug trade', *The Washington Quarterly*.

US State Department (1996) *International Narcotics Control Strategy Report*.

Wilkinson, P. (2000) *Terrorism Versus Democracy: The Liberal State Response*, Frank Cass.

Williams, P. (2000) 'Criminal cooperation: trends and patterns', *Jane's Conference on Transnational Organised Crime*, 20–21 September.

Williams, P. (2002) 'The changed landscape: from slime molds to terrorism', Powerpoint presentation, Kent Center, 23–24 May, http://www.markletaskforce.org (downloaded 17 August 2003).

The Global Dimension of Cybercrime
Peter Grabosky

It has become trite to suggest that cyberspace knows no boundaries. Indeed, cybercrime can be committed from the other side of the world as easily as from next door. The following pages review some of the basic forms of cybercrime, draw specific attention to the issues that arise when offences occur across borders and in relation to organised criminal groupings, and provide illustrations based on some of the more celebrated cases of the past few years.

In essence, cybercrime involves three types of case:

1. Conventional crimes committed with computers, such as digital child pornography, piracy, or intellectual property theft, and forgery.
2. Attacks on computer networks; and
3. Conventional criminal cases such as drug trafficking, in which evidence exists in digital form.

Cross-border offending may entail any of these types, but is most common in the first two.

Professor Peter Grabosky is a Professor in the Research School of Social Sciences, Australian National University.

Conventional Crimes Committed with Computers

Child Pornography

The use of computer networks to produce and distribute child pornography has become the subject of increasing attention. Today, these materials can be copied and transported across national borders at the speed of light[1]. In 2002, an investigation initiated by the German police resulted in the simultaneous execution of 37 search warrants in ten countries on members of a private Internet group exchanging and downloading child pornography over the internet [2].

Music, Video, and Software Piracy

Digital technology permits perfect reproduction and easy dissemination of print, graphics, sound, video, and multimedia combinations. The temptation to reproduce copyrighted material for personal use, for sale at a lower price, or indeed, for free distribution, has proven irresistible to many. US copyright industries estimate that they lose an estimated $20–22 billion annually due to piracy worldwide [3]. Pirated software may be bought and sold online all over the world [4]. The 'Drink or Die' Network, an international association of software pirates, was alleged to have pirated and distributed more than $50 million worth of movies, software and music in the three years prior to their disruption by Operation Buccaneer, an investigation resulting in simultaneous raids in six countries, in December 2001 [5].

Forgery

Identity theft has become an issue of great concern to countries around the world [6]. It too has been greatly facilitated by digital technology, which permits perfect reproduction of documents such as birth certificates or other papers. These in turn may be used to construct a false identity for use in a variety of criminal activities. Digital technology also facilitates the counterfeiting of currency and other negotiable instruments, as well as designer labels and logos.

Stalking

Computers can also be used for harassing, threatening or intrusive communications, from the traditional obscene telephone call to its contemporary manifestation in 'cyber-stalking', in which persistent messages are sent to an unwilling recipient [7]. The stalking can entail direct communication to the victim, or indirect communication through third parties. One man in Delhi is reported to have logged on to an internet chatroom using the identity of a woman. The offender allegedly used suggestive language, and disclosed the telephone number of the woman, who subsequently received harassing telephone calls, one from as far away as Kuwait. The offender was located through the IP address used in contacting the chatroom, and was subsequently arrested [8].

Attacks on Computer Networks

Attacks on computer networks arise from a variety of motives, and take a variety of forms.

Theft

Offenders who are motivated by monetary gain may obtain access to the computer networks of financial institutions in order to divert funds. In 1994, a Russian hacker, Vladimir Levin, operating from St Petersburg, accessed the computers of Citibank's central wire transfer department, and transferred funds from large corporate accounts to other accounts which had been opened by his accomplices in the United States, the Netherlands, Finland, Germany and Israel. Officials from one of the corporate victims, located in Argentina, notified the bank, and the suspect accounts, located in San Francisco, were frozen. The accomplice was arrested. Another accomplice was caught attempting to withdraw funds from an account in Rotterdam. Although Russian law precluded Levin's extradition, he was arrested during a visit to Britain, extradited from there to the United States, and subsequently convicted and imprisoned [9].

Another example of a transnational attack for profit was the work of Vasily Gorshkov and Alexey Ivanov. By exploiting a vulnerability in Windows NT, these residents of Chelyabinsk, Russia, launched a number of intrusions against Internet Service providers, online banks and e-commerce sites in the United States. The offenders succeeded in stealing over 56,000 credit card numbers and other personal financial information from the sites' customers. They then sought to extort money from the victims by threatening to publish customers' data and damage the companies' computers. They manipulated E-Bay auctions by using anonymous email accounts to be both seller and winning bidder in the one auction. The on-line payments system PayPal was also defrauded by using cash generated from stolen credit cards to pay for various products [10].

Espionage

Offenders may also attack computer systems in furtherance of espionage. The famous case of the Cuckoo's Egg involved German students, under contract to the KGB, hacking into US defence computers [11].

Some attacks appear to reflect curiosity or the desire to master complex technology. Toward the end of 1995, Julio Cesar Ardita, who lived at home in Buenos Aires with his parents and three younger brothers, used his PC and the facilities of Telecom Argentina to obtain unauthorised access to accounts in the Harvard University computer system. Ardita achieved this by installing a 'sniffer' program that captured the user ID and passwords of legitimate Harvard users. He then set about using these accounts to access other systems, including those of NASA, the US Department of Defense, and the Los Alamos National Laboratory, among others. While he did not appear to have gained access to highly classified material, Ardita was able to view and copy sensitive data on radar technology and aircraft design [12].

Political Statements, Vandalism, and Information Warfare

Attacks on computer systems may have political motives, whether expressive or instrumental. They range in severity from electronic graffiti to vandalism, terrorism, and electronic warfare. Individuals and protest groups have hacked the official web pages of many governmental and commercial organisations [13], creating a new art of 'electronic graffiti' [14]. Attempts have been made to disrupt the computer systems of the Sri Lankan Government [15] and of the North Atlantic Treaty Organisation during the 1999 bombing of Belgrade [16]. In March 2001, hackers based in South Korea caused the crash of a website at the Japanese Ministry of Education in protest against a newly approved history textbook [17].

In western industrial societies generally, and increasingly around the world, much national infrastructure is connected to the internet, and is potentially accessible to skilled hackers. What this means is that some systems that support essential services in advanced industrial societies are vulnerable to attack. Although such attacks have yet to occur on a sustained and widespread basis, we have seen examples of significant damage occasioned by isolated attacks. While none of them constitutes what might be termed 'cyberterrorism', some critical infrastructure systems remain vulnerable to concerted attack [18]. After all, defence planners around the world are investing substantially in information warfare, the means of disrupting the information technology infrastructure of defence systems [19].

Revenge

Persons who see themselves as aggrieved may seek to attack systems as an act of revenge. In 2001 a disgruntled former contractor was convicted of hacking into the computerised waste-management system of Maroochy Shire, Queensland, Australia, causing millions of litres of raw sewage to spill out into local rivers and parks [20].

Attention-seeking

Others will attack systems in search of celebrity (or notoriety). Such was the case of 'Mafiaboy', the 15-year-old Canadian youth whose attacks against Yahoo, Amazon.com and other prominent e-commerce sites in February 2000 earned him global attention. From his home in Canada, Mafiaboy harnessed the computing power of a number of systems, including those of the University of California at Santa Barbara, and used them to immobilise his target sites in what is termed a distributed denial of service attack. Mafiaboy was arrested after bragging in chatrooms about his exploits [21].

Other general forms of attack on computer systems include the insertion of worms and viruses. Generally referred to as malicious code, there are thousands of variations.

These may self-replicate and use up all the space in a computer system, or erase files. The impact of these may entail hundreds of millions of dollars in lost productivity and systems maintenance. The Melissa and ILOVEYOU viruses are two of the more prominent recent examples.

Much activity on the electronic frontier entails an element of adventure—the exploration of the unknown. The very fact that some activities in cyberspace are likely to elicit official condemnation is sufficient to attract the defiant, the rebellious, or the irresistibly curious. Given the degree of technical competence required to commit many computer-related crimes, there is one other motivational dimension worth noting here. This, of course, is the intellectual challenge of mastering complex systems. None of the above motivations is new. The element of novelty resides in the unprecedented capacity of technology to facilitate acting on these motivations.

Conventional Criminal Cases in which Evidence exists in Digital form

The rapid development and uptake of digital technology in the form of cell phones, palm pilots and other devices means that many ordinary crime scenes will contain some digital evidence. And just as legitimate organisations in the private and public sectors rely upon information systems for communications and record-keeping, so too are the efficiency and effectiveness of criminal organisations enhanced by technology.

The use of digital technology by terrorist organisations has also been noted. Well before September 11, 2001, CIA Director George Tenet testified that terrorist groups, 'including Hizbollah, HAMAS, the Abu Nidal organization, and Bin Laden's Al Qaeda organisation [were] using computerised files, e-mail, and encryption to support their operations' [22]. Even the use of information technology by criminals for basic record-keeping can have a transnational dimension. Incriminating documents can be stored on servers that are physically located in faraway places.

Challenges Arising from Cross-National Offending

The global reach of digital technology means that transnational offending is becoming more common. The cross-national nature of much cybercrime poses significant problems for law-enforcement and prosecuting authorities [23].

Where is the Crime?

Not the least of these challenges is to determine where the crime originated. This is not always apparent from the address and routing information. An attack that appears to have been launched from a nearby country may well have originated elsewhere, and been routed through numerous jurisdictions prior to its 'last address'. Skilled computer criminals will 'loop', or 'weave' through multiple sites in a variety of nations prior to reaching their target [24].

Ironically, offences that appear to have originated in far-flung countries may in fact have been launched from across town. Investigations by Hong Kong Police following a complaint from a local woman that she was the victim of a cyber-stalker led to a system in Colorado. Evidence obtained there revealed that the perpetrator in fact resided in Hong Kong, and the offending communications had been routed through the Colorado server [25].

When criminal activity originates in one country, transits one or more intermediate countries, and creates loss or damage in the destination country, where has the offence occurred? Sovereign states are free to define any behaviour as criminal, subject to whatever powers that are granted or constraints imposed by their constitutions. Traditionally, states have asserted jurisdiction in accordance with one or more of four principles [26]. According to the territoriality principle, states assert jurisdiction over behaviour occurring within their territorial borders. The vast majority of criminal laws do just that. In practice, with the vast majority of 'terrestrial' offences, the perpetrator, the victim and the act in question are all situated in the same jurisdiction.

According to the nationality principle (sometimes referred to as the extraterritoriality principle), states assert jurisdiction over behaviour involving their citizens as perpetrators, regardless of where the alleged conduct occurred. Citizens of the United States, Australia, and many other places can be prosecuted in their home countries for having had sex with children anywhere in the world, even in those countries where such conduct may not constitute a criminal offence.

Under the effects principle, countries assert jurisdiction over behaviour that affects their national interests, regardless of where the conduct may have taken place. Thus the United States prosecuted former president Manuel Noriega of Panama for drug-related offences. A person who, on foreign soil, engages in an act of terrorism against an Australian citizen, or who assists others in entering Australia illegally, is similarly liable to prosecution in Australia.

Under principles of universal jurisdiction, countries can establish mechanisms to prosecute a person for conduct, regardless of where it was committed, that is deemed to be a crime against humanity—i.e. genocide or slavery. This jurisdiction may also be asserted pursuant to a treaty, such as the Geneva Conventions of 1949.

Some countries are responding to the challenge of transnational cybercrime by expanding their jurisdiction. In Australia, the *Cybercrime Act 2001 (Cwlth)* asserts jurisdiction where

1. the conduct constituting the offence occurs partly in Australia or on board an Australian ship or aircraft;
2. the result of the conduct constituting the offence occurs partly in Australia or on board an Australian ship or aircraft; or
3. the person committing the offence is an Australian citizen or an Australian Company.

This legislation would appear to cover any offending behaviour with an Australian connection, with the exception of offences that are committed by foreign interests located outside of Australia against Australian interests on foreign soil.

Who is the Offender?

The next challenge is to assemble sufficient evidence to mobilise the law, that is, to obtain appropriate judicial authority for a physical search or for telecommunications interception. This is difficult enough when the offender is located within one's own borders. When the suspect himself is located abroad, these difficulties are compounded.

If an apparent crime is indeed worth investigating, assistance may be needed from authorities in the country where the offence originated; from authorities in the country or countries through which the offending activity may have transited on its way to the target; or where evidence of the crime may be situated. For various reasons, one or more of these authorities may be unwilling or unable to assist. They may lack the resources or technical capacity to investigate, they may lack the political will to assist, or they may simply have their own (and different) priorities.

When foreign authorities are able and willing to help, there are two basic elements to cooperation: informal investigator-to-investigator assistance, and formal mutual assistance. Informal assistance can be more expeditious, and is the preferred method of approach where compulsory powers (in other words, search warrants) are not required. It is based on good working relationships between police services of the countries in question, born of contacts made over time in the course of conferences, courtesy visits, and previous joint investigations. In the most advanced nations, arrangements for round the clock (24/7) contact points are in place.

Formal mutual assistance, on the other hand, is a more cumbersome process traditionally invoked pursuant to treaty arrangements between the countries in question, and involving the exchange of formal documents. It almost always requires that the offence in question be over a certain threshold of severity, and be a crime in both the requesting and the requested countries. This latter convention is referred to as 'dual criminality'. There exists a web of bilateral mutual assistance treaties between pairs of nations as well as multilateral agreements such as the London Extradition Scheme, which provides for the rendition of fugitive offenders among members of the Commonwealth of Nations.

In the Levin case noted above, mutual assistance arrangements were not in place between the US and Russia, but they were in place between the US and the United Kingdom, whence Levin was extradited. In other cases, mutual assistance arrangements may extend to investigation, but may not permit extradition. Under these circumstances, authorities in the country where the offender is physically situated may undertake the prosecution. For example, the investigation of Mafiaboy entailed close cooperation between Canadian and US authorities. But because Mafiaboy was a juvenile, and the extradition treaty between Canada and the US did not provide for the extradition of juveniles, he was prosecuted under Canadian law.

In cases where mutual assistance arrangements are weak or nonexistent, authorities may go to great lengths to lay their hands on a suspect and obtain incriminating evidence. In the Gorshkov/Ivanov matter discussed above, the suspects were resident in Russia and Russian authorities were disinclined to cooperate. To overcome this substantial impediment, FBI agents executed an undercover operation. Posing as representatives of a security firm called 'Invita', the agents made contact with Gorshkov and Ivanov in mid-2000, ostensibly to discuss employment opportunities in the United States. At the invitation of the agents, the two Russians demonstrated their hacking skills from Russia against a test network that had been established for the purpose. They were then invited to Seattle with the prospects of employment. The two flew to Seattle, all expenses paid, and were 'interviewed' about their computing skills. In the course of their presentation, Gorshkov accessed his computer system back in Russia. The interview took place in offices that were equipped with technologies that enabled the FBI to record their interviewees' keystrokes. The two were then arrested and charged with a spate of offences including fraud, extortion, and unauthorised computer intrusions. FBI investigators downloaded additional incriminating evidence remotely from Gorshkov's computer in Russia [27].

The legality of remote cross-border searches without the authority of the target country is questionable. If it is perceived as a violation of the target country's sovereignty, it may invite reciprocity [28].

Who will Prosecute?

Finally, where a spirit of cooperation does prevail, there remains the decision of whether to leave the matter to authorities in the country where the suspect is physically situated, or to seek extradition of the offender to deal with him under one's own law. The choice may depend on the relative heinousness with which authorities in the two countries regard the offending behaviour. Two illustrative cases involved offenders in Australia who violated laws of the United States. In May of 1999, Stephen George Hourmouzis, a resident of Melbourne, obtained access to a number of email servers and sent more than three million messages to addresses in Australia and the United States. The messages contained information purportedly reporting the results of research that predicted a 900 percent rise in the price of shares in a US corporation that was listed on the NASDAQ Exchange. The information was fraudulent. Rather than mobilise the federal criminal process and seek to extradite Hourmouzis, US authorities were happy to leave prosecution to Australia [29]. He was sentenced to prison for three years, to be released on probation after three months subject to good behaviour. US authorities chose not to incur the costs or risk the uncertainties for an outcome not significantly more severe than that likely to flow from the Australian criminal process.

By contrast, US authorities did seek to extradite an Australian who was an alleged member of the 'Drink or Die' Conspiracy. Criminal copyright violations attract much more severe sentences under US law than they do in Australia, and US authorities were intent on extracting the highest price they could for the offence [30].

Applying Substantive Criminal Law

The adequacy of the substantive criminal law is of great importance to the prosecution of cybercrime, whether domestic or cross-national. Prosecutions have foundered because inappropriate charges were laid, or because the offending conduct was not explicitly prohibited by law. The architect of the ILOVEYOU virus was resident in the Philippines, where criminal law at the time did not prohibit writing or releasing viruses. The lack of dual criminality precluded extradition to the United States, where it is likely that he would have been dealt with very severely. Moreover, the best charge that Philippine authorities could come up with was under the Access Devices Regulation Act—which made it a criminal offence to use a computer to obtain credit card or other personal information for a fraudulent purpose. When it became apparent that this bore no relationship to the acts that the suspect was alleged to have committed, charges were dropped.

Other issues relating to the substantive criminal law include issues relating to the charge of 'unauthorised access to a computer system'. A great deal of offending is done by persons who are authorised to access computer systems, but who do so for unauthorised purposes [31]. Inappropriate charges are likely to lead to these charges being dismissed. Similarly, if the law is not clear regarding what constitutes 'possession', this too may see the prosecution founder [32].

Other Considerations

Two other considerations posed by cybercrime are the use of encryption, and the volatility of evidence. At the dawn of the digital age, encryption technology required such computing power that it lay beyond the means of all but the largest organizations. The pioneering work of Diffie and Hellman led to the ultimate 'democratisation' of encryption technology [33]. Encryption, once the monopoly of security and national defence agencies, is now accessible to the ordinary consumer. Unfortunately, not all users of encryption are law-abiding citizens, and there are those users of encryption who use the technology to conceal communications in furtherance of criminal conspiracies, or to hide records of criminal transactions.

A nation's response to the use of encryption in furtherance of crime will depend on its constitutional constraints. In the United States, where individuals cannot be compelled to incriminate themselves, authorities may seek to use decryption technologies, or other intrusive surveillance methods [34]. One may also make it an additional offence to use encryption in the course of a crime. Those countries unconstrained by a bill of rights have devised a simpler solution to the challenge of encryption. They simply require individuals to disclose encryption keys or face criminal charges. In the United Kingdom, non-compliance can entail imprisonment for up to two years; in Australia, six months.

Another issue that tends to distinguish cybercrime from terrestrial crime is the volatility of evidence. The distinction is not perfect, for some digital evidence is durable despite the best efforts of the offender. Files that have been erased can subsequently be reconstructed [35]. Electronic footprints may be more robust than one might think. Nevertheless, the nature of some digital crime is such that rapid response is essential. Those cases requiring investigation in real time [36] do not make for leisurely inquiry. Even access to stored information may require timely action.

Internet service providers do not store transaction data forever, and requirements for retention, where they do exist, are limited.

Just as governments in terrestrial space can no longer afford to deploy police officers on every street corner, so too are law-enforcement resources limited in the digital world. The opportunity, indeed the necessity, for public/private collaboration in furtherance of security and prosperity in cyberspace, is with us. This is perhaps most visible in the area of digital piracy, where industry employees, including foreign nationals from corporate headquarters in another country, may play a major role in investigations and in providing technical assistance later at trial. Other commercial institutions, from the computer security industry to the insurance industry and private-sector specialists in forensic computing, are destined to play a wide role in the prevention and control of cybercrime. Many of these institutions are themselves multinationals, leading one to speculate on the prospects for the emergence of global, non-governmental, quasi-regulatory systems [37].

Future Directions

The borderless nature of cyberspace and the exponential take-up of digital technology throughout the world guarantee that transnational cybercrime will remain a challenge. Fortunately, many nations are rising to this challenge, individually and collectively. Initiatives such as those of the G8 and Council of Europe to harmonise substantive criminal law and to establish mechanisms for expedited mutual assistance constitute the most prominent examples.

Nevertheless, the web of international cooperation does have its holes. There are among the world's nations those whose substantive criminal laws and whose criminal procedure laws are still not attuned to the digital age, or which remain inconsistent with those of the G8 and the Council of Europe. 'Fast freeze' preservation of digital evidence, procedural law permitting real-time tracing across multiple jurisdictions, expansion of the 24/7 contact system, and more widespread arrangements for timely Mutual Legal Assistance and extradition are among the areas calling our for further development. Those nations that lag behind the leaders risk becoming havens for cybercriminals of the future.

Notes

[1] Grant et al. 'Child Pornography in the Digital Age'.
[2] US Customs Service, *Operation Artus*.
[3] International Intellectual Property Alliance, Press release, 30 April 2002.
[4] Microsoft, *Software Piracy*.
[5] US Department of Justice, 'Defendant Indicted in Connection with Operating Illegal Internet Software Piracy Group' 12 March 2003.
[6] See, for example, Smith, 'Identity related economic crime: risks and countermeasures'.
[7] Ogilvie, 'Cyberstalking'.
[8] Duggal, 'India's First Cyberstalking Case—Some Cyberlaw Perspectives'.

[9] Power, *Tangled Web*, 92–100.
[10] US Department of Justice, 'Russian Computer Hacker Convicted by Jury'.
[11] See, for a good account, Stoll, *The Cuckoo's Egg*.
[12] US Department of Justice, 'Federal Cybersleuthers Armed with First Ever Computer Wiretap Order Net International Hacker Charged with Illegally Entering Harvard and U.S. Military Computers'.
[13] Vatis, *Cyber Attacks During the War on Terrorism*.
[14] For some examples of electronic graffiti, see http://www.2600.com/hacked_pages/ (visited 27 October 2004).
[15] *AP*, 7 May 1998.
[16] *BBC*, 31 March 1999.
[17] *BBC*, 31 March 2001.
[18] Grabosky & Stohl, 'Cyberterrorism'.
[19] See Denning, *Information Warfare and Security*.
[20] Tagg, 'Aussie hacker jailed for sewage attacks'.
[21] *ZD Net*, 29 April 2000.
[22] Quoted in Freeh, *Statement Before the Senate Judiciary Committee, Subcommittee for the Technology, Terrorism, and Government Information*.
[23] See, for example, Goodman & Brenner, 'The Emerging Consensus on Criminal Conduct in Cyberspace'.
[24] Sussmann, 'The Critical Challenges from International High-tech and Computer-Related Crime at the Millennium'.
[25] Lo, 'Police Training for Cyber-Transformation'.
[26] Podgor, 'International Computer Fraud: A Paradigm for Limiting National Jurisdiction'.
[27] *C/net News.com*, 1 May 2001.
[28] Bellia, 'Chasing Bits Across Borders'.
[29] *R v Steven George Hourmouzis*, County Court, Melbourne.
[30] US Department of Justice, 'Defendant Indicted in Connection with Operating Illegal Internet Software Piracy Group'.
[31] *Director of Public Prosecutions v Bignell*.
[32] *Haynes v Hughes* (2001); *Atkins v Director of Public Prosecutions* (2000).
[33] Diffie & Hellman, 'New directions in cryptography'.
[34] The investigation of one Nicodemo S. Scarfo by agents of the US Government is illustrative. See http://www.epic.org/crypto/scarfo.html (visited 9 July 2003).
[35] *US v Upham* (1999).
[36] See Stoll, *The Cuckoo's Egg*.
[37] Braithwaite & Drahos, *Global Business Regulation*.

References

AP, 7 May 1998 http://www.augustachronicle.com/stories/050798/tec_124-1493.shtml (visited 27 October 2004).
Atkins v Director of Public Prosecutions (2000) EWHC Admin 302 (8 March 2000).
BBC, 31 March 1999 http://www.flora.org/flora.mai-not/10498 (visited 24 April 2003).
BBC, 31 March 2001 http://news.bbc.co.uk/hi/english/world/asia-pacific/newsid_1252000/1252965.stm (visited 2 May 2003).
Bellia, P. (2001) 'Chasing bits across borders', *University of Chicago Legal Forum*.
Braithwaite, J. & Drahos, P. (2000) *Global Business Regulation*, Cambridge University Press.
C/net News.com, 1 May 2001 http://news.com.com/2100-1001-256811.html (visited 27 October 2004).
Denning, D. (1999) *Information Warfare and Security*, Addison Wesley.

Diffie, W. & Hellman, M. (1976) 'New directions in cryptography', *IEEE Transactions on Information Theory*, p. 22.

Director of Public Prosecutions v Bignell (1988) 1 Cr.App.Rep. 1.

Duggal, S. (2001) 'India's first cyberstalking case—some cyberlaw perspectives' http://www. cyberlawindia.com/2CYBER27.htm (visited 29 March 2001).

Freeh, L. (2000) *Statement Before the Senate Judiciary Committee, Subcommittee for the Technology, Terrorism, and Government Information*, 28 March http://www.usdoj.gov/criminal/ cybercrime/freeh328.htm (visited 27 October 2004).

Goodman, M. & Brenner, S. (2002) 'The emerging consensus on criminal conduct in cyberspace', *UCLA Journal of Law & Technology*, vol. 3, http://www.lawtechjournal.com/articles/2002/ 03_020625_goodmanbrenner.php (visited 27 October 2004).

Grabosky, P. & Stohl, M. (2003) 'Cyberterrorism', *Reform*, p. 82.

Grant, A., David, F. & Grabosky, P. (1997) 'Child pornography in the digital age', *Transnational Organised Crime*, 3/4.

Haynes v Hughes (2001) WASCA 146 (9 May 2001).

International Intellectual Property Alliance, Press release, 30 April 2002 http://www.iipa.com/ pressreleases/2002_Apr30_USTR301.pdf

Lo, V., 'Police Training for Cyber-Transformation', paper presented at the Transnational Organised Crime Conference, Hong Kong, March 2002.

Microsoft (2003) *Software Piracy*, http://www.microsoft.com/piracy/basics/what/ip.asp (visited 4 July 2003).

Ogilvie, E. (2000) 'Cyberstalking', *Trends & Issues in Crime and Criminal Justice* No. 166 http://www. aic.gov.au/publications/tandi/tandi166.html (visited 27 October 2004).

Podgor, E. (2002) 'International computer fraud: a paradigm for limiting national jurisdiction', *UC Davis Law Review*, p. 35.

Power, R. (2000) *Tangled Web*, Cue Corporation.

R v Steven George Hourmouzis, County Court, Melbourne (Stott, J.) 30 October 2000 http://www. countycourt.vic.gov.au/judgments/hourmouz.htm (visited 29 December 2002).

Smith, R. (1999) 'Identity related economic crime: risks and countermeasures', *Trends & Issues in Crime and Criminal Justice*, No. 129 http://www.aic.gov.au/publications/tandi/ti129.pdf (visited 27 October 2004).

Stoll, C. (1991) *The Cuckoo's Egg*, Pan Books.

Sussmann, M. (1999) 'The critical challenges from international high-tech and computer-related crime at the millennium', *Duke Journal of Comparative and International Law*, 9/2.

Tagg, L. (2003) 'Aussie hacker jailed for sewage attacks', in: *Iafrica.com*, 1 November http://cooltech. iafrica.com/technews/archive/november/837110.htm (visited 27 October 2004).

US Customs Service (2002) *Operation Artus*, http://www.usdoj.gov/criminal/ceos/OperationArtus.htm

US Department of Justice, 'Federal Cybersleuthers Armed with First Ever Computer Wiretap Order Net International Hacker Charged with Illegally Entering Harvard and U.S. Military Computers', 29 March 1996 http://www.usdoj.gov/opa/pr/1996/March96/146.txt (visited 27 October 2004).

US Department of Justice, 'Russian Computer Hacker Convicted by Jury', 10 October 2001 http:// www.usdoj.gov/criminal/cybercrime/gorshkovconvict.htm (visited 27 October 2004).

US Department of Justice, 'Defendant Indicted in Connection with Operating Illegal Internet Software Piracy Group' 12 March 2003 http://www.cybercrime.gov/griffithsIndict.htm (visited 27 October 2004).

US v Upham 168 F.3d 532 (1999).

Vatis, M. (2003) *Cyber Attacks During the War on Terrorism*, http://www.ists.dartmouth.edu/ISTS/ counterterrorism/cyber_a1.pdf (visited 27 October 2004), Institute for Security Technology Studies.

ZD Net, 29 April 2000 http://www.zdnet.com/special/stories/defense/0,10459,2552467,00.html

INDEX